The Tale of Thorsteinn House-Power

Original Text, Translations, and Word Lists

Translated by
Matthew Leigh Embleton

Copyright ©2025 Matthew Leigh Embleton. All rights reserved.

The Tale of Thorsteinn House-Power

The Tale of Thorsteinn House-Power (*Old Norse*) 4
Word List *(Old Norse to English)*...46
Word List *(English to Old Norse)* 65
The Tale of Thorsteinn House-Power (*Old Icelandic*)..81
Word List *(Old Icelandic to English)* 123
Word List *(English to Old Icelandic)* 142
A Word Comparison of Old Norse and Old Icelandic Words 158

Cover: Old Norse text over an outline of Iceland. Author's design.

The original Old Norse and Old Icelandic texts are in the public domain.
These translations ©2022 Matthew Leigh Embleton
©2025 Matthew Leigh Embleton (This Edition)

Acknowledgments

I have long been fascinated by languages and history, and I am very grateful to the special people in my life who have supported and encouraged me in my work. Thank you for believing in me. You know who you are.

Introduction

Old Norse is a North Germanic language spoken by inhabitants of Scandinavia from about the 7th to the 15th centuries. Old Icelandic is a variety of Old West Norse that emerged during the Norse settlement of Iceland in the second half of the 9th century. The rich tradition of Icelandic literature survived by oral tradition over several centuries before being written down in the 13th Century. The Tale of Thorsteinn House-Power (*Þorsteins þáttr bæjarmagns*) is one of the many Tales of Icelanders or *Íslendingaþættir*. The word '*þáttr*' (plural: '*þættir*') translates as a strand of rope or a yarn, comparable to the word 'yarn' in English sometimes used to refer to a story.

This book contains:
- The Tale of Thorsteinn House-Power (*Þorsteins þáttr bæjarmagns*) (Old Norse Version)
- An Old Norse to English Word List
- An English to Old Norse Word List
- The Tale of Thorsteinn House-Power (*Þorsteins þáttr bæjarmagns*) (Old Icelandic Version)
- An Old Icelandic to English Word List
- An English to Old Icelandic Word List
- A Word Comparison of Old Norse and Old Icelandic words

The texts are presented in their original form, with a literal word-for-word line-by-line translation, and a Modern English translation, all side-by-side. In this way, it is possible to see and feel how the worked and how it has evolved. This book is designed to be of use and interest to anyone with a passion for the Old Norse or Old Icelandic language, Norse history, or languages and history in general.

The Tale of Thorsteinn House-Power (Old Norse)

The Tale of Thorsteinn House-Power (*Old Norse*)

Old Norse	Literal	English
1	**1**	**1**
Í þann tíma, er Hákon jarl Sigurðarson réð fyrir Noregi, bjó sá bóndi í Gaulardal, er Brynjólfr hét.	At that time, was Hakon earl Son-of-Sigurd ruled over Norway, lived there farmer in Gaulardale, was Brynjolf named.	About the time when Earl Hakon Sigurdson was ruler of Norway, there lived a farmer in Gaulardale, named Brynjolf.
Hann var kallaðr úlfaldi.	He was called Camel.	He was called Brynjolf Camel.
Hann var lendr maðr ok mikil kempa.	He was landed man and great warrior.	He was a landed man and a great warrior.
Kona hans hét Dagný; hún var dóttir Járnskeggja af Yrjum.	Wife his named Dagny she was daughter Iron-Beard of Yrjar.	His wife was named Dagny and she was the daughter of Iron-Beard of Yrjar.
Þau áttu einn son, er Þorsteinn hét.	They had one son, who Thorstein named.	They had one son who was named Thorstein.
Hann var mikill ok sterkr, harðúðigr ok óaflátssamr við hvern, sem eiga var.	He was great and strong, hard-minded and un-indulgent with everyone, as said-of was.	He was large and strong, strong-minded and unflinching with everyone that he spoke with.
Engi var jafnstórr í Noregi, ok trautt fengust þær dyrr, at honum væri hægt um at ganga, ok því var hann kallaðr bæjarmagn, því at hann þótti ofmagni bera flestum húsum.	None were equally-big in Norway, and scarcely got-they there door, that he would possible about to walk, and because was he called House-Power, because that he seemed to-overpower bear most houses.	No one was as big in all Norway, and there was scarcely a door that he could walk through, and he was called House-Power, because he seemed to overpower most houses.
Hann var óþýðr, ok fekk faðir hans honum því skip ok menn, ok var Þorsteinn þá ýmist í hernaði eða í kaupferðum, ok tókst honum hvárttveggja vel.	He was unfriendly, and got father his him therefore a-ship and men, and was Thorstein then either in raiding or in trading-journeys, and took he either well.	He was so unfriendly that his father gave him a ship with some men, and Thorstein was either raiding or trading, and he took to both well.

The Tale of Thorsteinn House-Power (Old Norse)

Old Norse	Literal	English
Í þenna tíma tók ríki í Noregi Óláfr konungr Tryggvason, en Hákon jarl var skorinn á háls af þræli sínum, þeim sem Þormóðr karkr hét.	In that time took kingdom in Norway Olaf the-king Tryggvason, when Hakon earl was cut in the-neck of servant his, then as Thormod Kark named.	It was about this time that King Olaf Tryggvason ruled the kingdom of Norway, when Earl Hakon had his throat slit by one of his servants, who was named Thormod Kark.
Þorsteinn bæjarmagn gerðist hirðmaðr Óláfs konungs.	Thorstein House-Power became court-man Olaf's the-king's.	Thorstein House-Power became a court man of King Olaf's.
Þótti konungi hann röskr maðr ok helt mikit til hans, en ekki var hann mjök kenndr af hirðmönnum.	Thought the-king he brave man and held much to him, but not was he much recognised of court-men.	The king thought he was a brave man and thought highly of him, but he was not liked by the other court-men.
Þótti þeim hann stríðlyndr ok óvæginn, ok hafði konungr hann mjök til þess at fara sendiferðir þær, sem aðrir töldust undan at fara.	Thought they he obstinate and ruthless, and had the-king he great for this to travel missions those, that others considered away from travelling.	They found him obstinate and ruthless, and the king had him going on great missions, that others were reluctant to travel on.
En stundum fór hann kaupferðir at afla konungnum gersema.	About awhile travelled he trading-voyages to provide the-king precious-things.	For a while he went on trading voyages to bring the king treasures.

2

Eitt sinn lá Þorsteinn austr fyrir Bálagarðssíðu, ok gaf honum eigi at sigla.	One occasion lay Thorstein east before Balagardsida, and gave him not to sail.	On one occasion Thorstein lay east near Balagardsida, and he was not given wind to sail.
Gekk hann á land einn morgin, ok er sól var í landsuðri, var Þorsteinn kominn í eitt rjóðr.	Went he to land one morning, and when the-sun was in South-East, was Thorstein coming to a clearing.	He went to land one morning, and when the sun was in the South-East, Thorstein came to a clearing.
Hóll fagr var í rjóðrinu.	Mound beautiful was in the-clearing.	There was a beautiful mound in the clearing.
Hann sá einn kollóttan pilt uppi á hólnum, ok mælti:	He saw a bald-headed boy up on the-mound, and spoke:	He saw a bald-headed boy up on the mound, and he spoke:
"Móðir mín",	"Mother mine",	"Mother mine",

The Tale of Thorsteinn House-Power (Old Norse)

Old Norse	Literal	English
segir hann, "fá þú mér út krókstaf minn ok bandvettlinga, því at ek vil á gandreið fara.	said he, "get you me out crooked-staff mine and mittens, because that I wish to witch-ride go.	he said, "get me my crooked staff and mittens, because I wish to go on a witch ride.
Er nú hátíð í heiminum neðra".	Is now festival in the-world under".	There is now a festival in the underworld".
Þá var snarat út ór hólnum einum krókstaf, sem eldsskara væri.	Then was twisted out from the-mound a crooked-staff, as fire-poker was.	Then a crooked staff was thrown out from the mound, shaped like a poker.
Hann stígr á stafinn ok dregr á sik vettlingana ok keyrir, sem börn eru vön at gera.	He climbed on the-staff and drew of his mitten and the-stick, as children are want to do.	He climbed on the staff and drew on his mittens and began riding the stick, as children often do.
Þorsteinn gengr á hólinn ok mælti slikum orðum sem piltrinn, ok var þegar út kastat staf ok vöttum ok mælt þetta:	Thorstein went to the-mound and spoke such words as the-boy, and was then out cast staff and gloves and spoke this:	Thorstein went to the mound and spoke the same words that the boy had, and then a staff and gloves were cast out and a voice asked:
"Hverr tekr nú við?"	"Who takes now with?"	"Who wants these now?".
"Bjálfi, sonr þinn",	"Bjalfi, son yours",	"Bjalfi, your son",
sagði Þorsteinn.	said Thorstein.	said Thorstein.
Síðan stígr hann á stafinn ok ríðr þar eptir, sem piltrinn fór undan.	Afterwards climbed he on the-staff and rode there after, as the-boy travelled away-from.	Afterwards he climbed on the staff and rode away after the boy.
Þeir kómu at einni móðu ok steyptu sér ofan í hana, ok var því líkast sem þeir væði reyk.	They came to a large-river and cast he down in it, and was it like as they waded-through smoke.	They came to a large river and cast down into it, and it was like they were wading through smoke.
Því næst birti þeim fyrir augum, ok kómu þeir at, sem á fell fram af hömrum.	Then near revealed they before eyes, and came they to, as a-river falling from off a-steep-cliff.	Then revealed before their eyes, they came to where a river was falling from a steep cliff.
Sér Þorsteinn þá byggð mikla ok borg stóra.	Saw Thorstein then settlements great and a-city great.	Thorstein then saw large settlements and a great city.
Þeir stefna til borgarinnar, ok sitr þar fólk yfir borðum.	They directed to the-city, and sat there folk across a-table.	They turned to the city, and there people were sat across a table.

The Tale of Thorsteinn House-Power (Old Norse)

Old Norse	Literal	English
Þeir gengu í höllina, ok var höll skipuð af fólki, ok var þar af engu drukkit utan af silfrkerum.	They went in the-hall, and was the-hall equipped of folk, and were they of nothing drinking except-for of silver.	They walked into the hall, and there were people filling the hall, and they were drinking from nothing but silver cups.
Trapiza stóð á gólfi.	Table stood on the-floor.	A table stood on the floor.
Allt sýndist þeim þar gullligt ok ekki drukkit nema vín.	All seemed they there gold and nothing drunk but wine.	Everything seemed to be gold, and everyone drunk nothing but wine.
Þat þóttist Þorsteinn skilja, at engi maðr sá þá.	That thought Thorstein such, that no man see then.	Then Thorstein realised that no man could see them.
Félagi hans fór með borðum ok henti allt þat, sem niðr fell.	Companion his went along the-tables and caught all that, as down fell.	His companion went along the tables and caught all that fell down from them.
Konungr sat þar í hásæti ok drottning.	The-king sat there in high-seat and the-queen.	The king sat there in the high seat with the queen.
Menn váru glaðir um höllina.	Men were glad about the-hall.	The men about the hall were glad.
Þessu næst sér Þorsteinn, at maðr kom í höllina ok kvaddi konung ok kveðst vera sendr til hans utan af Indíalandi ór fjalli því, er Lúkanus heitir, frá jarli þeim, er þar réð fyrir, ok segir konungi, at hann var huldumaðr.	This next saw Thorstein, that a-man came into the-hall and called the-king and greetings were sent to him out of India from mountains because, that Lucanus named, from the-earl they, that was advised for, and said the-king, that he was a-hidden-man.	Then Thorstein saw that a man had come into the hall and greeted the king, and he sent greetings from the mountains of India because the earl Lucanus ruled there, and he advised the king that he was an elf-man.
Hann færði honum einn gullhring.	He took to-him a gold-ring.	He presented him with a gold ring.
Eigi þóttist konungr betri hring sét hafa, ok fór hringrinn um höllina til sýnis, ok lofuðu hann allir.	Not thought the-king better ring seen had, and went the-ring about the-hall to his, and praised it all.	The king thought that he had not seen a better ring, and it was shown around the hall, and praised by all.
Hann var sundr tekinn í fjórum stöðum.	It was apart taken in four places.	This ring could be taken apart in four sections.
Annan grip sá Þorsteinn, er honum þótti mikils um vert.	Another-thing grabbed seeing Thorstein, that to-him thought much about worth.	Another thing grabbed Thorstein's sight, that he thought might be worth a lot.

The Tale of Thorsteinn House-Power (Old Norse)

Old Norse	Literal	English
Þat var dúkr sá, er lá á konungs borðinu.	It was table-cloth saw, that laid at the-king's table.	It was the table cloth that he saw, which was laid at the king's table.
Hann var með gullligum röndum ok í festir þeir tólf gimsteinar, sem beztir eru.	It was with gold stripes and on fastened there twelve precious-stones, that best were.	It had stripes of gold and was fastened with twelve of the best precious stones.
Gjarna vildi Þorsteinn dúkinn eiga.	Gladly willed Thorstein table-cloth to-own.	Thorstein gladly wished to own the table-cloth.
Kemr honum í hug at treysta á konungs hamingju ok vita, hvárt hann getr ekki nát hringnum.	Came he to think to reckon on the-king's luck and know, whether he get not get-hold-of the-ring.	He came to think about the king's luck and find out whether or not he could get hold of the ring.
Nú sér Þorsteinn, at konungrinn ætlar at draga hringinn á hönd sér.	Now saw Thorstein, that the-king intended to carry the-ring on hand his.	Now Thorstein saw that the king intended to carry the ring on his hand.
Þá greip Þorsteinn hringinn af honum, en annarri hendi tók hann dúkinn, ok fór allr matr í saur, en Þorsteinn hljóp á dyrr, en krókstafr hans varð honum eptir í höllinni.	Then grabbed Thorstein the-ring off him, then another hand took he the-table-cloth, and went all food in the-mud, then Thorstein ran to the-door, but crooked-stick his was him behind in the-hall.	Then Thorstein grabbed the ring off him, and then with his other hand he took the table cloth, and all the food fell in the mud, and then Thorstein ran to the door, but the crooked stick was behind him in the hall.
Verðr nú upphlaup mikit, hlaupa menn út síðan ok sjá, hvar Þorsteinn ferr, ok stefna eptir honum.	Became now uproar great, ran men out after and saw, where Thorstein went, and directed after him.	There now became a great uproar, and men ran out afterwards and saw where Thorstein went and started after him.
Sér hann nú, at þeir muni geta nát honum.	Saw he now, that they would get hold-of him.	He saw now that they would catch him.
Hann mælti þá:	He spoke then:	He then spoke:
"Ef þú ert svá góðr, Óláfr konungr, sem ek treysti mikit til þín, þá veittu mér lið".	"If you are so good, Olaf king, as I trust much to you, then grant me assistance".	"If you are so good king Olaf, as I trust you are, then grant me assistance".
En svá var Þorsteinn frár, at þeir kómust ekki fyrir hann, fyrr en hann kom at ánni, ok staldraði hann þá við.	Then so was Thorstein swift, that they came not for him, before that he came to the-river, and lingered he then with.	Then Thorstein was so fast, that they could not catch him before he came to the river, where he had to wait.

The Tale of Thorsteinn House-Power (Old Norse)

Old Norse	Literal	English
Þeir slógu hring um hann, en Þorsteinn varðist vel ok drap ótal marga, áðr förunautr hans kom ok færði honum stafinn, ok hurfu þeir þegar í móðuna.	They formed a-circle around him, and Thorstein defended well and killed countless many, after companion his came and brought him the-stick, and disappeared they straightaway into the-river.	They formed a circle around him, and Thorstein defended himself well killing a countless many of them, and afterwards his companion came and brought him the stick, and they disappeared straightaway into the river.
Komu þeir aptr á inn sama hól sem fyrr gátum vér, þá sól var í vestri.	Came they back to the same hill as before opening was, then the-sun was in the-west.	They came back to the same hill where the opening had been before, and then the sun was in the west.
Kastaði piltrinn þá inn stafnum ok klæðsekk þeim, sem hann hafði fylldan af góðum krásum, ok svá gerði Þorsteinn.	Cast the-boy then the stick and sack theirs, which he had filled of good food, and so did Thorstein.	The boy cast the stick and their sack, which he had filled with good food, and so did Thorstein.
Kollsveinn hljóp inn, en Þorsteinn nam staðar við glugginn.	The-boy ran in, but Thorstein took to-stand by the-skylight.	They boy ran inside, but Thorstein waited by a skylight window.
Hann sá þar tvær konur, ok vaf önnur guðvef, en önnur ruggaði barni.	He saw then two women, and wove one precious-cloth, and another rocking a-baby.	He then saw two women, and one wove precious cloth, and another was rocking a baby.
Sú mælti:	So spoke:	So they spoke:
"Hvat dvelr hann Bjálfa, bróður þinn?"	"What delays him Bjalfi, brother yours?"	"What delays your brother Bjalfi?".
"Ekki hefir hann mér fylgt í dag?"	"Not has he me followed to day?"	"Has he not followed me today?",
sagði hann.	said he.	he said.
"Hverr hefir þá farit með krókstafinn?"	"Who has then gone with the-crooked-stick?"	"Who has gone with the crooked-stick then?" she said.
segir hún.	said she.	"That was Thorstein House-Power",
"Þat var Þorsteinn bæjarmagn",	"That was Thorstein House-Power",	said Kollsvein,
segir Kollsveinn, "hirðmaðr Óláfs konungs.	said Kollsvein, "court-man Olaf's the-king's.	"a court man of King Olaf's.

The Tale of Thorsteinn House-Power (Old Norse)

Old Norse	Literal	English
Kom hann okkr í mikinn vanda, því at hann hafði ór undirheimum þau þing, at eigi munu slík í Noregi, ok var við því búit, at vit mundum drepnir, er hann kastaði stafnum í hendr þeim, ok eltu þeir hann til niðrgangs, ok þá færði ek honum stafinn, ok víst er hann hraustr maðr, því at eigi veit ek, hversu marga hann drap".	Came he us in much difficulty, because that he had away-from under-world their assembly, which not would-be such in Norway, and were with therefore prepared, to know would-be killed, when he cast stick in hand theirs, and chased they him to down-going, and then took I to-him the-stick, and certainly was he brave man, because that not know I, how-so many men killed".	He has brought us unto much difficulty by stealing from the assembly in the underworld, the like of which aren't to be found in Norway, and was nearly killed when he threw his stick into their hands, and they were chasing him to his death, and then I took the stick to him, and he certainly was a brave man, because I do not know how many men were killed".
Ok nú laukst aptr haugrinn.	And now closed back the-mound.	And now the mound closed.
Fór Þorsteinn nú til sinna manna, ok sigldu þaðan til Noregs, ok fann Óláf konung austr í Vík ok færði honum gersemi þessi ok sagði frá ferðum sínum, ok fannst mönnum mikit um.	Went Thorstein now to his men, and sailed from-there to Norway, and found Olaf the-king east in Vik and brought him treasures these and said from voyage his, and found men much about.	Thorstein now went to his men, and sailed from there to Norway, and found King Olaf at Vik in the east, and brought him the treasures and told him of his voyage, and people thought much about it.
Konungr bauð at gefa Þorsteini lén mikit, en hann kveðst enn vilja fara eina ferð í Austrveg.	The-king offered to give Thorstein a-fee great, but he said but wished travel one voyage to Eastern-Lands.	The king offered to give Thorstein a great fee but he said that he wished to travel on a voyage to the Eastern-Lands.
Var hann nú með konungi um vetrinn.	Was he now with the-king about winter.	He was now with the king over the winter.

3

At vári bjó Þorsteinn skip sitt.	In spring prepared Thorstein ship his.	In spring Thorstein prepared his ship.
Hann hafði snekkju ok fjóra menn ok tuttugu.	He had a-sailboat and four men and twenty.	He had a sailboat and twenty four men.
Ok er hann kom við Jamtaland, lá hann í höfn einn dag, ok gekk hann á land at skemmta sér.	And when he came to Jamtland, lay he in the-harbour one day, and went he to land to amuse himself.	And when he came to Jamtland, he lay in port one day, and he went ashore to amuse himself.
Hann kom í eitt rjóðr.	He came to a clearing.	He came to a clearing.

The Tale of Thorsteinn House-Power (Old Norse)

Old Norse	Literal	English
Þar var einn mikill steinn.	There was a large stone.	There was a large stone.
Skammt þaðan sá hann einn dverg furðuliga ljótan, ok grenjaði upp yfir sik.	A-short-distance from-there saw he a dwarf exceedingly hideous, and howling up over himself.	A short distance from there he saw a dwarf strangely ugly, and he was howling about himself.
Sýndist Þorsteini kjaptrinn snúinn út at eyranu, en öðrum megin nefit niðr at kjaptinum.	Thought Thorstein jaw twisted out at ears, on one side nose below the mouth.	It seemed to Thorstein that his jaw twisted up to the ear on one side and on the other side his nose overlapped his mouth.
Þorsteinn segir, hví hann léti svá heimsliga.	Thorstein said, why he made so foolishly.	Thorstein asked him why he was behaving so foolishly.
"Þú, góði maðr",	"You, good man",	"You, good man",
sagði hann, "undrast eigi.	said he, "wonder not.	he said,
Sér þú eigi þann mikla örn, er þar flýgr?	See you not that great eagle, that there flies?	"it is no wonder.
Hann hefir tekit son minn.	He had taken son mine.	Do you not see the great eagle that flies there? He's taken my son.
Ætla ek þat, at sá ófögnuðr sé sendr af Óðni, en ek spring, ef ek missi barnit".	Suppose I that, it so unhappy he-is sent of Odin, that I burst, if I lost child".	I think that the unhappy one was sent by Odin, but I will explode if I lose my child".
Þorsteinn skaut eptir erninum, ok kom undir vænginn, ok datt hann dauðr niðr, en Þorsteinn henti dvergsbarnit á lopti ok færði föðurnum, en dvergrinn varð feginn mjök ok mælti:	Thorstein shot after the-eagle, and came down the-wing, and fell he dead down, but Thorstein caught the-dwarf's-boy from-the-sky and brought to-the-father, the dwarf was relieved much and spoke:	Thorstein shot at the eagle, and it came down on the wing, and he fell down dead, but Thorstein caught the dwarf's boy as he fell from the sky, and brought it to his father, and the dwarf was relieved and spoke
"Þér á ek at launa lífgjöf ok sonr minn, ok kjós þér nú fyrir laun í gulli ok silfri".	"To-you that I to repay life-gift and son mine, and choose to-you now for to-repay in gold and silver".	"To you I owe a great debt for saving my son's life, and I choose to repay you in gold and silver".
"Græð þú fyrst son þinn",	"Tend-to you first son yours",	"Tend to your son first",
sagði Þorsteinn; "er ek eigi vanr at taka mútur á afli mínu".	said Thorstein "that I not accustomed to take payment for strength mine".	said Thorstein, "because I am not accustomed to taking payment for my strength".

The Tale of Thorsteinn House-Power (Old Norse)

Old Norse	Literal	English
"Eigi væri mér at óskyldara at launa",	"Not should-be to-me that less-should to repay",	"That should not make me repay you any less",
segir dvergrinn.	said the-dwarf.	said the dwarf.
"Mun þér ekki þykkja framboðligr serkr minn af sauða ullu, en eigi muntu á sundi mæðast ok eigi sár fá, ef þú hefir hann næst þér".	"Would you not value be-offered shirt mine of wether's wool, that not shall-you to swimming get-tired and not wound get, if you have it next to-you".	"Would you not value if I offered you my shirt of ram's wool, for you shall never get tired when swimming and never be wounded if you wear it next to your skin".
Þorsteinn fór í serkinn, ok var honum mátuligr, en honum sýndist dvergnum of lítill.	Thorstein went to the-shirt, and was he fitting, though to-him seemed the-dwarf of small.	Thorstein tried on the shirt, and it fit him, even though it seemed too small for the dwarf.
Hann tók ok silfrhring ór pungi sínum ok gaf Þorsteini ok bað hann vel geyma ok sagði honum aldri féfátt verða mundu, meðan hann ætti hringinn.	He took also silver-ring from pouch his and gave Thorstein and asked him well retain and said he never lack-of-money become would, as-long-as he had the-ring.	He also took a silver ring from his pouch and gave it to Thorstein and asked him to keep it safe saying that he would never lack money as long as he had the ring.
Síðan tók hann einn stein svartan ok gaf Þorsteini, "ok ef þú felr hann í lófa þér, sér þik engi.	Afterwards took he a stone black and gave Thorstein, "and if you fold it in promise to-you, see you none.	Afterwards he took a black stone and gave it to Thorstein: "and if you fold it in your hand in promise, no one shall see you.
Eigi hefi ek fleira, þat þér megi gagn at vera.	Not have I more, that to-you may benefit to be.	I do not have any more that may be of benefit to you.
Hall einn vil ek gefa þér til skemmtunar".	Piece-of-marble one will I give to-you for amusement".	There is a piece of marble that I will give to you for your amusement".
Tók hann þá hallinn ór pungi sínum.	Took he then the-piece-of-marble from pouch his.	He took the piece of marble then from his pouch.
Fylgdi honum einn stálbroddr.	Following it a steel-point.	There followed a steel point.
Hallrinn var þríhyrndr.	The-piece-of-marble was three-sided.	The piece of marble was three sided.
Hann var hvítr í miðju, en rauðr öðrum megin, en gul rönd utan um.	It was white in the-middle, and red other side, and gold around outside about.	It was white in the middle, red on one side, and gold around the outside.
Dvergrinn mælti:	The-dwarf said:	The dwarf said:

The Tale of Thorsteinn House-Power (Old Norse)

Old Norse	Literal	English
"Ef þú pjakkar broddinum á hallinn, þar sem hann er hvítr, þá kemr haglhríð svá mikil, at engi þorir móti at sjá.	"If you prick the-point of the-piece-of-marble, there where it is white, then comes hailstorm so great, that none dare to-meet to see.	"If you prick the point of the piece of marble where it is white, then there will come a hailstorm so great that none will dare to look towards it.
En ef þú vilt þíða þann snjó, þá skaltu pjakka þar, sem gulr er hallrinn, ok kemr þá sólskin, svá at allt bræðir.	Then if you wish thaw then snow, then shall-you prick there, where gold is the-marble, and comes then sunshine, so that all thaws.	Then if you wish to thaw the snow, then you should prick there, where the marble is gold, and then there will come sunshine, so that everything thaws.
En ef þú pjakkar þar í, sem rautt er, þá kemr þar ór eldr ok eimyrja með gneistaflaug, svá at engi má móti at sjá.	Then if you prick there in, where red is, then comes there out-of fire and embers with a-shower-of-sparks, so that none may meet to see.	Then if you prick there, where it is red, then there will come embers of fire with a shower of sparks, so much that none will dare to look towards
Þú mátt ok hæfa þat, sem þú vilt, með broddinum ok hallinum, ok hann kemr sjálfr aptr í hönd þér, þegar þú kallar.	You may also hit that, whatever you wish, with the-point and the-marble, and it comes itself back in hand to-you, as-soon-as you call.	You may also hit, whatever you wish, with the point and the marble, and it will come back by itself into your hand, as soon as you call for them.
Get ek nú ekki launat þér fleira at sinni".	Guess I now not repay you more than this".	I guess now that I cannot repay you more than this".
Þorsteinn þakkar honum gjafirnar.	Thorstein thanked him the-gifts.	Thorstein thanked him for the gifts.
Fór hann nú til sinna manna, ok var honum þessi ferð betr farin en ófarin.	Went he now to his men, and was to-him this journey better gone than unfinished.	He now went to his men, and to him the journey had gone better than when it was unfinished.
Þessu næst gefr þeim byr ok sigla í Austrveginn.	This next given them fair-wind and sailed to Eastern-Lands.	Next they were given a favourable wind and sailed to the Eastern-Lands.
Koma nú á fyrir þeim myrkr ok hafvillur, ok vita þeir ekki, hvar þeir fara, ok var þat hálfan mánuð, at þessi villa helzt.	Came now to before them fog and open-sea, and knew they not, where they travelled, and was that half a-month, that this lost-way held.	Now a fog came before them in the open sea, and they did not know where they travelled, and this held for half a month.

The Tale of Thorsteinn House-Power (Old Norse)

Old Norse	Literal	English
# 4	# 4	# 4
Þat var eitt kvöld, at þeir urðu varir við land.	It was one evening, that they became aware with land.	It was one evening that they were aware that they were close to land.
Köstuðu þeir nú akkerum ok lágu þar um nóttina.	Cast they now anchor and laid there about the-night.	They cast anchor and lay there overnight.
Um morguninn var gott veðr ok sólskin fagrt.	About morning was good weather and sunshine fair.	In the morning the weather was good with fair sunshine.
Váru þeir þá komnir á einn fjörð langan, ok sjá þeir þar hlíðir fagrar ok skóga.	Were they then come to a fjord long, and saw they there slope fair and forests.	They came to a long fjord, and saw fair slopes and forests.
Engi maðr var sá innanborðs, at þetta land þekkti.	No man was saw aboard, that this land knew.	There was no man aboard that saw the land and knew this land.
Ekki sáu þeir kvikt, hvárki dýr né fugla.	Not saw they living-thing, neither wild-animals nor birds.	They saw no living thing, neither animals nor birds.
Reistu þeir nú tjald á landi ok bjuggust vel um.	Raised they now tents on the-land and settled well about.	They now raised tents on the land and settled there well.
At morgni mælti Þorsteinn til sinna manna:	At morning spoke Thorstein to his men:	At morning Thorstein spoke to his men:
"Ek vil gera yðr kunnigt um ætlan mína.	"I wish to-make you know about intentions mine.	"I wish to let you know about my intentions.
Þér skuluð bíða mín hér sex nætr.	You should await me here six nights.	You should wait for me here for six nights.
Ætla ek mér at kanna land þetta".	Intend I me to explore the-land this".	It is my intention to explore this land.
Þeim þótti mikit fyrir því ok vilja með honum fara, en Þorsteinn vill þat eigi, "ok ef ek kem eigi aptr, áðr sjau sólir eru af himni",	They thought much for therefore and wished with him to-travel, but Thorstein wished that not, "and if I come not back, after seven suns they-are of the-sky",	They thought much of this because they also wished to travel with him, but Thorstein did not wish for that, "and if I do not come back before the seventh sunset in the sky",

The Tale of Thorsteinn House-Power (Old Norse)

Old Norse	Literal	English
segir hann, "þá skuluð þér sigla heim ok segja svá Óláfi konungi, at mér mun ekki auðit verða aptr at koma".	said he, "then should you sail home and tell so Olaf the-king, that I should not fated be return to come".	he said, "then you should sail home and tell King Olaf that I am not fated to return home".
Gengu þeir þá með honum upp á skóginn.	Went they then with him up to the-forests.	They went with him up to the forests.
Því næst hvarf hann þeim, ok fóru þeir aptr til skips ok breyttu eptir því, sem Þorsteinn bauð þeim.	Then next disappeared he from-them, and went they back to the-ships and behaved after accordingly, as Thorstein asked them.	Then next he disappeared from their sight, and they went back to the ships and behaved, as Thorstein had asked them.
Nú er at segja af Þorsteini, at allan þann dag gengr hann um mörkina ok verðr við ekki varr.	Now is to say that Thorstein, about all the day went he about the-trees and came with not aware.	Now is to say of Thorstein, that all day he went through the trees and was not aware of anything.
En at áliðnum degi kemr hann á eina braut breiða.	Then that following day came he to a way broad.	Then the following day he came to a broad road.
Hann gekk eptir brautinni, þangat til at aptnaði.	He went after turned-away, from-there to the the-evening.	He turned to follow it until the evening.
Gekk hann þá brott af brautinni ok víkr at einni stórri eik ok stígr upp í hana.	Went he then away of turning and moved towards a large oak and climbed up it he.	He turned off the track and moved towards a large oak tree and he climbed up it.
Var þar nóg rúm í at liggja.	Was there enough room of to lie-down.	There was enough room for him to lie down.
Sefr hann þar um nóttina.	Slept he there about the-night.	He slept there for the night.
En er sólin kom upp, heyrir hann dunur miklar ok manna mál.	When that sunrise came up, heard he a-din great and men's conversations.	When sunrise came, he heard a great din and men talking.
Sá hann þá, hvar margir menn ríða.	Saw he then, were many men riding.	He then saw that there were many man riding.
Þeir váru tveir ok tuttugu.	They were two and twenty.	There were twenty two.
Þá bar svá skjótt um fram.	Then bore so swiftly about from.	They came so swiftly past.
Undraðist Þorsteinn mjök vöxt þeira.	Surprised Thorstein much grown they-were.	Thorstein was surprised by how large they were.

The Tale of Thorsteinn House-Power (Old Norse)

Old Norse	Literal	English
Hafði hann eigi sét jafnstóra menn fyrr.	Had he not seen equally-large men before.	He had not seen men as large before.
Þorsteinn klæðir sik.	Thorstein clothed himself.	Thorstein clothed himself.
Líðr nú morgininn til þess, at sól er komin í landsuðr.	Passed now morning to this, that the-sun was coming to the-south-east.	Now the morning passed so that the sun was coming to the South-East.

5

Old Norse	Literal	English
Nú sér Þorsteinn þrjá menn ríða vel vápnaða ok svá stóra, at enga menn sá hann fyrr jafnstóra.	Now saw Thorstein three men riding well weaponed and saw great, that none men saw him before equally-as-big.	Now Thorstein saw three men riding well armed and very large, no men had he seen equally as big.
Sá var mestr, er í miðit reið, í gullskotnum klæðum á bleikum hesti, en hinir tveir riðu á grám hestum í rauðum skarlatsklæðum.	So was the-most, then in the-middle riding, in gold-trimmed clothes a pale horse, but the-other two rode on grey horses in red scarlet-clothing.	The most large, then riding in the middle, was in gold-trimmed clothes on a pale horse, but the other two rode on grey horses in red scarlet clothing.
En er þeir kómu þar gegnt, sem Þorsteinn var, mælti sá, sem fyrir þeim var, ok nam staðar:	And when they came there opposite, where Thorstein was, spoke so, as for they were, and took standing:	And when they came opposite where Thorstein was, they spoke where they were, and stood:
"Hvat er kvikt í eikinni?"	"What is alive in the-oak?"	"What is alive in that oak?"
Þorsteinn gekk þá á veginn fyrir þá ok heilsaði þeim, en þeir ráku upp hlátr mikinn, ok mælti inn mikli maðr:	Thorstein went then to the-road before-them then and greeted them, but they drove up laughter much, and spoke the larger man:	Thorstein then went to the road before them and then greeted them, but they erupted with much laughter, and the larger man spoke:
"Sjaldsénir eru oss þvílíkir menn, eða hvert er nafn þitt, eða hvaðan ertu?"	"Rarely-seen are us the-like men, but what is name yours, and from-where are-you?"	"Rarely have we seen the like of such a man, but what is your name, and where are you from?"
Þorsteinn nefndi sik ok kveðst vera kallaðr bæjarmagn, "en kyn mitt er í Noregi.	Thorstein named himself and said being called House-Power, "and kin mine is in Norway.	Thorstein named himself and said about-being called House-Power, "and my kin is in Norway.
Er ek hirðmaðr Óláfs konungs".	Am I court-man Olaf's the-king".	I am a court man of King Olaf".

The Tale of Thorsteinn House-Power (Old Norse)

Old Norse	Literal	English
Inn mikli maðr brosti ok mælti:	The largest man burst-out-laughing and said:	The largest man burst out laughing and said:
"Mest er logit frá hirðprýði hans, ef hann hefir engan vaskligri.	"Mostly is a-lie from court his, if he has no-one braver.	"Most about his court must be lies if he has no one braver.
Þykki mér þú heldr mega heita bæjarbarn en bæjarmagn".	Think me you rather may be-named House-Child than House-Power".	I think you may rather be called House-Child than House-Power".
"Lát nokkut fylgja nafnfesti",	"Have some following naming-gift",	"Give me a naming gift then",
segir Þorsteinn.	said Thorstein.	said Thorstein.
Inn mikli maðr tók fingrgull ok gaf Þorsteini.	The largest man took finger-gold and gave Thorstein.	The largest man took a gold ring from his finger and gave it to Thorstein.
Þat vá þrjá aura.	That was three ounces.	It was three ounces.
Þorsteinn mælti:	Thorstein spoke:	Thorstein spoke:
"Hvert er þitt nafn, eða hverrar ættar ertu, eða í hvert land er ek kominn?"	"What is your name, and whose lineage are-you, and in what land have I come?"	"What is your name, and whose lineage are you, and in what land have I come?"
"Goðmundr heiti ek.	"Godmund named I.	"I am named Godmund.
Ræð er þar fyrir, sem á Glæsisvöllum heitir.	Ruler am here over, which is Glasir-Plains named.	I rule over here, which is named Glasir-Plains.
Þar þjónar til þat land, er Risaland heitir.	There serve to that land, which Giant-Land named.	There serves to that land, which is named Giant-Land.
Ek er konungsson, en mínir sveinar heitir annarr Fullsterkr, en annarr Allsterkr, eða sáttu enga menn ríða hér um í morgin?"	I am a-king's-son, and my companions named one Full-Strong, and another All-Strong, and saw-you any men riding here about in the-morning?"	I am a king's son and my companions, one is named Full-Strong, and the other All-Strong, and did you see any men riding through here in the morning?"
Þorsteinn mælti:	Thorstein spoke:	Thorstein spoke:
"Hér riðu um tveir menn ok tuttugu ok létu eigi lítinn".	"Here rode about two men and twenty and had none little".	"Twenty two men rode through here and none were little".
"Þeir eru sveinar mínir",	"They were men mine",	"They were my men",

The Tale of Thorsteinn House-Power (Old Norse)

Old Norse	Literal	English
segir Goðmundr.	said Godmund.	said Godmund.
"Þat land liggr hér næst, er Jötunheimar heitir.	"That land lying here next-to, is Giant-Land named.	"That land lying next to here is named Giant-Land.
Þar ræðr sá konungr, er Geirröðr heitir.	There rules so the-king, who Geirrod named.	So there rules the king who is named Geirrod.
Undir hann erum vér skattgildir.	Under him are we tributaries.	We are tributaries under him.
Faðir minn hét Úlfheðinn trausti.	Father mine is-named Ulfhedin Trusty.	My father is named Ulfhedin Trusty.
Hann var kallaðr Goðmundr sem allir aðrir, þeir á Glæsisvöllum búa.	He was called Godmund as all others, they who Glasir-Plains live.	He was called Godmund as are all others who live in Glasir-Plains.
En faðir minn fór í Geirröðargarða at afhenda konungi skatta sína, ok í þeiri ferð fekk hann bana.	But father mine went to Geirrod's-Town to of-hand the-king tax his, and on their journey got he death.	But my father went to Geirrod's-Town to hand taxes to the king, but on their journey they got death.
Hefir konungr gert mér boð, at ek skyldi drekka erfi eptir föður minn ok taka slíkar nafnbætr sem faðir minn hafði, en þó unum vér illa við at þjóna Jötnum".	Has the-king made me an-invite, that I should drink inheritance after father mine and take such name-titles as father mine had, but though happy we badly with that serving Giants".	The king has made me an invite, for me to drink to his honour and take such titles that my father had, but we are not happy about serving giants".
"Hví riðu yðrir menn undan?"	"Why rode your men before?",	"Why did your men ride before?",
segir Þorsteinn.	said Thorstein.	said Thorstein.
"Mikil á skilr land vort",	"Great is separating land ours",	"There is a great separation of our land",
segir Goðmundr.	said Godmund.	said Godmund.
"Sú heitir Hemra.	"So named Hemra.	"It is called Hemra.
Hún er svá djúp ok ströng, at hana vaða engir hestar nema þeir, sem vér kumpánar eigum.	She is so deep and strong, that she wades no horses except they, which we fellows own.	It is so deep and strong, that no horses can wade it, except for the three which we are on.

The Tale of Thorsteinn House-Power (Old Norse)

Old Norse	Literal	English
Skulu hinir ríða fyrir uppsprettu árinnar, ok finnumst vér í kveld".	Shall others ride before up-spring the-river, and meet we in the-evening".	The others shall ride before the river spring, and we will meet in the evening".
"Þat mundi skemmtan at fara með yðr",	"That could-be amusement to travel with you",	"It could be an amusement to travel with you",
segir Þorsteinn, "ok sjá, hvat þar verðr til tíðenda".	said Thorstein, "and see, what there becomes to news".	said Thorstein, "and see what happens".
"Eigi veit ek, hversu þat hentar",	"Not know I, how-so that suits",	"I do not know how that suits",
segir Goðmundr, "því at þú munt kristinn".	said Godmund, "because that you must-be Christian".	said Godmund", because you must be a Christian".
"Ek mun mik ábyrgjast",	"I could myself take-care-of",	"I can take care of myself",
segir Þorsteinn.	said Thorstein.	said Thorstein.
"Ekki vilda ek þú hlytir vánt af mér",	"Not wish I you to-get difficulty from me",	"I do not wish for you to get any difficulty from me",
sagði Goðmundr, "en ef Óláfr konungr vill leggja gæfu á með oss, þá mundi ek framt á treysta, at þú færir".	said Godmund, "but if Olaf the-king will grant luck then with us, then should I provide to trust, that you travel".	said Godmund", but if King Olaf will grant you luck to travel with us, then I shall trust you to travel".
Þorsteinn segist því heita vilja.	Thorstein said accordingly promised he-wished.	Thorstein gave him his word as he wished.
Goðmundr biðr hann fara á bak með sér, ok svá gerði hann.	Godmund asked him to-travel on the-back with him, and so did he.	Godmund asked him to travel back with him, and so he did.
Ríða þeir nú til árinnar.	Rode they now to the-river.	They now rode to the river.
Var þar eitt hús, ok tóku þeir þar önnur klæði ok klæddu sik ok sína hesta.	Was there a house, and took they there other clothes and dressed themselves and their horses.	There was a house, and they took their other clothes and dressed themselves and their horses.
Þau klæði váru þeirar náttúru, at ekki festi vatn á þeim, en vatnit var svá kalt, at þegar hljóp drep í, ef nokkut vöknaði.	Their clothes were there natured, that not joined the-water to them, about the-water was so cold, that there ran gangrene to, if anything became-wet.	Their clothes were of a nature that the water could not touch them, because the water was so cold, that gangrene ran if anything became wet.
Riðu þeir nú yfir ána.	Rode they now across the-river.	They now rode across the river.

The Tale of Thorsteinn House-Power (Old Norse)

Old Norse	Literal	English
Hestarnir óðu sterkliga.	The-horses waded strongly.	The horses waded strongly.
Hestr Goðmundar rasaði, ok varð Þorsteinn vátr á tánni, ok hljóp þegar drep í.	Horse Godmund's tumbled, and became Thorstein water about toe, and ran there gangrene to.	Godmund's horse tumbled, and Thorstein's toe came into the water, and there ran gangrene.
En er þeir kómu af ánni, breiddu þeir niðr klæðin til þerris.	When that they came off the-river, spread they down clothes to dry.	When they came off the river, they spread their clothes to dry.
Þorsteinn hjó af sér tána, ok fannst þeim mikit um hreysti hans.	Thorstein hewed off his toe, and found they much about bravery his.	Thorstein cut his toe off, and they thought much of his bravery.
Ríða þeir nú sinn veg.	Rode they now their way.	They now rode on their way.
Bað Þorsteinn þá eigi fela sik, "því at ek kann at gera þann hulinshjálm, at mik sér engi".	Asked Thorstein then not hide him, "because that I can to make then helm-of-invisibility, that me see none".	Thorstein asked them not to hide him, "because I have a helm of invisibility, that none see me".
Goðmundr segir þat góða kunnáttu.	Godmund said that good skills.	Godmund said that was a good skill.
Kómu þeir nú til borgarinnar, ok kómu menn Goðmundar í móti honum.	Came they now to the-town, and came men Godmund's to meet him.	They now came to the town, and Godmund's men came to meet him.
Riðu þeir nú í borgina.	Rode they now into the-town.	They now rode into the town.
Mátti þar nú heyra alls háttar hljóðfæri, en ekki þótti Þorsteini af setning slegit.	Could they now hear all kinds musical-instruments, but not thought Thorstein of the-setting struck.	They could now hear all kinds of musical instruments, but Thorstein did not think much of the settings being played.
Geirröðr konungr kom nú í mót þeim ok fagnaði þeim vel, ok var þeim skipat eitt steinhús eða höll at sofa í ok menn til fengnir at leiða hesta þeira á stall.	Geirrod the-king came now to meet them and celebrated they well, and were they directed-to a stone-house and a-hall to sleep in and men to get to led horses there to stable.	King Geirrod now came to meet them and they were well welcomed, and they were directed to a stone house and a hall to sleep in, and men led their horses to a stable.
Var Goðmundr leiddr í konungshöll.	Was Godmund led to the-king's-hall.	Godmund was led to the king's hall.
Konungr sat í hásæti ok jarl sá hjá honum, er Agði hét.	The-king sat on a-high-seat and the-earl so beside him, was Agdi named.	The king sat on a high seat and the earl so beside him, was named Agdi.

The Tale of Thorsteinn House-Power (Old Norse)

Old Norse	Literal	English
Hann réð fyrir því heraði, er Grundir heita.	He ruled over therefore district, was Grundir named.	He ruled over the district, which was named Grundir.
Þat er á millum Risalands ok Jötunheima.	It was in between Giant-Land and Giant-Home.	It was in between Giant-Land and Giant-Home.
Hann hafði atsetu at Gnípalundi.	He had a-seat at Gnipalund.	He had an estate at Gnipalund.
Hann var fjölkunnigr, ok menn hans váru tröllum líkari en mönnum.	He was skilled-in-magic, and men his were trolls like than men.	He was skilled in magic, and his men were more like trolls than men.
Goðmundr settist á skörina fyrir öndvegit gagnvart konungi.	Godmund sat beside high-seat before opposite going-from the-king.	Godmund sat beside the high seat opposite the king.
Var sá siðr þeira, at konungsson skyldi ekki í hásæti sitja, fyrr en hann hafði tekit nafnbætr eptir föður sinn ok drukkit væri it fyrsta full.	Was so the-custom theirs, that the-king's-son should not in high-seat sit, before that he had taken name-titles after father his and drink-to was the first drunk.	It was their custom, that the king's son should not sit in the high seat, before he had taken his titles and the first drink to honour his father had been drunk.
Ríss þar nú upp in vænsta veizla, ok drukku menn glaðir ok kátir ok fóru síðan at sofa.	Rose there now up the good feast, and drank men gladly and merry and went then to sleep.	They now rose up and had a good feast, and the men drank gladly and merrily, and then went to sleep.
En er Goðmundr kom í hús sitt, sýndi Þorsteinn sik.	And when Godmund came to the-house his, showed Thorstein himself.	And when Godmund came to his house, Thorstein showed himself.
Hlógu þeir at honum.	Laughed they at him.	They laughed at him.
Goðmundr sagði mönnum sínum, hverr hann var, ok bað þá ekki hafa hann at hlátri.	Godmund told the-men his, who he was, and ordered then not have he to laughter.	Godmund told his men who he was and ordered them not to laugh at him.
Ok sofa þeir af um nóttina.	And slept they of through the-night.	And they slept through the night.

The Tale of Thorsteinn House-Power (Old Norse)

Old Norse	Literal	English
# 6	# 6	# 6
Nú er morginn kom, váru þeir snemma á fótum.	Now when morning came, were they early about feet.	Now when morning came, they were up early and on their feet.
Var Goðmundr leiddr til konungs hallar.	Was Godmund led to the-king's hall.	Godmund was led to the king's hall.
Konungr fagnaði honum vel.	The-king celebrated him well.	The king welcomed him well.
"Viljum vér nú vita",	"Wish we now know",	"We wish to know",
segir konungr, "hvárt þú vilt veita mér slíka hlýðni sem faðir þinn, ok vil ek þá auka þínar nafnbætr.	said the-king, "whether you wish to-grant me such homage as father yours, and wish I then extra your name-titles.	said the king, "whether you wish to grant me such homage as your father, and then I wish to give you more titles.
Skaltu þá halda Risalandi ok sverja mér eiða".	Shall-you then keep Giant-Land and swear to-me oath".	You shall then keep Giant-Land and swear an oath to me".
Goðmundr svarar:	Godmund answered:	Godmund answered:
"Ekki er þat lög at krefja svá unga menn til eiða".	"Not is that law that demand so young men to oath".	"It is not lawful to demand oaths from a man as young as me".
"Þat skal vera",	"That shall be",	"So it shall be",
sagði konungr.	said the-king.	said the king.
Síðan tók konungr guðvefjarskikkju ok lagði yfir Goðmund ok gaf honum konungsnafn, tók síðan horn mikit ok drakk til Goðmundi.	Then took the-king a-precious-cloak and laid over Godmund and gave him the-king's-name, took afterwards horn great and drank to Godmund.	Then the king took a precious cloak and laid it over Godmund and gave him the title of king, and then took a great horn and drank to Godmund.
Hann tók við horninu ok þakkaði konungi.	He took with the-horn and thanked the-king.	He took the horn and thanked the king.
Síðan stóð Goðmundr upp ok sté á stokkinn fyrir sæti konungs ok strengdi þess heit, at hann skal engum konungi þjóna né hlýðni veita, meðan Geirröðr konungr lifði.	Afterwards stood Godmund up and stepped onto the-footboard before seat the-king's and boldly this declared, that he shall no king serve nor homage grant, while Geirrod the-king lived.	Afterwards Godmund stood up and stepped onto the footboard before the king's seat and boldly declared, that he would serve no king nor grant homage, while King Geirrod lived.

The Tale of Thorsteinn House-Power (Old Norse)

Old Norse	Literal	English
Konungr þakkaði honum, sagði sér þat þykkja meira vert en þótt hann hefði eiða svarit.	The-king thanked him, told him that valued more worth that though he had oaths sworn.	The king thanked him, and told him that he would have valued more if he had sworn oaths.
Síðan drakk Goðmundr af horninu ok gekk til sætis síns.	Afterwards drank Godmund of the-horn and went to seat his.	Afterwards Godmund drank from the horn and went to his seat.
Váru menn þá glaðir ok kátir.	Were men then glad and merry.	Then the men were glad and merry.
Tveir menn eru nefndir með Agða jarli.	Two men were named with Agdi the-earl.	Two men were with Earl Agdi.
Hét annarr Jökull, en annarr Frosti.	Named one Jokul, and the-other Frosti.	One was named Jokul, and the other Frosti.
Þeir váru öfundsjúkir.	They were jealous.	They were jealous.
Jökull þreif upp uxahnútu ok kastaði í lið Goðmundar.	Jokul grabbed up ox-bone and threw at the-company-of Godmund.	Jokul grabbed an ox-bone and threw it at Godmund's company.
Þorsteinn sá þat ok henti á lopti ok sendi aptr, ok kom á nasir þeim, er Gustr hét, ok brotnaði í honum nefit ok ór honum allar tennrnar, en hann fell í óvit.	Thorstein saw that and caught in the-air and sent back, and came about nose them, was Gust named, and broke it his nose and through his all teeth, and he fell to unconscious.	Thorstein saw that, caught it in the air and sent it back, and it hit the nose of a man named Gust, and it broke his nose and all his teeth, and he fell unconscious.
Geirröðr konungr reiddist ok spurði, hverr berði beinum yfir hans borð.	Geirrod the-king rose and asked, who threw the-bone across his table.	Geirrod the king rose up and asked who threw the bone across the table.
Sagði hann, at reynt skyldi verða, hverr sterkastr væri í steinkastinu, áðr en úti væri.	Said he, that test should be, who strongest was in stone-throwing, after then out was.	He said that there should be a test to find out before it was over who was the strongest at stone throwing.
Síðan kallar konungr til tvá menn, Drött ok Hösvi:	Afterwards called the-king to two men, Drott and Hosvir:	Afterwards the king called two men, Drott and Hosvir:
"Farið þit ok sækið gullhnött minn ok berið hann hingat".	"Go you-two and seek gold-ball mine and bring it here".	"You two go and seek my gold ball and bring it here".
Þeir fóru ok kómu aptr með eitt selshöfuð, er stóð tíu fjórðunga.	They went and came back with a seal's-head, and weighed ten quarters.	They went and came back with a seal's head, which weighed ten quarters.

The Tale of Thorsteinn House-Power (Old Norse)

Old Norse	Literal	English
Þat var glóanda, svá at sindraði af svá sem ór afli, en fitan draup niðr sem glóanda bik.	It was glowing, so that sparkled of so as from a-forge, and fat dripped down as burning pitch.	It was glowing hot, so that sparks came off it as if from a forge, and fat dripped from it like burning pitch.
Konungr mælti:	The-king spoke:	The king spoke:
"Takið nú knöttinn ok kastið hverr at öðrum.	"Take now the-ball and throw each to other.	"Now take the ball and throw it to each other.
Hverr, sem niðr fellir, skal fara útlægr ok missa eignir sínar, en hverr eigi þorir at henda, skal heita níðingr".	Anyone, who down drops, shall go outlawed and lose property his, and anyone not daring to catch, shall be-named a-coward".	Anyone who drops it shall go outlawed and lose his property, and anyone who does not dare to catch, shall be named a coward.

7

Nú kastar Dröttr knettinum at Fullsterk.	Now threw Drott the-ball at Full-Strong.	Now Drott threw the ball at Full-Strong.
Hann greip á móti annarri hendi.	He gripped to meet one hand.	He gripped against it with one hand.
Þorsteinn sá, at honum varð orkufátt, ok hljóp undir knöttinn.	Thorstein saw, that he became low-energy, and ran behind the-ball.	Thorstein saw that his strength weakened, and got behind the ball.
Þeir snöruðu at Frosta, því at kapparnir stóðu fremstir við hvárntveggja bekkinn.	They threw at Frosti, because that champions stood foremost against either-side of-the-bench.	They threw it at Frosti, because the champions stood in front of the benches on either side.
Frosti tók mót sterkliga, ok kom svá nær andliti hans, at kinnbeinit rifnaði.	Frosti took against strongly, and came so near face his, that chin-bone split.	Frosti caught it strongly, and it came so near his face, that it split his chin bone.
Hann kastar knettinum at Allsterk.	He threw the-ball at All-Strong.	He threw the ball at All-Strong.
Hann tók í móti báðum höndum, ok lá við, at hann mundi kikna, áðr Þorsteinn studdi hann.	He received it against both hands, and had with, that he would-have bent-backwards, before Thorstein steadied him.	He caught it with both hands, and he would have bent backwards, before Thorstein steadied him.
Allsterkr snaraði at Agða jarli, en hann greip móti báðum höndum.	All-Strong turned-quickly at Agdi the-earl, and he grabbed against both hands.	All-Strong hurled the ball at Earl Agdi, and he caught it with both hands.

The Tale of Thorsteinn House-Power (Old Norse)

Old Norse	Literal	English
Fitan kom í skeggit á honum, ok logaði þat allt, ok var honum til þess annast at afhenda knöttinn ok fleygir at Goðmundi konungi.	Fat came to beard of his, and blazed that all, and was he to this he-took-care-of that off-handed the-ball and flew-it at Godmund the-king.	Burning fat went on to his beard, and it was all ablaze, and as he had to take care of that, he hurriedly threw the ball at King Godmund.
En Goðmundr snaraði at Geirröði konungi, en hann veik sér undan, ok urðu þeir fyrir Dröttr ok Hösvir, ok fengu þeir bana.	Then Godmund flew-it at Geirrod the-king, but he turned himself away, and came they for Drott and Hosvir, and caught them dead.	Then Godmund threw it at King Geirrod, but he turned out of the way, and it came to Drott and Hosvir, and killed them both.
En knöttrinn kom á glerglugg einn ok svá út í díki þat, sem grafit var um borgina, ok hljóp upp eldr logandi.	Then the-ball came to glass-window one and so out into the-moat that, which dug was about the-city, and ran up the-flames ablaze.	Then the ball went through a glass window and out into the moat, which was dug around the city, and the flames ran up in a blaze.
Var nú lokit þessu gamni.	Was now ended this game.	The game was now ended.
Tóku menn þá til drykkju.	Took men then to drinking.	The men took to drinking.
Sagði Agði jarl, at honum hrysi hugr við jafnan, er hann kom í flokk Goðmundar.	Said Agdi the-earl, that he trembled thought with every-time, that he came to band Godmund's.	Earl Agdi said that he thought he trembled every time he came to Godmund's company.
Um kveldit gekk Goðmundr at sofa ok hans menn.	About evening went Godmund to seep and his men.	In the evening Godmund went to sleep and so did his men.
Þökkuðu þeir Þorsteini hjástöðu, at þeim hefði slysalaust farit.	Thanked they Thorstein beside-standing, to them had accidents-without gone.	They thanked Thorstein for standing by them, so that they were without accidents.
Þorsteinn kvað lítit til reynt, "eða hvat mun til gamans haft á morgin?"	Thorstein said little to test, "but what should to games have in the-morning?"	Thorstein said it was nothing much, "but what sort of games will we have in the morning?"
"Konungr mun láta glíma",	"The-king should have wrestling",	"The king shall have wrestling",
segir Goðmundr, "ok munu þeir þá hefna sín, því at fjarstætt er um afl várt".	said Godmund, "and should they then avenge themselves, accordingly to far-away from about strength ours".	said Godmund, "and they shall avenge themselves accordingly because their strength is far more than ours".
"Konungs gæfa mun styrkja oss",	"The-king's luck should strengthen us",	"The king's luck shall strengthen us",

25

The Tale of Thorsteinn House-Power (Old Norse)

Old Norse	Literal	English
segir Þorsteinn.	said Thorstein.	said Thorstein.
"Hirðið eigi, þótt þér berizt þangat at, sem ek er fyrir".	"Take-care not, though you bear from-there that, which I am before".	"Take care not to bear it there, but bear towards me".
Sofa þeir af um nóttina.	Slept they of through night.	They slept through the night.
En at morgni fór hverr til sinnar skemmtunar, en matsveinar at dúka borð.	And at morning went each to his entertainment, while food-servants to tablecloths table.	And in the morning each went to his entertainment, while the food servants put the tablecloths on the table.
Geirröðr konungr spurði, hvárt menn vildu ekki glíma, en þeir sögðu, at hann skyldi ráða.	Geirrod the-king asked, which men wished not wrestling, and they said, as he should decide.	King Geirrod asked, which men wished to wrestle, and they said that he should decide.
Síðan afklæðast þeir ok tókust fangbrögðum.	Afterwards undressed they and took to-wrestling.	Then they undressed and took to wrestling.
Þorsteinn þóttist eigi sét hafa slíkan atgang, því at allt skalf, þá þeir fellu, ok lékst mjök á mönnum Agða jarls.	Thorstein thought not seen had such to-going, because that all shook, then they fell, and played much to men Agdi the-earl's.	Thorstein thought he had not seen such a clash, because everywhere shook, whenever they fell, and this happened often to Earl Agdi's men.
Frosti gekk nú fram á gólfit ok mælti:	Frosti went now to the floor and spoke:	Frosti now went to the floor and said:
"Hverr skal mér á móti?"	"Who shall me to meet?"	"Who shall oppose me?"
"Til mun verða einhverr",	"To should be someone",	"There will be someone",
sagði Fullsterkr.	said Full-Strong.	said Full-Strong.
Ráðast þeir nú á, ok váru með þeim miklar sviptingar, ok er Frosti miklu sterkari.	Arranged they now to, and were with they much tussle, and was Frosti much stronger.	They now attacked, and there were great upheavals with them, and Frosti was much stronger.
Berast þeir nú at Goðmundi.	Bore they now to Godmund.	They now arrived at Godmund.
Frosti tekr hann upp á bringu sér ok keiktist mjök.	Frosti took him up by the-chest his and bent much.	Frosti took him up by his chest and he had to bend his knees.

The Tale of Thorsteinn House-Power (Old Norse)

Old Norse	Literal	English
Þorsteinn slær fæti sínum á knésbætr honum, ok fell Frosti á bak aptr, en Fullsterkr á hann ofan.	Thorstein struck feet his about the-back-of-the-knees his, and fell Frosti on back back, but Full-Strong on him over.	Thorstein struck his foot on the back of his knees, and Frosti fell on his back, and Full-Strong fell on him.
Hnakkinn sprakk á Frosta ok olnbogarnir.	The-back-of-the-head broke of Frosti and elbows.	The back of Frosti's head was broken, and so were his elbows.
Hann stóð seint upp ok mælti:	He stood slowly up and spoke:	He slowly stood up and spoke:
"Ekki eru þér einir at gamninu, eða hví er svá fúlt í flokki yðrum?"	"Not are you alone in the-game, and what is so foul among men yours?"	"You are not alone in this game, and what is it that is so foul among your men?"
"Skammt á nefit at kenna ór kjaptinum",	"Short is nose to know from the-mouth",	"Your nose is too close to your own mouth",
sagði Fullsterkr.	said Full-Strong.	said Full-Strong.
Jökull stóð þá upp, ok Allsterkr réðst þá í móti honum, ok var þeira atgangr inn harðasti.	Jokul stood then up, and All-Strong moved then to oppose him, and were they to-going the hardest.	Jokul then stood up, and All-Strong moved to oppose him, and their clash was the hardest yet.
En þó var Jökull sterkari ok bar hann at bekk, þar sem Þorsteinn var fyrir.	But though was Jokul stronger and carried him to a-bench, there as Thorstein was before.	But Jokul was stronger and carried him to a bench, where Thorstein was.
Jökull vildi draga Allsterk frá bekknum ok togast við fast, en Þorsteinn helt honum.	Jokul wished-to drag All-Strong from the-bench and pulled against hard, but Thorstein held him.	Jokul tried had to drag All-Strong from the bench and pulled hard against him, but Thorstein held him.
Jökull tók svá fast, at hann sté í hallargólfit upp at ökkla, en Þorsteinn hratt Allsterk frá sér, ok fell Jökull á bak aptr, ok gekk ór liði á honum fótrinn.	Jokul tugged so hard, that he stepped in hall-floor up to ankles, then Thorstein pushed All-Strong away-from him, and fell Jokul on back back, and went out-of dislocated of his leg.	Jokul pulled so hard, that his feet sunk into the hall floor up to his ankles, then Thorstein pushed All-Strong away from him, and Jokul fell back and dislocated his leg.
Allsterkr gekk til bekkjar, en Jökull stóð upp seint ok mælti:	All-Strong went to bench, but Jokul stood up slowly and spoke:	All-Strong went back to his bench, but Jokul stood up slowly and spoke:
"Ekki sjáum vér alla þessa, sem á bekknum eru".	"Not see we all this, which on that-bench they-are".	"We cannot see everyone that is on that bench".

The Tale of Thorsteinn House-Power (Old Norse)

Old Norse	Literal	English
Geirröðr segir Goðmundi, hvárt hann vildi ekki glíma.	Geirrod said-to Godmund, whether he would not wrestle.	Geirrod asked Godmund if he would wrestle.
En hann kveðst aldri glímt hafa, en kveðst eigi vildu synjast.	And he said never wrestled had, but said not would refuse.	And he said that he had never wrestled, but he would not refuse.
Konungr bað Agða jarl hefna manna sinna.	The-king ordered Agdi the-earl avenge men his.	The king ordered Earl Agdi to avenge his men.
Hann kveðst löngu hafa af lagt, en segir konung ráða skyldu.	He said long had of left, but told the-king advice would.	He said that he had given up long ago, but he would do as the king decided.
Síðan afklæddust þeir.	Afterwards undressed they.	Then they undressed.
Eigi þóttist Þorsteinn sét hafa tröllsligri búk en á Agða.	Not thought Thorstein seen had troll-like thick-set than was Agdi.	Thorstein thought that he had not seen such a troll-like thick set man as Agdi.
Var hann blár sem hel.	Was he black as death.	He was black as death.
Goðmundr reis mót honum.	Godmund rose to-meet him.	Godmund rose to meet him.
Var hann hvítr á skinnslit.	Was he white in colour.	He was white in colour.
Agði jarl hösvaðist at honum ok lagði svá fast krummurnar at síðum hans, at allt gekk niðr at beini, ok bárust þeir víða um höllina.	Agdi the-earl went-for at him and had so fastened grabbed at sides his, that all went down to the-bone, and bore they widely about the-hall.	Earl Agdi went for him and grabbed at his sides so hard that it went down to the bone, and the carried widely around the hall.
Ok er þeir kómu þar, sem Þorsteinn var, þá brá Goðmundr jarli til sniðglímu ok sneri honum vakrliga.	And when they came there, where Thorstein was, then drew Godmund the-earl to hip-throw and turned him nimbly.	And when they came where Thorstein was, Godmund drew the earl into a hip throw and turned him nimbly.
Þorsteinn lagðist niðr fyrir fætr jarli, ok fell hann þá ok stakk niðr nösunum, ok brotnaði í honum þjófsnefit ok fjórar tennr.	Thorstein lay down before feet the-earl's, and fell he then and struck down on-the-nose, and broke was his thieving-nose and four teeth.	Thorstein lay down before the earl's feet, and then he fell and struck his nose, and his thieving nose was broken, and four teeth.
Jarl stóð upp ok mælti:	The-earl stood up and spoke:	The earl stood up and spoke:
"Þung verða gamalla manna föll, ok svá þyngst, at þrír gangi at einum".	"Heavy becomes the-old man falling, and so heaviest, when three go against one".	"Heavy becomes the old man falling, and heaviest, when it's three against one".

The Tale of Thorsteinn House-Power (Old Norse)

Old Norse	Literal	English
Fóru menn þá í klæði sín.	Went the-men then with-that clothed themselves.	With that the men clothed themselves.

8 | 8 | 8

Þessu næst fóru þeir konungr til borða.	This next went they the-king to the-tables.	After this the king and his guests went to the tables.
Töluðu þeir Agði jarl um, at þeir mundu einhvern prett við hafa haft, "því at mér býðr ávallt hita, er ek kem í þeira flokk".	Told they Agdi the-earl about, that they must-be some-way tricked against having had, "because that I invite always heat, when I come in their company".	Earl Agdi and the others said that they must have been tricked in some way, "because I always heat up, when I come in their company".
"Látum bíða",	"Leave-it abide",	"Let it be",
segir konungr, "sá mun koma, at okkr mun kunngera".	said the-king, "so shall come, that us should wiser".	said the king, "something will come and make us wiser".
Tóku menn þá at drekka.	Took men then to drinking.	Then the men took to drinking.
Þá váru borin inn tvau horn í höllina.	Then were brought in two horns into the-hall.	There were then two horns brought into the hall.
Þau átti Agði jarl, gersemar miklar, ok váru kölluð Hvítingar.	They had Agdi the-earl, treasured much, and were called Whitings.	They belonged to Earl Agdi, who treasured them, and they were called Whitings.
Þau váru tveggja álna há ok gulli búin.	They were two cubits high and gold prepared.	They were two cubits high and inlaid with gold.
Konungr lét sitt hornit ganga á hvárn bekk, "ok skal hverr drekka af í einu.	The-king had sat a-horn going to each bench, "and shall each drink of in one.	The king had set a horn on each bench, "and everyone shall drink from it in one.
Sá, sem því orkar eigi, skal fá byrlaranum eyri silfrs".	So, that accordingly able-to not, shall pay the-cup-bearer an-ounce-of silver".	So, therefore those not able to shall pay the cup bearer an ounce of silver".
Gekk engum af at drekka utan köppunum, en Þorsteinn gat svá til sét, at þeir, sem með Goðmundi váru, varð engi víttr.	Went none of to drink out-of the-cups, but Thorstein got so to seen, that they, which with Godmund were, became not bewitched.	No one was able to drink out of the cups, but Thorstein could see that those who were with Godmund did not become bewitched.

The Tale of Thorsteinn House-Power (Old Norse)

Old Norse	Literal	English
Drukku menn nú glaðir þat, sem eptir var dagsins, en um kveldit fóru menn at sofa.	Drank men now gladly that, as after was of-the-day, then about evening went men to sleep.	People now drank happily what was left of the day, but in the evening they went to sleep.
Goðmundr þakkaði Þorsteini fyrir góða hjástöðu.	Godmund thanked Thorstein for the-good beside-standing.	Godmund thanked Thorstein for his good help.
Þorsteinn spurði, nær endast mundi veizlan.	Thorstein asked, near ending would the-feast.	Thorstein asked, when the feast would end.
"At morgni skulu menn mínir ríða",	"At morning should men mine ride",	"In the morning my men shall ride",
segir Goðmundr.	said Godmund.	said Godmund.
"Veit ek, at nú lætr konungr allt við hafa.	"Know I, that now acts the-king all against have.	"I know that now the king will act against us with all he has.
Eru nú sýndar gersemar.	They-are now shown treasures.	When the treasures are shown.
Lætr konungr nú bera inn horn sitt it mikla.	Have the-king now brought in a-horn his this great.	Let the king now carry in his great horn.
Þat er kallat Grímr inn góði.	That is called Grim the Good.	That is called Grim the Good.
Þat er gersemi mikil ok þó galdrafullt ok búit með gull.	That is a-treasure great and though magic-full and inlaid with gold.	It is a great treasure, and magical and rich in gold.
Mannshöfuð er á stiklinum með holdi ok munni, ok þat mælir við menn ok segir fyrir óorðna hluti ok ef þat veit ófriðar ván.	A-man's-head is about the-narrow with flesh and a-mouth, and that speaks with men and said for unspoken lot and if that known un-peace is-expected.	A man's head is about the narrow end with flesh and a mouth, and it speaks to men and says unspoken things, and if war is expected.
Verðr þat bani vár, ef konungr veit, at kristinn maðr er með oss.	Becomes it the-death ours, if the-king knows, that a-Christian man is with us.	It will be the death of us if the king knows that a Christian man is with us.
Munum vér eigi þurfa at vera fésparir við hann".	Should we not need to be fee-sparing with him".	We should not need to spare wealth with him".
Þorsteinn sagði Grím eigi mæla fleira enn Óláfr konungr vildi, "en ek ætla, at Geirröðr sé feigr.	Thorstein said Grim not speak more than Olaf the-king wished, "and I suppose, that Geirrod is fated-to-die.	Thorstein said that Grim would not say to him any more than King Olaf wished, "and I suppose that Geirrod is a doomed man.

The Tale of Thorsteinn House-Power (Old Norse)

Old Norse	Literal	English
Þykki mér ráð, at þér hafið mín ráð heðan af.	Seems to-me advice, that you have my counsel from-hence of.	It seems to me to advise, that you do as I advise you from now on.
Skal ek sýna mik á morgin".	Shall I show myself in the-morning".	I shall show myself in the morning".
En þeir sögðu þat hættu ráð.	But they said that dangerous advice.	But they said that it was a dangerous decision.
Þorsteinn sagði, at Geirröðr vildi þá feiga, "eða hvat segir þú mér af Grími inum góða fleira?"	Thorstein said, that Geirrod wished then doomed, "but what say you to-me of Grim the Good more?"	Thorstein said that Geirrod wished them all doomed, "but what else can you tell me about Grim the Good"?
"Þat er frá honum at segja, at meðalmaðr má standa undir bugtinni á honum, en álnar breitt yfir beitina, ok er sá mestr drykkjumaðr í þeira liði, er drekkr beitina, en konungr drekkr af í einu.	"That is from him to say, that an-average-man may stand under the-curve of him, and a-yard broad across opening, and is so the-greatest drinking-man of their company, that drinks the-opening, but the-king drinks of all in-one.	"The first thing to say, is that an average man can stand under the curve of the horn, and it is a yard across at the opening, and the greatest drinking man in their company can drink deep into the horn, but only the king can drink it all in one.
Hverr maðr á at gefa Grími nokkura gersemi, en sú virðing þykkir honum sér mest ger, at í einu sé af drukkit.	Each man is to give Grim some treasure, but so worthy seems to-him to-see most done, that in one you of drink.	Each man has to give Grim something valuable, but most worthy honour to him is to drink it in one.
En ek veit, at mér ber fyrstum af at drekka, en þat er einskis manns þol at drekka þat í einu".	But I know, that I bear first of to drink, but that is nothing man endure than drink that in one".	But I know that I have to drink first, but it is no man's endurance to drink it at once".
Þorsteinn mælti:	Thorstein spoke:	Thorstein spoke:
"Þú skalt fara í serk minn, því at þér má þá ekki granda, þó at ólyfjan sé í drykknum.	"You shall go in shirt mine, because that you may then not to-injure, though that poison even if drink.	"You shall go in my shirt, because then you shall not come to injury, even if there is poison in the drink.
Tak kórónu af höfði þér ok gef Grími inum góða ok seg í eyra honum, at þú skalt gera honum miklu meira heiðr en Geirröðr, ok síðan skaltu láta sem þú drekkir.	Take the-crown off head yours and give Grim the Good and say in ear his, that you shall do him much more honour than Geirrod, and afterwards shall-you lay-out that you drink.	Take the crown off your head, and give it to Grim the Good, and say in his ear that you will do him much more honour than Geirrod, and afterwards shall you drink to that.

The Tale of Thorsteinn House-Power (Old Norse)

Old Norse	Literal	English
En eitr mun í horninu, ok skaltu steypa niðr næst þér, ok mun þik ekki saka.	Then poison should-be in the-horn, ad shall-you cast down near you, and shall you not injury.	Then should the poison be in the horn, you shall cast it down beside you, and you shall not be injured.
En þá er drykkjuskapr er úti, skaltu láta menn þína ríða".	But then when drinking is over, shall-you have men yours ride-away".	But when the drinking is over, have your men ride away".
Goðmundr sagði, at hann skuli ráða.	Godmund said, that he shall decide.	Godmund said, that he shall decide.
"En ef Geirröðr deyr, þá á ek alla Jötunheima, en ef hann lifir lengr, verðr þat bani vár".	"But if Geirrod dies, then with I all Giant-Home, but if he lives longer, becomes that death ours".	"But if Geirrod dies, then I own all the Giant-Home, but if he lives longer, that death will be ours".
Síðan sofa þeir af um nóttina.	Afterwards slept they of about the-night.	Afterwards they slept through the night.

9   9   9

Old Norse	Literal	English
Um morguninn eru þeir snemma á fótum ok taka sín klæði.	About morning were they soon about feet and took their clothes.	In the morning they got up early and took their clothes.
Þá kemr Geirröðr konungr til þeira ok biðr þá drekka velfaranda sinn.	Then came Geirrod the-king to them and asked them to-drink well-faring his.	Then King Geirrod came to them and asked them to drink their welfare.
Þeir gerðu svá.	They did so.	They did so.
Váru fyrst drukkin hornin Hvítingar næst máldrykkju skálum, en þá var drukkit minni Þórs ok Óðins.	Were first drunk the-horns Whitings next drinking bowls, and then were drunk in-memory Thor's and Odin's.	First the horns called Whitings were drunk from, next the drinking bowls, and they were drunk from in memory of Thor and Odin.
Því næst kómu inn margir slagir hljóðfæra, ok tveir menn, nokkuru minni en Þorsteinn, þeir báru Grím inn góða.	Then next came in many artful musical-instruments, and two men, somewhat smaller than Thorstein, they carried Grim the Good.	Then many kinds of instruments came in, and two men, somewhat smaller than Thorstein, brought in Grim the Good.
Allir stóðu upp ok fellu á kné fyrir honum.	All stood up and fell to knees before him.	Everyone stood up and fell on their knees before him.
Grímr var óhýrligr.	Grim was unfriendly-looking.	Grim was hideous.

The Tale of Thorsteinn House-Power (Old Norse)

Old Norse	Literal	English
Geirröðr mælti til Goðmundar:	Geirrod spoke to Godmund:	Geirrod said to Godmund:
"Tak við Grími inum góða, ok er þetta þín handsals skál".	"Take with Grim the Good, and be this your binding shall".	"Take Grim the Good and let this toast be your binding pledge".
Goðmundr gekk at Grími ok tók af sér gullkórónu ok setti á hann ok mælti í eyra honum, sem Þorsteinn hafði sagt honum.	Godmund went to Grim and took off himself gold-crown and set on him and spoke in ear his, as Thorstein had told him.	Godmund went to Grim, took off his gold crown, set it upon him, and spoke in his ear, as Thorstein had told him.
Síðan lét hann renna af horninu ofan í serk sér, ok var eitr í.	Then had he ran of the-horn over into shirt his, and was poison in.	Then he ran the horn over into his shirt, and poured the poisonous drink in.
Hann drakk til Geirröði konungi ok kyssti á stikilinn, ok fór Grímr hlæjandi frá honum.	He drank to Geirrod the-king and kissed the horn-point, and went Grim smiling went-from him.	He drank to King Geirrod and kissed the point of the horn, and Grim was taken away from him with a smile on his face.
Tók Geirröðr þá við fullu horninu ok bað Grím með góðri heill koma ok bað hann kunngera sér, ef nokkurr háski væri nær.	Took Geirrod then with the-full horn and asked Grim with luck whole coming and asked him to-announce to-him, if something dangerous was near.	Geirrod took the full horn and asked Grim to bring him good luck and asked him if there was anything dangerous near.
"Hefi ek opt sét þik með betra bragði".	"Have I often seen you with better looking".	"I have often seen you in a better mood".
Tók hann gullmen af sér ok gaf Grími, drakk síðan til Agða jarli, ok þótti því líkast sem boði felli á sker, er niðr rann eptir hálsinum á honum, ok drakk af allt.	Took he gold-necklace off himself and gave Grim, drank afterwards to Agdi the-earl, and seemed therefore like as breaking wave on a-rock, as down ran after throat of him, and drank of all.	He took a gold necklace off himself and gave it to Grim, and drank afterwards to Earl Agdi, and it was like a wave breaking on a rock, as the drink ran down his throat, and he drank all of it.
Grímr hristi höfuðit, ok var hann borinn Agða jarli, ok gaf hann honum tvá gullhringa ok bað sér miskunnar ok drakk síðan af í þremr ok fekk byrlaranum.	Grim shook his-head, and was he carried Agdi the-earl, and gave it to-him two gold-rings and asked his mercy and drank afterwards of in three and went the-cup-bearer.	Grim shook his head, and he was carried to Earl Agdi who gave him two gold rings and asked for his mercy, and he drank in three draughts and then returned it to the cup-bearer.
Grímr mælti:	Grim said:	Grim said:

The Tale of Thorsteinn House-Power (Old Norse)

Old Norse	Literal	English
"Svá ergist hverr sem eldist".	"The feebler each who oldest".	"The older the man, the feebler"
Þá var hornit fyllt, ok skyldu þeir drekka af tveir, Jökull ok Fullsterkr.	Then was the horn, filled and should they drink of, Jokul and Full-Strong.	The horn was filled again so that Jokul and Full-Strong would drink from it.
Fullsterkr drakk fyrr.	Full-Strong drank before.	Full-Strong drank before.
Jökull tók við ok leit í hornit ok kvað lítilmannliga drukkit ok sló Fullsterk með horninu.	Jokul took with and had in horn and said weakly drank and struck Full-Strong with the-horn.	Jokul took the horn and said that Full-Strong drank like a weakling, and struck him with the horn.
En hann rak hnefann á nasir Jökli, svá at þjófshakan brotnaði, en ór hrutu tennrnar.	But he drove fist to nose Jokul's, so that thievish-chin broken, then out-of erupted the-teeth.	But he drove his first into Jokul's nose, so that his thievish chin was broken, and then teeth erupted out of his mouth.
Var þá upphlaup mikit.	Was then uproar much.	There was much uproar.
Geirröðr bað menn eigi láta þetta spyrjast, at þeir skildi svá illa.	Geirrod asked men not have this was-heard, that they separated so ill.	Geirrod asked the men not to have it heard that they had separated on bad terms.
Váru þeir þegar sáttir, ok var Grímr inn góði burt borinn.	Were they straightaway agreed, and was Grim the Good away carried.	They were reconciled straight away and Grim the Good was carried away.

10

Litlu síðar kom maðr gangandi í höllina.	Little afterwards came a-man walking into the-hall.	A little afterwards a man came walking into the hall.
Allir undruðust, hversu lítill hann var.	All wondered, how-so little he was.	Everyone wondered at how little he was.
Þat var Þorsteinn bæjarbarn.	That was Thorstein House-Child.	It was Thorstein House-Child.
Hann veik at Goðmundi ok sagði, at hestar væru til reiðu.	He turned to Godmund and told, him horses were to ride.	He turned to Godmund and told him to prepare the horses to ride.
Geirröðr spurði, hvat barn at þat væri.	Geirrod asked, who the-child that it was.	Geirrod asked who the child was.
Goðmundr segir:	Godmund said:	Godmund said:

The Tale of Thorsteinn House-Power (Old Norse)

Old Norse	Literal	English
"Þat er smásveinn minn, er Óðinn konungr sendi mér, ok er konungs gersemi ok kann marga smáleika, ok ef yðr þætti nokkuru neytr, þá vil ek gefa yðr hann".	"That is little-boy mine, that Odin the-king sent me, and is the-king's treasure and knows many small-games, and if you seem some good-use, then will I give you him".	"This is my little boy that king Odin sent me, and is the king's treasure, and he knows many tricks, and if you think he may be of use then I will give him to you".
"Þat er svipmikill drengr",	"That is a-striking fellow",	"That is a striking fellow",
segir konungr, "ok vil ek sjá fimleika hans",	said the-king, "and wish I to-see tricks his",	said the king, "and I wish to see his tricks",
ok bað Þorstein leika nokkurn smáleik.	and asked Thorstein play some small-games.	and asked Thorstein to play some tricks.
Þorsteinn tók hall sinn ok brodd ok pjakkar þar í, sem hvítt er.	Thorstein took marble his and point and pricked there in, where white was.	Thorstein took his marble and point and pricked where it was white.
Kemr haglhríð svá mikil, at engi þorir í móti at sjá, ok varð svá mikil fönn í höllinni, at tók í ökkla.	Came hailstorm so great, that none dared to meet to see, and was so great snow in the-hall, that took at ankles.	There came a hailstorm so great, that none dared to meet it with their eyes, and the snow was so great in the hall that it was up to everyone's ankles".
Konungr hló at.	The-king laughed at.	The king laughed at this.
Nú stangaði Þorsteinn hallinn, þar sem hann var gulr.	Now stabbed Thorstein the-marble, there where it was yellow.	Now Thorstein stabbed at the marble where it was yellow.
Kom þá sólskin svá heitt, at snjórinn bráðnaði allr á lítilli stundu.	Came then sunshine so hot, that the-snow melted all in little while.	Then came sunshine so hot that the snow melted in a short while.
Þar fylgdi sætr ilmr, en Geirröðr kvað hann var listamann.	There followed mountain-pastures sweet-smell, and Geirrod said he was a-skilled-craftsman.	There followed the sweet smell of mountain pastures, and Geirrod said that he was a skilled craftsman.
En Þorsteinn segir eptir einn leikinn, er heitir svipuleikr.	Then Thorstein said after one trick, that called the-scourge.	Then Thorstein said that there remained one trick which was called the scourge.
Konungr segist hann sjá vilja.	The-king said he to-see wished.	The king said he wished to see it.

The Tale of Thorsteinn House-Power (Old Norse)

Old Norse	Literal	English
Þorsteinn stóð á miðju hallargólfi ok pjakkar þar í hallinn, sem rautt er.	Thorstein stood in the-middle hall-floor and pricked there in the-marble, where red was.	Thorstein stood in the middle of the hall floor and pricked the marble where it was red.
Stökkva þar ór gneistar.	Jumped there of sparks.	Then sparks jumped from it.
Síðan hleypr hann um höllina fyrir hvert sæti.	Afterwards ran he about the-hall before each seat.	Afterwards he ran about the hall in front of each seat.
Tókust þá at vaxa gneistaflaugin, svá at hverr maðr varð at geyma sín augu.	Took then to grow sparks-flying, so that each man was to to-mind their eyes.	Then the fling sparks grew so that every man had to mind his eyes.
En Geirröðr konungr hló at.	Then Geirrod the-king laughed at.	Then King Geirrod laughed at this.
Tók þá at vaxa eldrinn, svá at öllum þótti við of um.	Took then to grow the-fire, so that all thought against of about.	The fires grew so that all thought against it.
Þorsteinn hafði sagt Goðmundi fyrir, at hann skyldi út ganga ok fara á hest.	Thorstein had told Godmund before, that he should out go and travel with horses.	Thorstein had told Godmund before, that he should go and travel with the horses.
Þorsteinn hleypr fyrir Geirröð ok mælti:	Thorstein ran before Geirrod and said:	Thorstein ran before Geirrod and said:
"Vili þér láta auka leikinn?"	"Wish you to-have more games?"	"Do you wish to have more games?"
"Lát sjá, sveinn",	"Let see, boy",	"Let's see, boy",
sagði hann.	said he.	he said.
Pjakkar Þorsteinn þá í fastara lagi.	Pricked Thorstein then to harder thrust.	Thorstein then pricked harder.
Kemr þá í auga Geirröði konungi.	Came then in eyes Geirrod's the-king.	Then came sparks into King Geirrod's eyes.
Þorsteinn hleypr til dyranna ok snaraði hallinum ok broddinum, ok kom í sitt auga hvárt á Geirröði konungi, ok steyptist hann dauðr á gólfit, en Þorsteinn gekk út.	Thorstein ran to the-door and threw the-marble and point, and came to his eyes each that Geirrod the-king, and knocked him dead on the-floor, then Thorstein went out.	Thorstein ran to the door and threw the marble and the point, and each came to King Geirrod's eyes, and he was knocked dead on the floor, then Thorstein went out.
Var Goðmundr þá kominn á hest.	When Godmund then came to horses.	Godmund had then come on horseback.

The Tale of Thorsteinn House-Power (Old Norse)

Old Norse	Literal	English
Þorsteinn bað þá ríða, "því at nú er ekki deigum vært".	Thorstein bid then to-ride, "because that now is not weak short".	Thorstein then bid then that they ride away, "because now is not the time for weakness".
Þeir ríða til árinnar.	They rode to the-river.	They rode to the river
Var þá aptr kominn hallrinn ok broddrinn.	Was then back coming the-marble and the-point.	Then the marble and point was coming back.
Þorsteinn segir, at Geirröðr var dauðr.	Thorstein said, that Geirrod was dead.	Thorstein said that Geirrod was dead.
Ríða þeir nú yfir ána ok þangat, sem þeir höfðu fundizt.	Rode they now across the river from-there, where they had met.	They now rode across the river from there, where they had met.
Þá mælti Þorsteinn:	Then spoke Thorstein:	Then Thorstein spoke:
"Hér munum vér nú skilja, ok mun mönnum mínum mál þykkja, at ek komi til þeira".	"Forces should we now separate, and should men mine the-matter think, that I come to them".	"Our forces should now separate, and my men think that I should come to them.
"Far heim með mér",	"Travel home with me",	"Travel home with me",
sagði Goðmundr, "ok skal ek launa þér góða fylgd".	said Godmund, "and shall I repay you good following".	said Godmund, "and I shall repay you for your good help".
"Síðan mun ek þess vitja",	"Afterwards should I this visit",	"Afterwards I should visit",
segir Þorsteinn, "en aptr skalt þú fara með fjölmenni í Geirröðargarða.	said Thorstein, "but back shall you travel with following-men to Geirrod's-Town.	said Thorstein, "but you should travel back to Geirrod's-Town with a following of men.
Er nú landit í yðru valdi".	Is now the-land in your control".	Now the land is in your control".
"Þú munt ráða",	"You should reckon",	"Whatever you reckon"
sagði Goðmundr, "en Óláfi konungi skaltu færa kveðju mína".	said Godmund, "then Olaf the-king shall be-brought greetings mine".	said Godmund, "then King Olaf shall be brought my greetings".

The Tale of Thorsteinn House-Power (Old Norse)

Old Norse	Literal	English
Tók hann þá eitt gullker ok silfrdisk ok tvítugt handklæði gullofit ok sendi konungi, en bað Þorstein vitja sín, ok skildu með kærleikum.	Took he then a golden-bowl and silver-dish and twenty hand-cloths gold-woven and sent the-king, and asked Thorstein visit him, and separated with friendly-terms.	He then took a golden bowl and a silver dish and twenty gold woven towels also to send to the king, and he asked Thorstein to visit him, and they separated on friendly terms.

11

Old Norse	Literal	English
En nú sér Þorsteinn, hvar Agði jarl ferr í allmiklum jötunmóð.	And now saw Thorstein, where Agdi the-earl travelling in all-mighty giant's-wrath.	And now saw Thorstein, where Earl Agdi was travelling in an almighty giant's wrath.
Þorsteinn ferr eptir honum.	Thorstein went after him.	Thorstein went after him.
Sér hann þá mikinn húsabæ, er Agði átti.	Saw he then great farmstead, which Agdi owned.	He then saw a great farmstead, which Agdi owned.
Aldingarðr var við grindhliðit, ok stóð þar við ein jungfrú.	Orchard was with gate, and stood there with a young-woman.	There was an orchard, and at the gate there stood a young woman.
Hún var dóttir Agða ok hét Goðrún.	She was daughter Agdi's and named Gudrun.	She was Agdi's daughter and was named Gudrun.
Mikil var hún ok fríð.	Tall was she and peaceful.	She was tall and fair.
Hún heilsaði föður sínum ok spurði tíðenda.	She greeted father hers and asked of-news.	She greeted her father and asked him the news.
"Nóg eru tíðendi",	"Enough is news",	"There is news enough",
segir hann.	said he.	he said.
"Geirröðr konungr er dauðr, ok hefir Goðmundr af Glæsisvöllum svikit oss alla ok hefir leynt þar kristnum manni, ok heitir sá Þorsteinn bæjarmagn.	"Geirrod the-king is dead, and has Godmund of Glasir-Plains tricked us all and has hidden there Christian man, and named so Thorstein House-Power.	"King Geirrod is dead, and Godmund of Glasir-Plains has tricked us all and has hidden a Christian man there, and he is named Thorstein House-Power.
Hann hefir ausit eldi í augu oss.	He has thrown fire in eyes ours.	He has thrown fire in our eyes.
Skal ek nú drepa menn hans".	Shall I now kill men his".	I shall now kill his men".

The Tale of Thorsteinn House-Power (Old Norse)

Old Norse	Literal	English
Kastar hann þar niðr hornunum Hvítingum ok hljóp til skógar, sem hann væri galinn.	Threw he there down the-horn Whitings and ran to the-forest, as-if he was mad.	There he threw down the horn called Whitings and ran to the forest as if he was mad.
Þorsteinn gekk at Goðrúnu.	Thorstein went to Gudrun.	Thorstein went to Gudrun.
Hún heilsaði honum ok spurði hann at nafni.	She greeted him and asked him of name.	She greeted him and asked him his name.
Hann kvaðst Þorsteinn bæjarbarn heita, hirðmaðr Óláfs konungs.	He said Thorstein House-Child named, court-man Olaf's the-king.	He said he was named Thorstein House-Child, a court man of King Olaf.
"Stórr mun þar inn stærsti, sem þú ert barnit",	"Big must there the biggest, if you are the-child",	"His big must be the biggest, if you are the child",
sagði hún.	said she.	she said.
"Viltu fara með mér",	"Will-you travel with me",	"Will you travel with me",
segir Þorsteinn, "ok taka við trú?"	said Thorstein, "and take with the-faith?"	said Thorstein, "and take the faith?".
"Við lítit yndi á ek hér at skiljast",	"With little happiness that I here to separate",	"With little happiness here to separate from", she said,
segir hún, "því at móðir mín er dauð.	said she, "because that mother mine is dead.	"because my mother is dead.
Hún var dóttir Óttars jarls af Hólmgörðum, ok váru þau ólík at skapsmunum, því at faðir minn er mjök tröllaukinn, ok sé ek nú, at hann er feigr.	She was daughter Ottar's the-earl of Novgorod, and were they unlike in mood-mind, as that father mine is much troll-possessed, and see I now, that he is doomed.	She was the daughter of Earl Ottar of Novgorod, and they were unlike in temperament, as my father who is troll-possessed, and I see now that he is doomed.
En ef þú vilt fylgja mér aptr hingat, þá mun ek fara með þér".	Then if you will follow me back here, then shall I travel with you".	Then if you will follow back here with me, then I shall travel with you".
Síðan tók hún þing sín, en Þorsteinn tók hornin Hvítinga.	Afterwards took she things hers, and Thorstein took the-horn Whitings.	Afterwards she took her things, and Thorstein took the horn called Whitings.
Síðan gengu þau á skóginn ok sáu, hvar Agði fór.	Afterwards went they into the-forest and saw, where Agdi went.	Afterwards they went into the forest and saw, where Agdi went.

The Tale of Thorsteinn House-Power (Old Norse)

Old Norse	Literal	English
Hann grenjaði mjök ok helt fyrir augun.	He screamed much and held before eyes.	He screamed a lot and held his hands before his eyes.
Hafði þat saman borit, þegar hann sá skip Þorsteins, hljóp sá verkr í þjófsaugun á honum, at hann sá eigi.	Had that together borne, as-soon-as he saw ship Thorstein's, ran so pain in thief's-eyes of his, that he saw not.	That had happened together with, as soon as he saw Thorstein's ship, a pain ran in his thief's eyes, so that he could not see.
Var þá komit at sólarfalli, er þau komu til skips.	Was then coming to sunset, when they came to ships.	It was approaching sunset, when they came to the ships.
Váru menn Þorsteins þá burt búnir, en er þeir sáu Þorstein, urðu þeir fegnir.	When men Thorstein's then away prepared, then when they saw Thorstein, became they joyful.	When Thorstein's men were preparing to journey away, then they saw Thorstein and became joyful.
Sté Þorsteinn þá á skip, ok sigldu burt.	Stepped Thorstein then onto the-ship, and sailed away.	Thorstein stepped onto the ship, and they sailed away.
Er eigi getit um ferð hans, fyrr en hann kom heim í Noreg.	Is nothing told-of about the-journey his, before that he came home to Norway.	Nothing is told of his journey, before he came home to Norway.

12

Þenna vetr sat Óláfr konungr í Þrándheimi.	That winter sat Olaf the-king in Trondheim.	That winter King Olaf sat at Trondheim.
Þorsteinn fann konung at jólum ok færði honum gripi þá, sem Goðmundr sendi honum, ok hornin Hvítinga ok marga aðra gripi.	Thorstein met the-king at Yule and brought him treasure then, which Godmund sent him, and the-horn Whitings and many other treasures.	Thorstein met the king at Yule and brought him treasure, which Godmund had sent him, and the horn called Whitings, and many other treasures.
Sagði hann konungi frá ferðum sínum ok sýndi honum Goðrúnu.	Told he the-king from voyage his and showed him Gudrun.	He told the king of his voyages and showed him Gudrun.
Konungr þakkaði honum, ok lofuðu allir hans hreysti ok þótti mikils um vert.	The-king thanked him, and praised all his valour and thought much about worthy.	The king thanked him, and praised all his valour and thought much of his worthiness.
Síðan lét konungr skíra Goðrúnu ok kenna trú.	Afterwards had the-king baptised Gudrun and taught the-faith.	Afterwards the king had Gudrun baptised and taught the faith.

The Tale of Thorsteinn House-Power (Old Norse)

Old Norse	Literal	English
Þorsteinn lék svipuleik um jólin, ok þótti mönnum þat skemmtan mikil.	Thorstein played the-scourge about Yule, and thought men that amusement great.	Thorstein played the scourge through Yule, and men thought it was great amusement.
Hvítingar gengu í minnum, ok váru tveir menn um hvárt horn.	Whitings went in came, and were two men about each horn.	The Whitings were brought in, and two men shared each horn.
En ker þat, sem Goðmundr hafði sent konungi, gekk engum af at drekka utan Þorsteini bæjarbarni.	The vessel that, which Godmund had sent the-king, went none of of drinking except Thorstein House-Child.	The cup that Godmund had sent the king, was not drunk from except by Thorstein House-Child.
Handklæðit brann eigi, þótt því væri í eld kastat, ok var hreinna eptir en áðr.	Hand-cloth burned not, though that was in fire cast, and was cleaner after than before.	The hand-cloth did not burn, even though it was cast in fire, and was cleaner than before.
Þorsteinn talar um við konung, at hann vildi gera brullaup til Goðrúnar, en konungr veitti honum þat, ok var þat sæmilig veizla.	Thorstein talked through with the-king, that he wished to-make wedding-proposal to Gudrun, and the-king granted him that, and was that well feast.	Thorstein talked through with the king, that he wished to make a wedding proposal to Gudrun, and the king granted him that, and was there a splendid feast.
Ok ina fyrstu nótt, er þau kómu í eina sæng ok niðr var hleypt fortjaldinu, þá brast upp þilfjöl at höfðum Þorsteins, ok var þar kominn Agði jarl ok ætlaði at drepa hann.	And the first night, when they came to one bed and down was cast the-curtain, then burst up decks over head Thorstein's, and was then come Agdi the-earl and intended to kill him.	And on the first night, when they came to bed together, the curtain was cast down, and then the decks over Thorstein's head burst open, and there had come Earl Agdi intending to kill him.
En þar laust í móti hita svá miklum, at hann þorði eigi inn at ganga.	But then loosed in opposition heat so great, that he dared not in to go.	But then was released so great a heat against him, that he dared not go in.
Sneri hann þá í burtu.	Turned he then to away.	He turned away.
Þá kom konungr at ok sló hann með gullbúnu refði í höfuðit, en hann steyptist niðr í jörðina.	Then came the-king to and struck him with gold-plated staff about head, then he fell down to the-ground.	Then the king came and struck him with a gold plated staff on the head, then he fell face down on the ground.
Helt konungr vörð um nóttina, en um morguninn váru horfin hornin Hvítingar.	Held the-king guard about the-night, then about morning were disappeared the-horns Whitings.	The king held guard through the night, and then in the morning the horns called Whitings had disappeared.
Gekk veizlan vel fram.	Went the-feast well from-there.	The feast went well from there.

The Tale of Thorsteinn House-Power (Old Norse)

Old Norse	Literal	English
Sat Þorsteinn með konungi um vetrinn, ok unnust þau Goðrún vel.	Sat Thorstein with the-king through winter, and loved they Gudrun well.	Thorstein sat with the king through the winter, and he and Gudrun loved each other well.
Um várit beiddi Þorsteinn orlofs at sigla í Austrveginn ok finna Goðmund konung.	About spring asked Thorstein vacation to sail to Eastern-Lands and find Godmund the-king.	In the spring Thorstein asked for a vacation to sail to the Eastern-Lands to find King Godmund.
En konungr sagðist þat eigi gera, utan hann lofaði at koma aptr.	But the-king said that not to-do, without him pledging to come back.	But the king said that he should not do it without promising to come back.
Þorsteinn hét því.	Thorstein promised accordingly.	Thorstein promised accordingly.
Konungr bað hann halda trú sína vel, "ok eig meira undir þér en þeim austr þar".	The-king asked him keep faith his well, "and have more behind you than they Eastern-Lands there".	The king asked him to keep his faith well: "and have more behind you than those in the Eastern-Lands there".
Skildust þeir með kærleikum, ok báðu allir vel fyrir honum, því at Þorsteinn var orðinn vinsæll.	Separated they with friendship, and bid all well for him, because that Thorstein was became popular.	They separated with friendship, and all bid him well, for Thorstein had become popular.
Sigldi hann í Austrveg, ok er eigi getit annars en sú ferð færist vel.	Sailed he to Eastern-Lands, and was nothing told-of other than so travelled the-journey well.	He sailed to the Eastern-Lands, and nothing was told other than that he travelled the journey well.
Kom hann á Glæsisvöllu, ok fagnaði Goðmundr honum vel.	Came he to Glasir-Plains, and welcomed Godmund him well.	He came to Glasir-Plains, and Godmund welcomed him well.
Þorsteinn mælti:	Thorstein spoke:	Thorstein spoke:
"Hvat hafið þér frétt ór Geirröðargörðum?"	"What have you news of Geirrod's-Town?"	"What news do you have of Geirrod's-Town?"
"Þangat fór ek",	"There travelled I",	"I travelled there",
segir Goðmundr, "ok gáfu þeir landit í mitt vald, ok ræðr þar fyrir Heiðrekr úlfhamr, sonr minn".	said Godmund, "and gave they land to me power, and rules there over Heidrek Wolf-Skin, son mine".	said Godmund, "and they gave me power over the land, and ruling over there is Heidrek Wolf-Skin, my son".
"Hvar er Agði jarl?"	"What of Agdi the-earl?"	"What of Earl Agdi?"
segir Þorsteinn.	said Thorstein.	said Thorstein.

The Tale of Thorsteinn House-Power (Old Norse)

Old Norse	Literal	English
"Hann lét gera sér haug, þá þér fóruð",	"He had done himself a-burial-mound, when you travelled",	"He had made himself a burial mound, when you travelled",
segir Goðmundr, "ok gekk þar í með mikit fé, en þeir Jökull ok Frosti drukknuðu í ánni Hemru, er þeir fóru frá veizlunni, en ek hefi nú vald yfir heraðinu á Grundum".	said Godmund, "and went there in with much wealth, but they Jokul and Frosti drowned in the-river Hemra, as they travelled from the-feast, then I have now power across the-district of Grundir".	said Godmund", and retired there with much wealth, and Jokul and Frosti drowned in the river Hemra, as they travelled from the feast, and I now have power across the district of Grundir".
"Þar er nú mikit undir",	"There is now much under",	"There is now a lot under it",
segir Þorsteinn, "hverju þú vilt mér af skipta, því at mér þykkir Goðrún eiga arf allan eptir föður sinn, Agða jarl".	said Thorstein, "how you will me to give, because that to-me seems Gudrun my-wife inheritance all after father his, Agdi the-earl".	said Thorstein, "how much you wish to let me have, because it seems to me that my wife Gudrun is entitled to all the inheritance after he father, Earl Agdi".
"Ef þú vilt vera minn maðr",	"If you will be my man",	"If you will be my man",
sagði Goðmundr.	said Godmund.	said Godmund.
"Þá muntu ekki vanda um trú mína",	"Then should not custom about the-faith mine",	"Then you will not have any problems with my faith",
segir Þorsteinn.	said Thorstein.	said Thorstein.
"Þat vil ek",	"That will I",	"That I will",
sagði Goðmundr.	said Godmund.	said Godmund.
Sídan fóru þeir til Grunda, ok tók Þorsteinn heraðit undir sik.	Afterwards travelled they to Grundir, and took Thorstein the-district under himself.	Afterwards they travelled to Grundir, and Thorstein took the district under himself.

13   13   13

Old Norse	Literal	English
Þorsteinn reisti bú at Gnípalundi, því at Agði jarl hafði gengit aptr ok eytt bæinn.	Thorstein raised the-dwelling at Gnipalund, because that Agdi the-earl had come back and devastated the-dwelling.	Thorstein raised the house at Gnipalund, as Earl Agdi had come back and devastated the old house.
Gerðist Þorsteinn höfðingi mikill.	Became Thorstein a-chieftain great.	Thorstein became a great chieftain.

The Tale of Thorsteinn House-Power (Old Norse)

Old Norse	Literal	English
Goðrún fæddi sveinbarn mikit litlu síðar, ok hét Brynjólfr.	Gudrun raised a-baby-boy large little since, and named Brynjolf.	Gudrun gave birth to a big baby boy, and he was named Brynjolf.
Ekki var traust, at Agði jarl glettist eigi við Þorstein.	Not was trusted, that Agdi the-earl playing-tricks not against Thorstein.	There was no confidence that Earl Agdi would not play-tricks against Thorstein.
Eina nótt gekk Þorsteinn af sæng sinni ok sá, hvar at Agði fór.	One night went Thorstein to bed his and saw, where that Agdi moving.	One night Thorstein got out of his bed and saw where Agdi was moving.
Hann þorði hvergi inn í hliðin, því at kross var fyrir hverjum dyrum.	He dared neither in the the-gates, because that the-cross was before each doorway.	He dared not enter the gates, for there was a cross at every door.
Þorsteinn gekk til haugsins.	Thorstein went to burial-mound-his.	Thorstein went to the mound.
Hann var opinn, ok gekk hann inn ok tók burt hornin Hvítinga.	It was open, and went he inside and took away the-horns Whitings.	It was open, and he went inside and took away the horns called Whitings.
Þá kom Agði jarl í hauginn, en Þorsteinn hljóp út hjá honum ok setti kross í dyrrnar, ok laukst aptr haugrinn, ok hefir ekki orðit vart við Agða síðan.	Then came Agdi the-earl into the-mound, and Thorstein ran out beside him and set the-cross in the-door, and closed afterwards the-mound, and has no word was of Agdi since..	Then Earl Agdi came to the mound, but Thorstein ran out beside him and put a cross in the door, and the mound was closed, and Agdi has not been seen since.
Um sumarit eptir fór Þorsteinn til Noregs ok færði Óláfi konungi hornin Hvítinga.	About summer after went Thorstein to Norway and brought Olaf the-king the-horns Whitings.	The following summer Thorstein went to Norway, and brought King Olaf the horns called Whitings.
Síðan fekk hann orlof ok sigldi til eigna sinna.	Then got he leave to sail to possessions his.	Then he took leave and sailed to his possessions.
Bauð konungr honum halda vel trú sína.	Asked the-king him hold well faith his.	The king commanded him to keep his faith well.
Höfum vér eigi frétt síðan til Þorsteins.	Have we not news since of Thorstein's.	We have not heard from Thorstein since.
En þá Óláfr konungr hvarf af Orminum langa, hurfu hornin Hvítingar.	But when Olaf the-king disappeared from The-Serpent Long, vanished the-horns Whitings.	But when King Olaf disappeared from the Long Serpent, the horns of the Whites disappeared.

The Tale of Thorsteinn House-Power (Old Norse)

Old Norse	Literal	English
Lúkum vér þar þætti Þorsteins bæjarbarns.	End we there the-story Thorstein's House-Child.	We end there the tale of Thorstein House-Child.

Word List *(Old Norse to English)*

Old Norse	English
A, a	
aðra	other
aðrir	others
af	drink, from, from, of, of, off, that, to, to
afhenda	off-handed, of-hand
afklæðast	undressed
afklæddust	undressed
afl	strength
afla	provide
afli	a-forge, strength
agða	Agdi (name), Agdi (name), Agdi's (name)
agði	Agdi (name), Agdi (name)
akkerum	anchor
aldingarðr	orchard
aldri	never, never
alla	all, all
allan	all
allar	all
allir	all, all
allmiklum	all-mighty
allr	all, all
alls	all
allsterk	All-Strong (name)
allsterkr	All-Strong (name)
allt	all, all
andliti	face
annan	another-thing
annarr	another, one, one, the-other
annarri	another, one
annars	other
annast	he-took-care-of
aptnaði	the-evening
aptr	afterwards, back, back, return
arf	inheritance
at	about, against, as, at, at, from, him, in, in, it, of, of, over, than, than, that, that, the, the, to, to, towards, when, which
atgang	to-going
atgangr	to-going
atsetu	a-seat
auðit	fated
auga	eyes, eyes
augu	eyes, eyes
augum	eyes
augun	eyes
auka	extra, more
aura	ounces
ausit	thrown
austr	east, east, Eastern-Lands (place)
austrveg	Eastern-Lands (place)
austrveginn	Eastern-Lands (place)
Á, á	
á	a, about, a-river, at, beside, by, for, from, in, into, is, of, on, onto, that, the, then, to, was, who, with
ábyrgjast	take-care-of
áðr	after, before
áliðnum	following
álna	cubits
álnar	a-yard
ána	the, the-river
ánni	the-river, the-river
árinnar	the-river, the-river
átti	had, owned
áttu	had
ávallt	always

Word List (Old Norse to English)

Old Norse	English
Æ, æ	
ætla	intend, suppose
ætlaði	intended
ætlan	intentions
ætlar	intended
ættar	lineage
ætti	had

Old Norse	English
B, b	
bað	asked, bid, ordered
báðu	bid
báðum	both
bæinn	the-dwelling
bæjarbarn	House-Child (name)
bæjarbarni	House-Child (name)
bæjarbarns	House-Child (name)
bæjarmagn	House-Power (name)
bak	back, the-back
bálagarðssíðu	Balagardsida (place)
bana	dead, death
bandvettlinga	mittens
bani	death, the-death
bar	bore, carried
barn	the-child
barni	a-baby
barnit	child, the-child
báru	carried
bárust	bore
bauð	asked, offered
beiddi	asked
beini	the-bone
beinum	the-bone
beitina	opening, the-opening
bekk	a-bench, bench
bekkinn	of-the-bench
bekkjar	bench
bekknum	that-bench, the-bench
ber	bear
bera	bear, brought
berast	bore
berði	threw
berið	bring
berizt	bear
betr	better
betra	better
betri	better
beztir	best
bíða	abide, await
biðr	asked
bik	pitch
birti	revealed
bjálfa	Bjalfi
bjálfi	Bjalfi
bjó	lived, prepared
bjuggust	settled
blár	black
bleikum	pale
boð	an-invite
boði	breaking
bóndi	farmer
borð	table
borða	the-tables
borðinu	table
borðum	a-table, the-tables
borg	a-city
borgarinnar	the-city, the-town
borgina	the-city, the-town
borin	brought
borinn	carried
borit	borne
börn	children
brá	drew
bráðnaði	melted
bræðir	thaws
bragði	looking
brann	burned
brast	burst
braut	way
brautinni	turned-away, turning
breiða	broad
breiddu	spread
breitt	broad
breyttu	behaved
bringu	the-chest
brodd	point
broddinum	point, the-point
broddrinn	the-point

Word List (Old Norse to English)

Old Norse	English
bróður	brother
brosti	burst-out-laughing
brotnaði	broke, broken
brott	away
brullaup	wedding-proposal
brynjólfr	Brynjolf (name)
bú	the-dwelling
búa	live
bugtinni	the-curve
búin	prepared
búit	inlaid, prepared
búk	thick-set
búnir	prepared
burt	away
burtu	away
býðr	invite
byggð	settlements
byr	fair-wind
byrlaranum	the-cup-bearer

D, d

Old Norse	English
dag	day
dagný	Dagny (name)
dagsins	of-the-day
datt	fell
dauð	dead
dauðr	dead
degi	day
deigum	weak
deyr	dies
díki	the-moat
djúp	deep
dóttir	daughter
draga	carry, drag
drakk	drank
drap	killed
draup	dripped
dregr	drew
drekka	drink, drinking, they, to-drink
drekkir	drink
drekkr	drinks
drengr	fellow
drep	gangrene
drepa	kill
drepnir	killed
drött	Drott (name)
drottning	the-queen
dröttr	Drott (name)
drukkin	drunk
drukkit	drank, drink, drinking, drink-to, drunk
drukknuðu	drowned
drukku	drank
drykkju	drinking
drykkjumaðr	drinking-man
drykkjuskapr	drinking
drykknum	drink
dúka	tablecloths
dúkinn	table-cloth, the-table-cloth
dúkr	table-cloth
dunur	a-din
dvelr	delays
dverg	dwarf
dvergnum	the-dwarf
dvergrinn	dwarf, the-dwarf
dvergsbarnit	the-dwarf's-boy
dýr	wild-animals
dyranna	the-door
dyrr	door, the-door
dyrrnar	the-door
dyrum	doorway

E, e

Old Norse	English
eða	and, but, or
ef	if
eiða	oath, oaths
eig	have
eiga	my-wife, said-of, to-own
eigi	none, not, nothing
eigna	possessions
eignir	property
eigum	own
eik	oak
eikinni	the-oak
eimyrja	embers

Word List (Old Norse to English)

Old Norse	English
ein	a
eina	a, one
einhvern	some-way
einhverr	someone
einir	alone
einn	a, one
einni	a
einskis	nothing
einu	in-one, one
einum	a, one
eitr	poison
eitt	a, one
ek	I
ekki	no, not, nothing
eld	fire
eldi	fire
eldist	oldest
eldr	fire, the-flames
eldrinn	the-fire
eldsskara	fire-poker
eltu	chased
en	about, and, but, on, than, that, the, then, though, when, while
endast	ending
enga	any, none
engan	no-one
engi	no, none, not
engir	no
engu	nothing
engum	no, none
enn	but, than
eptir	after, behind
er	am, and, as, be, from, have, is, of, that, then, was, when, which, who
erfi	inheritance
ergist	feebler
erninum	the-eagle
ert	are
ertu	are-you
eru	are, is, they-are, were
erum	are
eyra	ear
eyranu	ears
eyri	an-ounce-of
eytt	devastated

F, f

Old Norse	English
fá	get, pay
faðir	father
fæddi	raised
færa	be-brought
færði	brought, took
færir	travel
færist	the-journey
fæti	feet
fætr	feet
fagnaði	celebrated, welcomed
fagr	beautiful
fagrar	fair
fagrt	fair
fangbrögðum	to-wrestling
fann	found, met
fannst	found
far	travel
fara	go, to-travel, travel, travelled, travelling
farið	go
farin	gone
farit	gone
fast	fastened, hard, hard
fastara	harder
fé	wealth
féfátt	lack-of-money
feginn	relieved
fegnir	joyful
feiga	doomed
feigr	doomed, fated-to-die
fekk	got, went
fela	hide
félagi	companion
fell	falling, fell
felli	wave
fellir	drops
fellu	fell
felr	fold
fengnir	get
fengu	caught

Word List (Old Norse to English)

Old Norse	English
fengust	got-they
ferð	journey, the-journey, travelled, voyage
ferðum	voyage
ferr	travelling, went
fésparir	fee-sparing
festi	joined
festir	fastened
fimleika	tricks
fingrgull	finger-gold
finna	find
finnumst	meet
fitan	fat
fjalli	mountains
fjarstætt	far-away
fjölkunnigr	skilled-in-magic
fjölmenni	following-men
fjóra	four
fjórar	four
fjörð	fjord
fjórðunga	quarters
fjórum	four
fleira	more
flestum	most
fleygir	flew-it
flokk	band, company
flokki	men
flýgr	flies
föður	father
föðurnum	to-the-father
fólk	folk
fólki	folk
föll	falling
fönn	snow
fór	moving, travelled, went
fortjaldinu	the-curtain
fóru	travelled, went
fóruð	travelled
förunautr	companion
fótrinn	leg
fótum	feet
frá	away-from, from, went-from
fram	from, from-there, to
framboðligr	be-offered
framt	provide
frár	swift
fremstir	foremost
frétt	news
fríð	peaceful
frosta	Frosti (name)
frosti	Frosti, Frosti (name)
fugla	birds
full	drunk
fullsterk	Full-Strong (name)
fullsterkr	Full-Strong (name)
fullu	the-full
fúlt	foul
fundizt	met
furðuliga	exceedingly
fylgd	following
fylgdi	followed, following
fylgja	follow, following
fylgt	followed
fylldan	filled
fyllt	horn
fyrir	before, before-them, for, over
fyrr	before
fyrst	first
fyrsta	first
fyrstu	first
fyrstum	first

G, g

Old Norse	English
gæfa	luck
gæfu	luck
gaf	gave
gáfu	gave
gagn	benefit
gagnvart	going-from
galdrafullt	magic-full
galinn	mad
gamalla	the-old
gamans	games
gamni	game
gamninu	the-game
gandreið	witch-ride
ganga	go, going, walk

50

Word List (Old Norse to English)

Old Norse	English
gangandi	walking
gangi	go
gat	got
gátum	opening
gaulardal	Gaulardale (place)
gef	give
gefa	give
gefr	given
gegnt	opposite
geirröð	Geirrod (name)
geirröðargarða	Geirrod's-Town (place)
geirröðargörðum	Geirrod's-Town (place)
geirröði	Geirrod (name), Geirrod's (name)
geirröðr	Geirrod (name)
gekk	went
gengit	come
gengr	went
gengu	went
ger	done
gera	do, done, make, to-do, to-make
gerði	did
gerðist	became
gerðu	did
gersema	precious-things
gersemar	treasured, treasures
gersemi	a-treasure, treasure, treasures
gert	made
get	guess
geta	get
getit	told-of
getr	get
geyma	retain, to-mind
gimsteinar	precious-stones
gjafirnar	the-gifts
gjarna	gladly
glaðir	glad, gladly
glæsisvöllu	Glasir-Plains (place)
glæsisvöllum	Glasir-Plains (place)
glerglugg	glass-window
glettist	playing-tricks
glíma	wrestle, wrestling
glímt	wrestled
glóanda	burning, glowing
glugginn	the-skylight
gneistaflaug	a-shower-of-sparks
gneistaflaugin	sparks-flying
gneistar	sparks
gnípalundi	Gnipalund (place)
góða	good, Good (name), the-good
góði	good, Good (name)
goðmund	Godmund (name)
goðmundar	Godmund (name), Godmund's (name)
goðmundi	Godmund (name)
goðmundr	Godmund, Godmund (name)
góðr	good
góðri	luck
goðrún	Gudrun (name)
goðrúnar	Gudrun (name)
goðrúnu	Gudrun (name)
góðum	good
gólfi	the-floor
gólfit	floor, the-floor
gott	good
græð	tend-to
grafit	dug
grám	grey
granda	to-injure
greip	grabbed, gripped
grenjaði	howling, screamed
grím	Grim (name)
grími	Grim (name)
grímr	Grim (name)
grindhliðit	gate
grip	grabbed
gripi	treasure, treasures
grunda	Grundir (place)
grundir	Grundir (place)
grundum	Grundir (place)
guðvef	precious-cloth
guðvefjarskikkju	a-precious-cloak
gul	gold
gull	gold
gullbúnu	gold-plated
gullhnött	gold-ball

Word List (Old Norse to English)

Old Norse	English
gullhring	gold-ring
gullhringa	gold-rings
gulli	gold
gullker	golden-bowl
gullkórónu	gold-crown
gullligt	gold
gullligum	gold
gullmen	gold-necklace
gullofit	gold-woven
gullskotnum	gold-trimmed
gulr	gold, yellow
gustr	Gust

H, h

Old Norse	English
há	high
hæfa	hit
hægt	possible
hættu	dangerous
hafa	had, had, have, having
hafði	had
hafið	have
haft	had, have
hafvillur	open-sea
haglhríð	hailstorm
hákon	Hakon (name)
halda	hold, keep
hálfan	half
hall	marble, piece-of-marble
hallar	hall
hallargólfi	hall-floor
hallargólfit	hall-floor
hallinn	the-marble, the-piece-of-marble
hallinum	the-marble
hallrinn	the-marble, the-piece-of-marble
háls	the-neck
hálsinum	throat
hamingju	luck
hana	he, it, she
handklæði	hand-cloths
handklæðit	hand-cloth
handsals	binding
hann	he, him, it, men
hans	him, his
harðasti	hardest
harðúðigr	hard-minded
hásæti	a-high-seat, high-seat
háski	dangerous
hátíð	festival
háttar	kinds
haug	a-burial-mound
hauginn	the-mound
haugrinn	the-mound, the-mound
haugsins	burial-mound-his
heðan	from-hence
hefði	had
hefi	have
hefir	had, has, have
hefna	avenge
heiðr	honour
heiðrekr	Heidrek (name)
heill	whole
heilsaði	greeted
heim	home
heiminum	the-world
heimsliga	foolishly
heit	declared
heita	be-named, named, promised
heiti	named
heitir	called, named
heitt	hot
hel	death
heldr	rather
helt	held
helzt	held
hemra	Hemra (place)
hemru	Hemra (place)
henda	catch
hendi	hand
hendr	hand
hentar	suits
henti	caught
hér	forces, here
heraði	district
heraðinu	the-district

Word List (Old Norse to English)

Old Norse	English
heraðit	the-district
hernaði	raiding
hest	horses
hesta	horses
hestar	horses
hestarnir	the-horses
hesti	horse
hestr	horse
hestum	horses
hét	is-named, named, promised
heyra	hear
heyrir	heard
himni	the-sky
hingat	here
hinir	others, the-other
hirðið	take-care
hirðmaðr	court-man
hirðmönnum	court-men
hirðprýði	court
hita	heat
hjá	beside
hjástöðu	beside-standing
hjó	hewed
hlæjandi	smiling
hlátr	laughter
hlátri	laughter
hlaupa	ran
hleypr	ran
hleypt	cast
hliðin	the-gates
hlíðir	slope
hljóðfæra	musical-instruments
hljóðfæri	musical-instruments
hljóp	ran
hló	laughed
hlógu	laughed
hluti	lot
hlýðni	homage
hlytir	to-get
hnakkinn	the-back-of-the-head
hnefann	fist
höfði	head
höfðingi	a-chieftain
höfðu	had
höfðum	head
höfn	the-harbour
höfuðit	head, his-head
höfum	have
hól	hill
holdi	flesh
hólinn	the-mound
hóll	mound
höll	a-hall, the-hall
höllina	the-hall
höllinni	the-hall
hólmgörðum	Novgorod (place)
hólnum	the-mound
hömrum	a-steep-cliff
hönd	hand
höndum	hands
honum	he, him, his, it, to-him
horfin	disappeared
horn	a-horn, horn, horns
hornin	the-horn, the-horns
horninu	horn, the-horn
hornit	a-horn, horn, the
hornunum	the-horn
hösvaðist	went-for
hösvi	Hosvir (name)
hösvir	Hosvir (name)
hratt	pushed
hraustr	brave
hreinna	cleaner
hreysti	bravery, valour
hring	a-circle, ring
hringinn	the-ring
hringnum	the-ring
hringrinn	the-ring
hristi	shook
hrutu	erupted
hrysi	trembled
hug	think
hugr	thought
huldumaðr	a-hidden-man
hulinshjálm	helm-of-invisibility
hún	she
hurfu	disappeared, vanished
hús	house, the-house
húsabæ	farmstead
húsum	houses

53

Word List (Old Norse to English)

Old Norse	English
hvaðan	from-where
hvar	were, what, where
hvarf	disappeared
hvárki	neither
hvárn	each
hvárntveggja	either-side
hvárt	each, whether, which
hvárttveggja	either
hvat	what, who
hvergi	neither
hverju	how
hverjum	each
hvern	everyone
hverr	anyone, each, who
hverrar	whose
hversu	how-so
hvert	each, what
hví	what, why
hvítinga	Whitings (name)
hvítingar	Whitings (name)
hvítingum	Whitings (name)
hvítr	white
hvítt	white

I, i

Old Norse	English
illa	badly, ill
ilmr	sweet-smell
in	the
ina	the
indíalandi	India
inn	in, inside, the
innanborðs	aboard
inum	the
it	the, this

Í, í

Old Norse	English
í	about, all, among, at, if, in, into, it, of, on, the, to, was, with-that

J, j

Old Norse	English
jafnan	every-time
jafnstóra	equally-as-big, equally-large
jafnstórr	equally-big
jamtaland	Jamtland (place)
jarl	earl, the-earl
jarli	the-earl, the-earl's
jarls	the-earl, the-earl's
járnskeggja	Iron-Beard (name)
jökli	Jokul's (name)
jökull	Jokul (name)
jólin	Yule (name)
jólum	Yule (name)
jörðina	the-ground
jötnum	giants
jötunheima	Giant-Home (place)
jötunheimar	Giant-Land (place)
jötunmóð	giant's-wrath
jungfrú	young-woman

K, k

Old Norse	English
kærleikum	friendly-terms, friendship
kallaðr	called
kallar	call, called
kallat	called
kalt	cold
kann	can, knows
kanna	explore
kapparnir	champions
karkr	Kark (name)
kastaði	cast, threw
kastar	threw
kastat	cast
kastið	throw
kátir	merry
kaupferðir	trading-voyages
kaupferðum	trading-journeys
keiktist	bent
kem	come
kempa	warrior

Word List (Old Norse to English)

Old Norse	English
kemr	came, comes
kenna	know, taught
kenndr	recognised
ker	vessel
keyrir	the-stick
kikna	bent-backwards
kinnbeinit	chin-bone
kjaptinum	mouth, the-mouth
kjaptrinn	jaw
kjós	choose
klæddu	dressed
klæði	clothed, clothes
klæðin	clothes
klæðir	clothed
klæðsekk	sack
klæðum	clothes
kné	knees
knésbætr	the-back-of-the-knees
knettinum	the-ball
knöttinn	the-ball
knöttrinn	the-ball
kollóttan	bald-headed
kollsveinn	Kollsvein (name), the-boy
kölluð	called
kom	came
koma	came, come, coming
komi	come
komin	coming
kominn	came, come, coming
komit	coming
komnir	come
komu	came
kómu	came
kómust	came
kona	wife
konung	the-king
konungi	king, the-king
konungnum	the-king
konungr	king, the-king
konungrinn	the-king
konungs	the-king, the-king's
konungshöll	the-king's-hall
konungsnafn	the-king's-name
konungsson	a-king's-son, the-king's-son
konur	women
köppunum	the-cups
kórónu	the-crown
köstuðu	cast
krásum	food
krefja	demand
kristinn	a-Christian, Christian
kristnum	Christian
krókstaf	crooked-staff
krókstafinn	the-crooked-stick
krókstafr	crooked-stick
kross	the-cross
krummurnar	grabbed
kumpánar	fellows
kunnáttu	skills
kunngera	to-announce, wiser
kunnigt	know
kvað	said
kvaddi	called
kvaðst	said
kveðju	greetings
kveðst	greetings, said
kveld	the-evening
kveldit	evening
kvikt	alive, living-thing
kvöld	evening
kyn	kin
kyssti	kissed

L, l

Old Norse	English
lá	had, laid, lay
lætr	acts, have
lagði	had, laid
lagðist	lay
lagi	thrust
lagt	left
lágu	laid
land	land, the-land
landi	the-land
landit	land, the-land
landsuðr	the-south-east
landsuðri	South-East
langa	Long (name)
langan	long

Word List (Old Norse to English)

Old Norse	English
lát	have, let
láta	have, lay-out, to-have
látum	leave-it
laukst	closed
laun	to-repay
launa	repay
launat	repay
laust	loosed
leggja	grant
leiða	led
leiddr	led
leika	play
leikinn	games, trick
leit	had
lék	played
lékst	played
lén	a-fee
lendr	landed
lengr	longer
lét	had
léti	made
létu	had
leynt	hidden
lið	assistance, the-company-of
liði	company, dislocated
líðr	passed
lifði	lived
lífgjöf	life-gift
lifir	lives
liggja	lie-down
liggr	lying
líkari	like
líkast	like
listamann	a-skilled-craftsman
lítill	little, small
lítilli	little
lítilmannliga	weakly
lítinn	little
lítit	little
litlu	little
ljótan	hideous
lófa	promise
lofaði	pledging
lofuðu	praised
lög	law
logaði	blazed
logandi	ablaze
logit	a-lie
lokit	ended
löngu	long
lopti	the-air, the-sky
lúkanus	Lucanus (name)
lúkum	end

M, m

Old Norse	English
má	may
maðr	a-man, man
mæðast	get-tired
mæla	speak
mælir	speaks
mælt	spoke
mælti	said, spoke
mál	conversations, the-matter
máldrykkju	drinking
manna	man, men, men, men's
manni	man
manns	man
mannshöfuð	a-man's-head
mánuð	a-month
marga	many
margir	many
matr	food
matsveinar	food-servants
mátt	may
mátti	could
mátuligr	fitting
með	along, with
meðalmaðr	an-average-man
meðan	as-long-as, while
mega	may
megi	may
megin	side
meira	more
menn	men, the-men
mér	I, me, to-me
mest	most, mostly
mestr	the-greatest, the-most

Word List (Old Norse to English)

Old Norse	English
miðit	the-middle
miðju	the-middle
mik	me, myself
mikil	great, tall
mikill	great, large
mikils	much
mikinn	great, much
mikit	great, large, much
mikla	great
miklar	great, much
mikli	larger, largest
miklu	much
miklum	great
millum	between
mín	me, mine, my
mína	mine
mínir	mine, my
minn	mine, my
minni	in-memory, smaller
minnum	came
mínu	mine
mínum	mine
miskunnar	mercy
missa	lose
missi	lost
mitt	me, mine
mjök	great, much
móðir	mother
móðu	large-river
móðuna	the-river
mönnum	men, the-men
morgin	morning, the-morning
morgininn	morning
morginn	morning
morgni	morning
morguninn	morning
mörkina	the-trees
mót	against, meet, to-meet
móti	against, meet, oppose, opposition, to-meet
mun	could, must, shall, should, should-be, would
mundi	could-be, should, would, would-have
mundu	must-be, would
mundum	would-be
muni	would
munni	a-mouth
munt	must-be, should
muntu	shall-you, should
munu	should, would-be
munum	should
mútur	payment
myrkr	fog

N, n

Old Norse	English
nær	near
næst	near, next, next-to
nætr	nights
nafn	name
nafnbætr	name-titles
nafnfesti	naming-gift
nafni	name
nam	took
nasir	nose
nát	get-hold-of, hold-of
náttúru	natured
né	nor
neðra	under
nefit	nose
nefndi	named
nefndir	named
nema	but, except
neytr	good-use
níðingr	a-coward
niðr	below, down
niðrgangs	down-going
nóg	enough
nokkura	some
nokkurn	some
nokkurr	something
nokkuru	some, somewhat
nokkut	anything, some
noreg	Norway (place)
noregi	Norway (place)
noregs	Norway (place)

Word List (Old Norse to English)

Old Norse	*English*
nösunum	on-the-nose
nótt	night
nóttina	night, the-night
nú	now

O, o

of	of
ofan	down, over
ofmagni	to-overpower
ok	ad, also, and, filled, river, to
okkr	us, us
olnbogarnir	elbows
opinn	open
opt	often
orðinn	became
orðit	word
orðum	words
orkar	able-to
orkufátt	low-energy
orlof	leave
orlofs	vacation
orminum	The-Serpent (name)
oss	ours, us

Ó, ó

óaflátssamr	un-indulgent
óðinn	Odin (name)
óðins	Odin's (name)
óðni	Odin (name)
óðu	waded
ófarin	unfinished
ófögnuðr	unhappy
ófriðar	un-peace
óhýrligr	unfriendly-looking
óláf	Olaf (name)
ólafi	Olaf (name)
Óláfr	Olaf (name)
óláfs	Olaf's (name)
ólík	unlike
ólyfjan	poison
óorðna	unspoken

Old Norse	*English*
ór	away-from, from, of, out-of, through
óskyldara	less-should
ótal	countless
óþýðr	unfriendly
óttars	Ottar's (name)
óvæginn	ruthless
óvit	unconscious

Ö, ö

öðrum	one, other
öfundsjúkir	jealous
ökkla	ankles
öllum	all
öndvegit	opposite
önnur	another, one, other
örn	eagle

P, p

pilt	boy
piltrinn	the-boy
pjakka	prick
pjakkar	prick, pricked
prett	tricked
pungi	pouch

R, r

ráð	advice, counsel
ráða	advice, decide, reckon
ráðast	arranged
ræð	ruler
ræðr	rules
rak	drove
ráku	drove
rann	ran
rasaði	tumbled
rauðr	red
rauðum	red
rautt	red

Word List (Old Norse to English)

Old Norse	English
réð	advised, ruled
réðst	moved
refði	staff
reið	riding
reiddist	rose
reiðu	ride
reis	rose
reisti	raised
reistu	raised
renna	ran
reyk	smoke
reynt	test
ríða	ride, ride-away, riding, rode, to-ride
ríðr	rode
riðu	rode
rifnaði	split
ríki	kingdom
risaland	Giant-Land (place)
risalandi	Giant-Land (place)
risalands	Giant-Land (place)
ríss	rose
rjóðr	clearing
rjóðrinu	the-clearing
rönd	around
röndum	stripes
röskr	brave
ruggaði	rocking
rúm	room

S, s

Old Norse	English
sá	saw, see, seeing, so, there
sækið	seek
sæmilig	well
sæng	bed
sæti	seat
sætis	seat
sætr	mountain-pastures
sagði	said, said, told, told
sagðist	said
sagt	told, told
saka	injury
sama	same
saman	together
sár	wound
sat	sat
sáttir	agreed
sáttu	saw-you
sáu	saw
sauða	wether's
saur	the-mud
sé	even, he-is, is, see, you
sefr	slept
seg	say
segir	said, said-to, say, told
segist	said
segja	say, tell
seint	slowly
selshöfuð	seal's-head
sem	as, as-if, if, that, whatever, where, which, who
sendi	sent
sendiferðir	missions
sendr	sent
sent	sent
sér	he, him, himself, his, saw, see, to-him, to-see
serk	shirt
serkinn	the-shirt
serkr	shirt
sét	seen
setning	the-setting
setti	set
settist	sat
sex	six
sídan	afterwards
síðan	after, afterwards, since, since., then
síðar	afterwards, since
siðr	the-custom
síðum	sides
sigla	sail, sailed
sigldi	sail, sailed
sigldu	sailed
sigurðarson	Son-of-Sigurd (name)
sik	him, himself, his, themselves

Word List (Old Norse to English)

Old Norse	English
silfrdisk	silver-dish
silfrhring	silver-ring
silfri	silver
silfrkerum	silver
silfrs	silver
sín	hers, him, their, themselves
sína	his, their
sínar	his
sindraði	sparkled
sinn	his, occasion, their
sinna	his
sinnar	his
sinni	his, this
síns	his
sínum	hers, his
sitja	sit
sitr	sat
sitt	his, sat
sjá	saw, see, to-see
sjaldsénir	rarely-seen
sjálfr	itself
sjau	seven
sjáum	see
skal	shall
skál	shall
skalf	shook
skalt	shall
skaltu	shall, shall-you
skálum	bowls
skammt	a-short-distance, short
skapsmunum	mood-mind
skarlatsklæðum	scarlet-clothing
skatta	tax
skattgildir	tributaries
skaut	shot
skeggit	beard
skemmta	amuse
skemmtan	amusement
skemmtunar	amusement, entertainment
sker	a-rock
skildi	separated
skildu	separated
skildust	separated
skilja	separate, such
skiljast	separate
skilr	separating
skinnslit	colour
skip	a-ship, ship, the-ship
skipat	directed-to
skips	ships, the-ships
skipta	give
skipuð	equipped
skíra	baptised
skjótt	swiftly
skóga	forests
skógar	the-forest
skóginn	the-forest, the-forests
skörina	high-seat
skorinn	cut
skuli	shall
skulu	shall, should
skuluð	should
skyldi	should
skyldu	and, would
slær	struck
slagir	artful
slegit	struck
slík	such
slíka	such
slíkan	such
slíkar	such
slikum	such
sló	struck
slógu	formed
slysalaust	accidents-without
smáleik	small-games
smáleika	small-games
smásveinn	little-boy
snaraði	flew-it, threw, turned-quickly
snarat	twisted
snekkju	a-sailboat
snemma	early, soon
sneri	turned
sniðglímu	hip-throw
snjó	snow
snjórinn	the-snow
snöruðu	threw
snúinn	twisted

Word List (Old Norse to English)

Old Norse	English
sofa	seep, sleep, slept
sögðu	said
sól	the-sun
sólarfalli	sunset
sólin	sunrise
sólir	suns
sólskin	sunshine
son	son
sonr	son
sprakk	broke
spring	burst
spurði	asked
spyrjast	was-heard
staðar	standing, to-stand
stærsti	biggest
staf	staff
stafinn	the-staff, the-stick
stafnum	stick
stakk	struck
stálbroddr	steel-point
staldraði	lingered
stall	stable
standa	stand
stangaði	stabbed
sté	stepped
stefna	directed
stein	stone
steinhús	stone-house
steinkastinu	stone-throwing
steinn	stone
sterkari	stronger
sterkastr	strongest
sterkliga	strongly
sterkr	strong
steypa	cast
steyptist	fell, knocked
steyptu	cast
stígr	climbed
stikilinn	horn-point
stiklinum	the-narrow
stóð	stood, weighed
stóðu	stood
stöðum	places
stokkinn	the-foot-board
stökkva	jumped
stóra	great
stórr	big
stórri	large
strengdi	boldly
stríðlyndr	obstinate
ströng	strong
studdi	steadied
stundu	while
stundum	awhile
styrkja	strengthen
sú	so
sumarit	summer
sundi	swimming
sundr	apart
svá	saw, so, the
svarar	answered
svarit	sworn
svartan	black
sveinar	companions, men
sveinbarn	a-baby-boy
sveinn	boy
sverja	swear
svikit	tricked
svipmikill	a-striking
sviptingar	tussle
svipuleik	the-scourge
svipuleikr	the-scourge
sýna	show
sýndar	shown
sýndi	showed
sýndist	seemed, thought
sýnis	his
synjast	refuse

T, t

Old Norse	English
tak	take
taka	take, took
takið	take
talar	talked
tána	toe
tánni	toe
tekinn	taken
tekit	taken
tekr	takes, took

Word List (Old Norse to English)

Old Norse	English
tennr	teeth
tennrnar	teeth, the-teeth
tíðenda	news, of-news
tíðendi	news
til	for, of, to
tíma	time
tíu	ten
tjald	tents
togast	pulled
tók	received, took, tugged
tókst	took
tóku	took
tókust	took
töldust	considered
tólf	twelve
töluðu	told
trapiza	table
traust	trusted
trausti	Trusty (name)
trautt	scarcely
treysta	reckon, trust
treysti	trust
tröllaukinn	troll-possessed
tröllsligri	troll-like
tröllum	trolls
trú	faith, the-faith
tryggvason	Tryggvason (name)
tuttugu	twenty
tvá	two
tvær	two
tvau	two
tveggja	two
tveir	of, two
tvítugt	twenty

Þ, þ

Old Norse	English
þá	them, then, when
þaðan	from-there
þær	there, those
þætti	seem, the-story
þakkaði	thanked, thanked
þakkar	thanked
þangat	from-there, there
þann	that, the, then
þar	here, then, then, there, they, was
þat	it, that
þau	their, they
þegar	as-soon-as, straightaway, then, there
þeim	from-them, theirs, them, then, they
þeir	should, them, there, they
þeira	their, theirs, them, there, they, they-were
þeirar	there
þeiri	their
þekkti	knew
þenna	that
þér	to-you, you, yours
þerris	dry
þess	this
þessa	this
þessi	these, this
þessu	this
þetta	this
þíða	thaw
þik	you
þilfjöl	decks
þín	you, your
þína	yours
þínar	your
þing	assembly, things
þinn	yours
þit	you-two
þitt	your, yours
þjófsaugun	thief's-eyes
þjófshakan	thievish-chin
þjófsnefit	thieving-nose
þjóna	serve, serving
þjónar	serve
þó	though
þökkuðu	thanked
þol	endure
þorði	dared
þorir	dare, dared, daring
þormóðr	Thormod (name)
þórs	Thor's (name)

Word List (Old Norse to English)

Old Norse	English
þorstein	Thorstein (name)
þorsteini	Thorstein (name)
þorsteinn	Thorstein (name)
þorsteins	Thorstein's (name)
þótt	though
þótti	seemed, thought
þóttist	thought
þræli	servant
þrándheimi	Trondheim (place)
þreif	grabbed
þremr	three
þríhyrndr	three-sided
þrír	three
þrjá	three
þú	you
þung	heavy
þurfa	need
því	accordingly, as, because, it, that, then, therefore
þvílíkir	the-like
þykki	seems, think
þykkir	seems
þykkja	think, value, valued
þyngst	heaviest

U, u

Old Norse	English
ullu	wool
um	about, around, through
undan	away, away-from, before
undir	behind, down, under
undirheimum	under-world
undraðist	surprised
undrast	wonder
undruðust	wondered
unga	young
unnust	loved
unum	happy
upp	up
upphlaup	uproar
uppi	up
uppsprettu	up-spring
urðu	became, came
utan	except, except-for, out, out-of, outside, without
uxahnútu	ox-bone

Ú, ú

Old Norse	English
úlfaldi	camel
úlfhamr	Wolf-Skin (name)
úlfheðinn	Ulfhedin (name)
út	out
úti	out, over
útlægr	outlawed

V, v

Old Norse	English
vá	was
vaða	wades
væði	waded-through
vænginn	the-wing
vænsta	good
væri	should-be, was, would
vært	short
væru	were
vaf	wove
vakrliga	nimbly
vald	power
valdi	control
ván	is-expected
vanda	custom, difficulty
vanr	accustomed
vánt	difficulty
vápnaða	weaponed
var	was, were, when
vár	ours
varð	became, was
varðist	defended
vári	spring
varir	aware
várit	spring
varr	aware
vart	was

Word List (Old Norse to English)

Old Norse	English
várt	ours
váru	were, when
vaskligri	braver
vatn	the-water
vatnit	the-water
vátr	water
vaxa	grow
veðr	weather
veg	way
veginn	the-road
veik	turned
veit	know, known, knows
veita	grant, to-grant
veitti	granted
veittu	grant
veizla	feast
veizlan	the-feast
veizlunni	the-feast
vel	well
velfaranda	well-faring
vér	was, we
vera	be, being, were
verða	be, become, becomes
verðr	became, becomes, came
verkr	pain
vert	worth, worthy
vestri	the-west
vetr	winter
vetrinn	winter
vettlingana	mitten
við	against, by, of, to, with
víða	widely
vík	Vik (place)
víkr	moved
vil	will, wish
vilda	wish
vildi	willed, wished, wished-to, would
vildu	wished, would
vili	wish
vilja	he-wished, wished
viljum	wish
vill	will, wished
villa	lost-way

Old Norse	English
vilt	will, wish
viltu	will-you
vín	wine
vinsæll	popular
virðing	worthy
víst	certainly
vit	know
vita	knew, know
vitja	visit
víttr	bewitched
vöknaði	became-wet
vön	want
vörð	guard
vort	ours
vöttum	gloves
vöxt	grown

Y, y

Old Norse	English
yðr	you
yðrir	your
yðru	your
yðrum	yours
yfir	across, over
yndi	happiness
yrjum	Yrjar (place)

Ý, ý

Old Norse	English
ýmist	either

Word List (English to Old Norse)

Word List *(English to Old Norse)*

English	Old Norse	English	Old Norse
		alive	kvikt
A, a		all	alla, allan, allar, allir, allr, alls, allt, í, öllum
a	á, ein, eina, einn, einni, einum, eitt	all-mighty	allmiklum
		All-Strong (name)	allsterk, allsterkr
a-baby	barni	alone	einir
a-baby-boy	sveinbarn	along	með
a-bench	bekk	also	ok
abide	bíða	always	ávallt
ablaze	logandi	am	er
able-to	orkar	a-man	maðr
aboard	innanborðs	a-man's-head	mannshöfuð
about	á, at, en, í, um	among	í
a-burial-mound	haug	a-month	mánuð
accidents-without	slysalaust	a-mouth	munni
accordingly	því	amuse	skemmta
accustomed	vanr	amusement	skemmtan, skemmtunar
a-chieftain	höfðingi		
a-Christian	kristinn	an-average-man	meðalmaðr
a-circle	hring	anchor	akkerum
a-city	borg	and	eða, en, er, ok, skyldu
a-coward	níðingr	an-invite	boð
across	yfir	ankles	ökkla
acts	lætr	another	annarr, annarri, önnur
ad	ok	another-thing	annan
a-din	dunur	an-ounce-of	eyri
advice	ráð, ráða	answered	svarar
advised	réð	any	enga
a-fee	lén	anyone	hverr
a-forge	afli	anything	nokkut
after	áðr, eptir, síðan	apart	sundr
afterwards	aptr, sídan, síðan, síðar	a-precious-cloak	guðvefjarskikkju
		are	ert, eru, erum
against	at, mót, móti, við	are-you	ertu
Agdi (name)	agða, agði	a-river	á
Agdi's (name)	agða	a-rock	sker
agreed	sáttir	around	rönd, um
a-hall	höll	arranged	ráðast
a-hidden-man	huldumaðr	artful	slagir
a-high-seat	hásæti	as	at, er, sem, því
a-horn	horn, hornit	a-sailboat	snekkju
a-king's-son	konungsson	a-seat	atsetu
a-lie	logit	a-ship	skip

65

Word List (English to Old Norse)

English	Old Norse
a-short-distance	skammt
a-shower-of-sparks	gneistaflaug
as-if	sem
asked	bað, bauð, beiddi, biðr, spurði
a-skilled-craftsman	listamann
as-long-as	meðan
assembly	þing
assistance	lið
as-soon-as	þegar
a-steep-cliff	hömrum
a-striking	svipmikill
at	á, at, í
a-table	borðum
a-treasure	gersemi
avenge	hefna
await	bíða
aware	varir, varr
away	brott, burt, burtu, undan
away-from	frá, ór, undan
awhile	stundum
a-yard	álnar

B, b

English	Old Norse
back	aptr, bak
badly	illa
Balagardsida (place)	bálagarðssíðu
bald-headed	kollóttan
band	flokk
baptised	skíra
be	er, vera, verða
bear	ber, bera, berizt
beard	skeggit
beautiful	fagr
be-brought	færa
became	gerðist, orðinn, urðu, varð, verðr
became-wet	vöknaði
because	því
become	verða
becomes	verða, verðr
bed	sæng
before	áðr, fyrir, fyrr, undan
before-them	fyrir
behaved	breyttu
behind	eptir, undir
being	vera
below	niðr
be-named	heita
bench	bekk, bekkjar
benefit	gagn
bent	keiktist
bent-backwards	kikna
be-offered	framboðligr
beside	á, hjá
beside-standing	hjástöðu
best	beztir
better	betr, betra, betri
between	millum
bewitched	víttr
bid	bað, báðu
big	stórr
biggest	stærsti
binding	handsals
birds	fugla
Bjalfi	bjálfa, bjálfi
black	blár, svartan
blazed	logaði
boldly	strengdi
bore	bar, bárust, berast
borne	borit
both	báðum
bowls	skálum
boy	pilt, sveinn
brave	hraustr, röskr
braver	vaskligri
bravery	hreysti
breaking	boði
bring	berið
broad	breiða, breitt
broke	brotnaði, sprakk
broken	brotnaði
brother	bróður
brought	bera, borin, færði
Brynjolf (name)	brynjólfr
burial-mound-his	haugsins
burned	brann
burning	glóanda

Word List (English to Old Norse)

English	Old Norse
burst	brast, spring
burst-out-laughing	brosti
but	eða, en, enn, nema
by	á, við

C, c

English	Old Norse
call	kallar
called	heitir, kallaðr, kallar, kallat, kölluð, kvaddi
came	kemr, kom, koma, kominn, komu, kómu, kómust, minnum, urðu, verðr
camel	úlfaldi
can	kann
carried	bar, báru, borinn
carry	draga
cast	hleypt, kastaði, kastat, köstuðu, steypa, steyptu
catch	henda
caught	fengu, henti
celebrated	fagnaði
certainly	víst
champions	kapparnir
chased	eltu
child	barnit
children	börn
chin-bone	kinnbeinit
choose	kjós
Christian	kristinn, kristnum
cleaner	hreinna
clearing	rjóðr
climbed	stígr
closed	laukst
clothed	klæði, klæðir
clothes	klæði, klæðin, klæðum
cold	kalt
colour	skinnslit
come	gengit, kem, koma, komi, kominn, komnir
comes	kemr
coming	koma, komin, kominn, komit
companion	félagi, förunautr
companions	sveinar
company	flokk, liði
considered	töldust
control	valdi
conversations	mál
could	mátti, mun
could-be	mundi
counsel	ráð
countless	ótal
court	hirðprýði
court-man	hirðmaðr
court-men	hirðmönnum
crooked-staff	krókstaf
crooked-stick	krókstafr
cubits	álna
custom	vanda
cut	skorinn

D, d

English	Old Norse
Dagny (name)	dagný
dangerous	hættu, háski
dare	þorir
dared	þorði, þorir
daring	þorir
daughter	dóttir
day	dag, degi
dead	bana, dauð, dauðr
death	bana, bani, hel
decide	ráða
decks	þilfjöl
declared	heit
deep	djúp
defended	varðist
delays	dvelr
demand	krefja
devastated	eytt
did	gerði, gerðu
dies	deyr
difficulty	vanda, vánt
directed	stefna
directed-to	skipat
disappeared	horfin, hurfu, hvarf
dislocated	liði
district	heraði

Word List (English to Old Norse)

English	*Old Norse*
do	gera
done	ger, gera
doomed	feiga, feigr
door	dyrr
doorway	dyrum
down	niðr, ofan, undir
down-going	niðrgangs
drag	draga
drank	drakk, drukkit, drukku
dressed	klæddu
drew	brá, dregr
drink	af, drekka, drekkir, drukkit, drykknum
drinking	drekka, drukkit, drykkju, drykkjuskapr, máldrykkju
drinking-man	drykkjumaðr
drinks	drekkr
drink-to	drukkit
dripped	draup
drops	fellir
Drott (name)	drótt, dróttr
drove	rak, ráku
drowned	drukknuðu
drunk	drukkin, drukkit, full
dry	þerris
dug	grafit
dwarf	dverg, dvergrinn

E, e

each	hvárn, hvárt, hverjum, hverr, hvert
eagle	örn
ear	eyra
earl	jarl
early	snemma
ears	eyranu
east	austr
Eastern-Lands (place)	austr, austrveg, austrveginn
either	hvárttveggja, ýmist
either-side	hvárntveggja
elbows	olnbogarnir
embers	eimyrja
end	lúkum
ended	lokit
ending	endast
endure	þol
enough	nóg
entertainment	skemmtunar
equally-as-big	jafnstóra
equally-big	jafnstórr
equally-large	jafnstóra
equipped	skipuð
erupted	hrutu
even	sé
evening	kveldit, kvöld
everyone	hvern
every-time	jafnan
exceedingly	furðuliga
except	nema, utan
except-for	utan
explore	kanna
extra	auka
eyes	auga, augu, augum, augun

F, f

face	andliti
fair	fagrar, fagrt
fair-wind	byr
faith	trú
falling	fell, föll
far-away	fjarstætt
farmer	bóndi
farmstead	húsabæ
fastened	fast, festir
fat	fitan
fated	auðit
fated-to-die	feigr
father	faðir, föður
feast	veizla
feebler	ergist
fee-sparing	fésparir
feet	fæti, fætr, fótum
fell	datt, fell, fellu, steyptist
fellow	drengr

Word List (English to Old Norse)

English	Old Norse
fellows	kumpánar
festival	hátíð
filled	fylldan, ok
find	finna
finger-gold	fingrgull
fire	eld, eldi, eldr
fire-poker	eldsskara
first	fyrst, fyrsta, fyrstu, fyrstum
fist	hnefann
fitting	mátuligr
fjord	fjörð
flesh	holdi
flew-it	fleygir, snaraði
flies	flýgr
floor	gólfit
fog	myrkr
fold	felr
folk	fólk, fólki
follow	fylgja
followed	fylgdi, fylgt
following	áliðnum, fylgd, fylgdi, fylgja
following-men	fjölmenni
food	krásum, matr
food-servants	matsveinar
foolishly	heimsliga
for	á, fyrir, til
forces	hér
foremost	fremstir
forests	skóga
formed	slógu
foul	fúlt
found	fann, fannst
four	fjóra, fjórar, fjórum
friendly-terms	kærleikum
friendship	kærleikum
from	á, af, at, er, frá, fram, ór
from-hence	heðan
from-them	þeim
from-there	fram, þaðan, þangat
from-where	hvaðan
Frosti	frosti
Frosti (name)	frosta, frosti
Full-Strong (name)	fullsterk, fullsterkr

G, g

English	Old Norse
game	gamni
games	gamans, leikinn
gangrene	drep
gate	grindhliðit
Gaulardale (place)	gaulardal
gave	gaf, gáfu
Geirrod (name)	geirröð, geirröði, geirröðr
Geirrod's (name)	geirröði
Geirrod's-Town (place)	geirröðargarða, geirröðargörðum
get	fá, fengnir, geta, getr
get-hold-of	nát
get-tired	mæðast
Giant-Home (place)	jötunheima
Giant-Land (place)	jötunheimar, risaland, risalandi, risalands
giants	jötnum
giant's-wrath	jötunmóð
give	gef, gefa, skipta
given	gefr
glad	glaðir
gladly	gjarna, glaðir
Glasir-Plains (place)	glæsisvöllu, glæsisvöllum
glass-window	glerglugg
gloves	vöttum
glowing	glóanda
Gnipalund (place)	gnípalundi
go	fara, farið, ganga, gangi
Godmund	goðmundr
Godmund (name)	goðmund, goðmundar, goðmundi, goðmundr
Godmund's (name)	goðmundar
going	ganga
going-from	gagnvart
gold	gul, gull, gulli, gullligt, gullligum, gulr
gold-ball	gullhnött
gold-crown	gullkórónu
golden-bowl	gullker

Word List (English to Old Norse)

English	Old Norse	English	Old Norse
gold-necklace	gullmen	hand	hendi, hendr, hönd
gold-plated	gullbúnu	hand-cloth	handklæðit
gold-ring	gullhring	hand-cloths	handklæði
gold-rings	gullhringa	hands	höndum
gold-trimmed	gullskotnum	happiness	yndi
gold-woven	gullofit	happy	unum
gone	farin, farit	hard	fast
good	góða, góði, góðr, góðum, gott, vænsta	harder	fastara
		hardest	harðasti
Good (name)	góða, góði	hard-minded	harðúðigr
good-use	neytr	has	hefir
got	fekk, gat	have	eig, er, hafa, hafið, haft, hefi, hefir, höfum, lætr, lát, láta
got-they	fengust		
grabbed	greip, grip, krummurnar, þreif		
		having	hafa
grant	leggja, veita, veittu	he	hana, hann, honum, sér
granted	veitti		
great	mikil, mikill, mikinn, mikit, mikla, miklar, miklum, mjök, stóra	head	höfði, höfðum, höfuðit
		hear	heyra
		heard	heyrir
greeted	heilsaði	heat	hita
greetings	kveðju, kveðst	heaviest	þyngst
grey	grám	heavy	þung
Grim (name)	grím, grími, grímr	Heidrek (name)	heiðrekr
gripped	greip	he-is	sé
grow	vaxa	held	helt, helzt
grown	vöxt	helm-of-invisibility	hulinshjálm
Grundir (place)	grunda, grundir, grundum	Hemra (place)	hemra, hemru
		here	hér, hingat, þar
guard	vörð	hers	sín, sínum
Gudrun (name)	goðrún, goðrúnar, goðrúnu	he-took-care-of	annast
		hewed	hjó
guess	get	he-wished	vilja
Gust	gustr	hidden	leynt
		hide	fela

H, h

English	Old Norse	English	Old Norse
		hideous	ljótan
		high	há
had	ætti, átti, áttu, hafa, hafði, haft, hefði, hefir, höfðu, lá, lagði, leit, lét, létu	high-seat	hásæti, skörina
		hill	hól
		him	at, hann, hans, honum, sér, sik, sín
hailstorm	haglhríð	himself	sér, sik
Hakon (name)	hákon	hip-throw	sniðglímu
half	hálfan		
hall	hallar		
hall-floor	hallargólfi, hallargólfit		

Word List (English to Old Norse)

English	Old Norse
his	hans, honum, sér, sik, sína, sínar, sinn, sinna, sinnar, sinni, síns, sínum, sitt, sýnis
his-head	höfuðit
hit	hæfa
hold	halda
hold-of	nát
homage	hlýðni
home	heim
honour	heiðr
horn	fyllt, horn, horninu, hornit
horn-point	stikilinn
horns	horn
horse	hesti, hestr
horses	hest, hesta, hestar, hestum
Hosvir (name)	hösvi, hösvir
hot	heitt
house	hús
House-Child (name)	bæjarbarn, bæjarbarni, bæjarbarns
House-Power (name)	bæjarmagn
houses	húsum
how	hverju
howling	grenjaði
how-so	hversu

I, i

English	Old Norse
I	ek, mér
if	ef, í, sem
ill	illa
in	á, at, í, inn
India	indíalandi
inheritance	arf, erfi
injury	saka
inlaid	búit
in-memory	minni
in-one	einu
inside	inn
intend	ætla
intended	ætlaði, ætlar
intentions	ætlan
into	á, í
invite	býðr
Iron-Beard (name)	járnskeggja
is	á, er, eru, sé
is-expected	ván
is-named	hét
it	at, hana, hann, honum, í, þat, því
itself	sjálfr

J, j

English	Old Norse
Jamtland (place)	jamtaland
jaw	kjaptrinn
jealous	öfundsjúkir
joined	festi
Jokul (name)	jökull
Jokul's (name)	jökli
journey	ferð
joyful	fegnir
jumped	stökkva

K, k

English	Old Norse
Kark (name)	karkr
keep	halda
kill	drepa
killed	drap, drepnir
kin	kyn
kinds	háttar
king	konungi, konungr
kingdom	ríki
kissed	kyssti
knees	kné
knew	þekkti, vita
knocked	steyptist
know	kenna, kunnigt, veit, vit, vita
known	veit
knows	kann, veit
Kollsvein (name)	kollsveinn

Word List (English to Old Norse)

English	*Old Norse*

L, l

English	Old Norse
lack-of-money	féfátt
laid	lá, lagði, lágu
land	land, landit
landed	lendr
large	mikill, mikit, stórri
larger	mikli
large-river	móðu
largest	mikli
laughed	hló, hlógu
laughter	hlátr, hlátri
law	lög
lay	lá, lagðist
lay-out	láta
leave	orlof
leave-it	látum
led	leiða, leiddr
left	lagt
leg	fótrinn
less-should	óskyldara
let	lát
lie-down	liggja
life-gift	lífgjöf
like	líkari, líkast
lineage	ættar
lingered	staldraði
little	lítill, lítilli, lítinn, lítit, litlu
little-boy	smásveinn
live	búa
lived	bjó, lifði
lives	lifir
living-thing	kvikt
long	langan, löngu
Long (name)	langa
longer	lengr
looking	bragði
loosed	laust
lose	missa
lost	missi
lost-way	villa
lot	hluti
loved	unnust
low-energy	orkufátt
Lucanus (name)	lúkanus
luck	gæfa, gæfu, góðri, hamingju
lying	liggr

M, m

English	Old Norse
mad	galinn
made	gert, léti
magic-full	galdrafullt
make	gera
man	maðr, manna, manni, manns
many	marga, margir
marble	hall
may	má, mátt, mega, megi
me	mér, mik, mín, mitt
meet	finnumst, mót, móti
melted	bráðnaði
men	flokki, hann, manna, menn, mönnum, sveinar
men's	manna
mercy	miskunnar
merry	kátir
met	fann, fundizt
mine	mín, mína, mínir, minn, mínu, mínum, mitt
missions	sendiferðir
mitten	vettlingana
mittens	bandvettlinga
mood-mind	skapsmunum
more	auka, fleira, meira
morning	morgin, morgininn, morginn, morgni, morguninn
most	flestum, mest
mostly	mest
mother	móðir
mound	hóll
mountain-pastures	sætr
mountains	fjalli
mouth	kjaptinum
moved	réðst, víkr
moving	fór

Word List (English to Old Norse)

English	Old Norse
much	mikils, mikinn, mikit, miklar, miklu, mjök
musical-instruments	hljóðfæra, hljóðfæri
must	mun
must-be	mundu, munt
my	mín, mínir, minn
myself	mik
my-wife	eiga

N, n

English	Old Norse
name	nafn, nafni
named	heita, heiti, heitir, hét, nefndi, nefndir
name-titles	nafnbætr
naming-gift	nafnfesti
natured	náttúru
near	nær, næst
need	þurfa
neither	hvárki, hvergi
never	aldri
news	frétt, tíðenda, tíðendi
next	næst
next-to	næst
night	nótt, nóttina
nights	nætr
nimbly	vakrliga
no	ekki, engi, engir, engum
none	eigi, enga, engi, engum
no-one	engan
nor	né
Norway (place)	noreg, noregi, noregs
nose	nasir, nefit
not	eigi, ekki, engi
nothing	eigi, einskis, ekki, engu
Novgorod (place)	hólmgörðum
now	nú

O, o

English	Old Norse
oak	eik
oath	eiða
oaths	eiða
obstinate	stríðlyndr
occasion	sinn
Odin (name)	óðinn, óðni
Odin's (name)	óðins
of	á, af, at, er, í, of, ór, til, tveir, við
off	af
offered	bauð
off-handed	afhenda
of-hand	afhenda
of-news	tíðenda
often	opt
of-the-bench	bekkinn
of-the-day	dagsins
Olaf (name)	óláf, óláfi, Óláfr
Olaf's (name)	óláfs
oldest	eldist
on	á, en, í
one	annarr, annarri, eina, einn, einu, einum, eitt, öðrum, önnur
on-the-nose	nösunum
onto	á
open	opinn
opening	beitina, gátum
open-sea	hafvillur
oppose	móti
opposite	gegnt, öndvegit
opposition	móti
or	eða
orchard	aldingarðr
ordered	bað
other	aðra, annars, öðrum, önnur
others	aðrir, hinir
Ottar's (name)	óttars
ounces	aura
ours	oss, vár, várt, vort
out	út, utan, úti
outlawed	útlægr
out-of	ór, utan
outside	utan
over	at, fyrir, ofan, úti, yfir
own	eigum
owned	átti

Word List (English to Old Norse)

English	Old Norse
ox-bone	uxahnútu

P, p

English	Old Norse
pain	verkr
pale	bleikum
passed	líðr
pay	fá
payment	mútur
peaceful	fríð
piece-of-marble	hall
pitch	bik
places	stöðum
play	leika
played	lék, lékst
playing-tricks	glettist
pledging	lofaði
point	brodd, broddinum
poison	eitr, ólyfjan
popular	vinsæll
possessions	eigna
possible	hægt
pouch	pungi
power	vald
praised	lofuðu
precious-cloth	guðvef
precious-stones	gimsteinar
precious-things	gersema
prepared	bjó, búin, búit, búnir
prick	pjakka, pjakkar
pricked	pjakkar
promise	lófa
promised	heita, hét
property	eignir
provide	afla, framt
pulled	togast
pushed	hratt

Q, q

English	Old Norse
quarters	fjórðunga

R, r

English	Old Norse
raiding	hernaði
raised	fæddi, reisti, reistu
ran	hlaupa, hleypr, hljóp, rann, renna
rarely-seen	sjaldsénir
rather	heldr
received	tók
reckon	ráða, treysta
recognised	kenndr
red	rauðr, rauðum, rautt
refuse	synjast
relieved	feginn
repay	launa, launat
retain	geyma
return	aptr
revealed	birti
ride	reiðu, ríða
ride-away	ríða
riding	reið, ríða
ring	hring
river	ok
rocking	ruggaði
rode	ríða, ríðr, riðu
room	rúm
rose	reiddist, reis, ríss
ruled	réð
ruler	ræð
rules	ræðr
ruthless	óvæginn

S, s

English	Old Norse
sack	klæðsekk
said	kvað, kvaðst, kveðst, mælti, sagði, sagðist, segir, segist, sögðu
said-of	eiga
said-to	segir
sail	sigla, sigldi
sailed	sigla, sigldi, sigldu
same	sama
sat	sat, settist, sitr, sitt

Word List (English to Old Norse)

English	Old Norse	English	Old Norse
saw	sá, sáu, sér, sjá, svá	sides	síðum
saw-you	sáttu	silver	silfri, silfrkerum, silfrs
say	seg, segir, segja	silver-dish	silfrdisk
scarcely	trautt	silver-ring	silfrhring
scarlet-clothing	skarlatsklæðum	since	síðan, síðar
screamed	grenjaði	since.	síðan
seal's-head	selshöfuð	sit	sitja
seat	sæti, sætis	six	sex
see	sá, sé, sér, sjá, sjáum	skilled-in-magic	fjölkunnigr
seeing	sá	skills	kunnáttu
seek	sækið	sleep	sofa
seem	þætti	slept	sefr, sofa
seemed	sýndist, þótti	slope	hlíðir
seems	þykki, þykkir	slowly	seint
seen	sét	small	lítill
seep	sofa	smaller	minni
sent	sendi, sendr, sent	small-games	smáleik, smáleika
separate	skilja, skiljast	smiling	hlæjandi
separated	skildi, skildu, skildust	smoke	reyk
separating	skilr	snow	fönn, snjó
servant	þræli	so	sá, sú, svá
serve	þjóna, þjónar	some	nokkura, nokkurn, nokkuru, nokkut
serving	þjóna	someone	einhverr
set	setti	something	nokkurr
settled	bjuggust	some-way	einhvern
settlements	byggð	somewhat	nokkuru
seven	sjau	son	son, sonr
shall	mun, skal, skál, skalt, skaltu, skuli, skulu	Son-of-Sigurd (name)	sigurðarson
shall-you	muntu, skaltu	soon	snemma
she	hana, hún	South-East	landsuðri
ship	skip	sparkled	sindraði
ships	skips	sparks	gneistar
shirt	serk, serkr	sparks-flying	gneistaflaugin
shook	hristi, skalf	speak	mæla
short	skammt, vært	speaks	mælir
shot	skaut	split	rifnaði
should	mun, mundi, munt, muntu, munu, munum, skulu, skuluð, skyldi, þeir	spoke	mælt, mælti
		spread	breiddu
		spring	vári, várit
should-be	mun, væri	stabbed	stangaði
show	sýna	stable	stall
showed	sýndi	staff	refði, staf
shown	sýndar	stand	standa
side	megin	standing	staðar
		steadied	studdi

Word List (English to Old Norse)

English	Old Norse	English	Old Norse
steel-point	stálbroddr	taught	kenna
stepped	sté	tax	skatta
stick	stafnum	teeth	tennr, tennrnar
stone	stein, steinn	tell	segja
stone-house	steinhús	ten	tíu
stone-throwing	steinkastinu	tend-to	græð
stood	stóð, stóðu	tents	tjald
straightaway	þegar	test	reynt
strength	afl, afli	than	at, en, enn
strengthen	styrkja	thanked	þakkaði, þakkar, þökkuðu
stripes	röndum		
strong	sterkr, ströng	that	á, af, at, en, er, sem, þann, þat, þenna, því
stronger	sterkari		
strongest	sterkastr	that-bench	bekknum
strongly	sterkliga	thaw	þíða
struck	slær, slegit, sló, stakk	thaws	bræðir
such	skilja, slík, slíka, slíkan, slíkar, slikum	the	á, ána, at, en, hornit, í, in, ina, inn, inum, it, svá, þann
suits	hentar	the-air	lopti
summer	sumarit	the-back	bak
sunrise	sólin	the-back-of-the-head	hnakkinn
suns	sólir	the-back-of-the-knees	knésbætr
sunset	sólarfalli	the-ball	knettinum, knöttinn, knöttrinn
sunshine	sólskin		
suppose	ætla	the-bench	bekknum
surprised	undraðist	the-bone	beini, beinum
swear	sverja	the-boy	kollsveinn, piltrinn
sweet-smell	ilmr	the-chest	bringu
swift	frár	the-child	barn, barnit
swiftly	skjótt	the-city	borgarinnar, borgina
swimming	sundi	the-clearing	rjóðrinu
sworn	svarit	the-company-of	lið
		the-crooked-stick	krókstafinn
		the-cross	kross
		the-crown	kórónu

T, t

English	Old Norse	English	Old Norse
		the-cup-bearer	byrlaranum
table	borð, borðinu, trapiza	the-cups	köppunum
table-cloth	dúkinn, dúkr	the-curtain	fortjaldinu
tablecloths	dúka	the-curve	bugtinni
take	tak, taka, takið	the-custom	siðr
take-care	hirðið	the-death	bani
take-care-of	ábyrgjast	the-district	heraðinu, heraðit
taken	tekinn, tekit	the-door	dyranna, dyrr, dyrrnar
takes	tekr	the-dwarf	dvergnum, dvergrinn
talked	talar	the-dwarf's-boy	dvergsbarnit
tall	mikil		

Word List (English to Old Norse)

English	Old Norse	English	Old Norse
the-dwelling	bæinn, bú	the-moat	díki
the-eagle	erninum	the-morning	morgin
the-earl	jarl, jarli, jarls	the-most	mestr
the-earl's	jarli, jarls	the-mound	hauginn, haugrinn, hólinn, hólnum
the-evening	aptnaði, kveld		
the-faith	trú	the-mouth	kjaptinum
the-feast	veizlan, veizlunni	themselves	sik, sín
the-fire	eldrinn	the-mud	saur
the-flames	eldr	then	á, en, er, síðan, þá, þann, þar, þegar, þeim, því
the-floor	gólfi, gólfit		
the-foot-board	stokkinn		
the-forest	skógar, skóginn	the-narrow	stiklinum
the-forests	skóginn	the-neck	háls
the-full	fullu	the-night	nóttina
the-game	gamninu	the-oak	eikinni
the-gates	hliðin	the-old	gamalla
the-gifts	gjafirnar	the-opening	beitina
the-good	góða	the-other	annarr, hinir
the-greatest	mestr	the-piece-of-marble	hallinn, hallrinn
the-ground	jörðina	the-point	broddinum, broddrinn
the-hall	höll, höllina, höllinni	the-queen	drottning
the-harbour	höfn	there	sá, þær, þangat, þar, þegar, þeir, þeira, þeirar
the-horn	hornin, horninu, hornunum		
		therefore	því
the-horns	hornin	the-ring	hringinn, hringnum, hringrinn
the-horses	hestarnir		
the-house	hús	the-river	ána, ánni, árinnar, móðuna
their	sín, sína, sinn, þau, þeira, þeiri		
		the-road	veginn
theirs	þeim, þeira	the-scourge	svipuleik, svipuleikr
the-journey	færist, ferð	these	þessi
the-king	konung, konungi, konungnum, konungr, konungrinn, konungs	The-Serpent (name)	orminum
		the-setting	setning
		the-ship	skip
the-king's	konungs	the-ships	skips
the-king's-hall	konungshöll	the-shirt	serkinn
the-king's-name	konungsnafn	the-sky	himni, lopti
the-king's-son	konungsson	the-skylight	glugginn
the-land	land, landi, landit	the-snow	snjórinn
the-like	þvílíkir	the-south-east	landsuðr
them	þá, þeim, þeir, þeira	the-staff	stafinn
the-marble	hallinn, hallinum, hallrinn	the-stick	keyrir, stafinn
		the-story	þætti
the-matter	mál	the-sun	sól
the-men	menn, mönnum	the-table-cloth	dúkinn
the-middle	miðit, miðju	the-tables	borða, borðum

Word List (English to Old Norse)

English	Old Norse	English	Old Norse
the-teeth	tennrnar	to-grant	veita
the-town	borgarinnar, borgina	to-have	láta
the-trees	mörkina	to-him	honum, sér
the-water	vatn, vatnit	to-injure	granda
the-west	vestri	told	sagði, sagt, segir, töluðu
the-wing	vænginn		
the-world	heiminum	told-of	getit
they	drekka, þar, þau, þeim, þeir, þeira	to-make	gera
		to-me	mér
they-are	eru	to-meet	mót, móti
they-were	þeira	to-mind	geyma
thick-set	búk	took	færði, nam, taka, tekr, tók, tókst, tóku, tókust
thief's-eyes	þjófsaugun		
thieving-nose	þjófsnefit	to-overpower	ofmagni
thievish-chin	þjófshakan	to-own	eiga
things	þing	to-repay	laun
think	hug, þykki, þykkja	to-ride	ríða
this	it, sinni, þess, þessa, þessi, þessu, þetta	to-see	sér, sjá
		to-stand	staðar
Thormod (name)	Þormóðr	to-the-father	föðurnum
Thor's (name)	Þórs	to-travel	fara
Thorstein (name)	Þorstein, Þorsteini, Þorsteinn	towards	at
		to-wrestling	fangbrögðum
Thorstein's (name)	Þorsteins	to-you	þér
those	þær	trading-journeys	kaupferðum
though	en, þó, þótt	trading-voyages	kaupferðir
thought	hugr, sýndist, þótti, þóttist	travel	færir, far, fara
		travelled	fara, ferð, fór, fóru, fóruð
three	þremr, þrír, þrjá		
three-sided	þríhyrndr	travelling	fara, ferr
threw	berði, kastaði, kastar, snaraði, snöruðu	treasure	gersemi, gripi
		treasured	gersemar
throat	hálsinum	treasures	gersemar, gersemi, gripi
through	ór, um		
throw	kastið	trembled	hrysi
thrown	ausit	tributaries	skattgildir
thrust	lagi	trick	leikinn
time	tíma	tricked	prett, svikit
to	á, af, at, fram, í, ok, til, við	tricks	fimleika
		troll-like	tröllsligri
to-announce	kunngera	troll-possessed	tröllaukinn
to-do	gera	trolls	tröllum
to-drink	drekka	Trondheim (place)	Þrándheimi
toe	tána, tánni	trust	treysta, treysti
to-get	hlytir	trusted	traust
together	saman	Trusty (name)	trausti
to-going	atgang, atgangr		

Word List (English to Old Norse)

English	Old Norse
Tryggvason (name)	tryggvason
tugged	tók
tumbled	rasaði
turned	sneri, veik
turned-away	brautinni
turned-quickly	snaraði
turning	brautinni
tussle	sviptingar
twelve	tólf
twenty	tuttugu, tvítugt
twisted	snarat, snúinn
two	tvá, tvær, tvau, tveggja, tveir

U, u

English	Old Norse
Ulfhedin (name)	úlfheðinn
unconscious	óvit
under	neðra, undir
under-world	undirheimum
undressed	afklæðast, afklæddust
unfinished	ófarin
unfriendly	óþýðr
unfriendly-looking	óhýrligr
unhappy	ófögnuðr
un-indulgent	óaflátssamr
unlike	ólík
un-peace	ófriðar
unspoken	óorðna
up	upp, uppi
uproar	upphlaup
up-spring	uppsprettu
us	okkr, oss

V, v

English	Old Norse
vacation	orlofs
valour	hreysti
value	þykkja
valued	þykkja
vanished	hurfu
vessel	ker
Vik (place)	vík
visit	vitja
voyage	ferð, ferðum

W, w

English	Old Norse
waded	óðu
waded-through	væði
wades	vaða
walk	ganga
walking	gangandi
want	vön
warrior	kempa
was	á, er, í, þar, vá, væri, var, varð, vart, vér
was-heard	spyrjast
water	vátr
wave	felli
way	braut, veg
we	vér
weak	deigum
weakly	lítilmannliga
wealth	fé
weaponed	vápnaða
weather	veðr
wedding-proposal	brullaup
weighed	stóð
welcomed	fagnaði
well	sæmilig, vel
well-faring	velfaranda
went	fekk, ferr, fór, fóru, gekk, gengr, gengu
went-for	hösvaðist
went-from	frá
were	eru, hvar, væru, var, váru, vera
wether's	sauða
what	hvar, hvat, hvert, hví
whatever	sem
when	at, en, er, þá, var, váru
where	hvar, sem
whether	hvárt
which	at, er, hvárt, sem
while	en, meðan, stundu
white	hvítr, hvítt
Whitings (name)	hvítinga, hvítingar, hvítingum

Word List (English to Old Norse)

English	Old Norse
who	á, er, hvat, hverr, sem
whole	heill
whose	hverrar
why	hví
widely	víða
wife	kona
wild-animals	dýr
will	vil, vill, vilt
willed	vildi
will-you	viltu
wine	vín
winter	vetr, vetrinn
wiser	kunngera
wish	vil, vilda, vili, viljum, vilt
wished	vildi, vildu, vilja, vill
wished-to	vildi
witch-ride	gandreið
with	á, með, við
without	utan
with-that	í
Wolf-Skin (name)	úlfhamr
women	konur
wonder	undrast
wondered	undruðust
wool	ullu
word	orðit
words	orðum
worth	vert
worthy	vert, virðing
would	mun, mundi, mundu, muni, skyldu, væri, vildi, vildu
would-be	mundum, munu
would-have	mundi
wound	sár
wove	vaf
wrestle	glíma
wrestled	glímt
wrestling	glíma

English	Old Norse
you	sé, þér, þik, þín, þú, yðr
young	unga
young-woman	jungfrú
your	þín, þínar, þitt, yðrir, yðru
yours	þér, þína, þinn, þitt, yðrum
you-two	þit
Yrjar (place)	yrjum
Yule (name)	jólin, jólum

Y, y

English	Old Norse
yellow	gulr

The Tale of Thorsteinn House-Power (*Old Icelandic*)

Old Icelandic	Literal	English
1	**1**	**1**
Í þann tíma, er Hákon jarl Sigurðarson réð fyrir Noregi, bjó sá bóndi í Gaulardal, er Brynjólfur hét.	At that time, was Hakon earl Son-of-Sigurd ruled over Norway, lived there farmer in Gaulardale, was Brynjolf named.	About the time when Earl Hakon Sigurdson was ruler of Norway, there lived a farmer in Gaulardale, named Brynjolf.
hann var kallaður úlfaldi.	he was called Camel.	He was called Brynjolf Camel.
hann var lendur maður og mikil kempa.	he was landed man and great warrior.	He was a landed man and a great warrior.
kona hans hét Dagný hún var dóttir Járnskeggja af Yrjum.	wife his named Dagny she was daughter Iron-Beard of Yrjar.	His wife was named Dagny and she was the daughter of Iron-Beard of Yrjar.
þau áttu einn son, er Þorsteinn hét.	they had one son, who Thorstein named.	They had one son who was named Thorstein.
hann var mikill og sterkr, harðúðigr og óaflátssamr við hvern, sem eiga var.	he was great and strong, hard-minded and un-indulgent with everyone, as said-of was.	He was large and strong, strong-minded and unflinching with everyone that he spoke with.
engi var jafnstórr í Noregi, og trautt fengust þær dyrr, að honum væri hægt um að ganga, og því var hann kallaður Bæjarmagn, því að hann þótti ofmagni bera flestum húsum.	none were equally-big in Norway, and scarcely got-they there door, that he would possible about to walk, and because was he called House-Power, because that he seemed to-overpower bear most houses.	No one was as big in all Norway, and there was scarcely a door that he could walk through, and he was called House-Power, because he seemed to overpower most houses.
hann var óbýður, og fekk faðir hans honum því skip og menn, og var Þorsteinn þá ýmist í hernaði eða í kaupferðum, og tókst honum hvárttveggja vel.	he was unfriendly, and got father his him therefore a-ship and men, and was Thorstein then either in raiding or in trading-journeys, and took he either well.	He was so unfriendly that his father gave him a ship with some men, and Thorstein was either raiding or trading, and he took to both well.

The Tale of Thorsteinn House-Power (Old Icelandic)

Old Icelandic	Literal	English
Í þenna tíma tók ríki í Noregi Óláfur konungr Tryggvason, en Hákon jarl var skorinn á háls af þræli sínum, þeim sem Þormóður Karkr hét.	in that time took kingdom in Norway Olaf the-king Tryggvason, when Hakon earl was cut in the-neck of servant his, then as Thormod Kark named.	It was about this time that King Olaf Tryggvason ruled the kingdom of Norway, when Earl Hakon had his throat slit by one of his servants, who was named Thormod Kark.
Þorsteinn Bæjarmagn gerðist hirðmaður Óláfs konungs.	Thorstein House-Power became court-man Olaf's the-king's.	Thorstein House-Power became a court man of King Olaf's.
þótti konungi hann röskr maður og helt mikið til hans, en ekki var hann mjög kenndur af hirðmönnum.	thought the-king he brave man and held much to him, but not was he much recognised of court-men.	The king thought he was a brave man and thought highly of him, but he was not liked by the other court-men.
þótti þeim hann stríðlyndur og óvæginn, og hafði konungr hann mjög til þess að fara sendiferðir þær, sem aðrir töldust undan að fara.	thought they he obstinate and ruthless, and had the-king he great for this to travel missions those, that others considered away from travelling.	They found him obstinate and ruthless, and the king had him going on great missions, that others were reluctant to travel on.
en stundum fór hann kaupferðir að afla konungnum gersema.	about awhile travelled he trading-voyages to provide the-king precious-things.	For a while he went on trading voyages to bring the king treasures.

2

eitt sinn lá Þorsteinn austr fyrir Bálagarðssíðu, og gaf honum eigi að sigla.	one occasion lay Thorstein east before Balagardsida, and gave him not to sail.	On one occasion Thorstein lay east near Balagardsida, and he was not given wind to sail.
gekk hann á land einn morgin, og er sól var í landsuðri, var Þorsteinn kominn í eitt rjóður.	went he to land one morning, and when the-sun was in South-East, was Thorstein coming to a clearing.	He went to land one morning, and when the sun was in the South-East, Thorstein came to a clearing.
hóll fagr var í rjóðrinu.	mound beautiful was in the-clearing.	There was a beautiful mound in the clearing.
hann sá einn kollóttan pilt uppi á hólnum, og mælti:	he saw a bald-headed boy up on the-mound, and spoke:	He saw a bald-headed boy up on the mound, and he spoke:
"móðir mín",	"mother mine",	"Mother mine",

The Tale of Thorsteinn House-Power (Old Icelandic)

Old Icelandic	Literal	English
segir hann, "fá þú mér út krókstaf minn og bandvettlinga, því að ek vil á gandreið fara.	said he, "get you me out crooked-staff mine and mittens, because that I wish to witch-ride go.	he said, "get me my crooked staff and mittens, because I wish to go on a witch ride.
er nú hátíð í heiminum neðra".	is now festival in the-world under".	There is now a festival in the underworld".
þá var snarað út ór hólnum einum krókstaf, sem eldsskara væri.	then was twisted out from the-mound a crooked-staff, as fire-poker was.	Then a crooked staff was thrown out from the mound, shaped like a poker.
hann stígr á stafinn og dregr á sik vettlingana og keyrir, sem börn eru vön að gera.	he climbed on the-staff and drew of his mitten and the-stick, as children are want to do.	He climbed on the staff and drew on his mittens and began riding the stick, as children often do.
Þorsteinn gengr á hólinn og mælti slikum orðum sem piltrinn, og var þegar út kastað staf og vöttum og mælt þetta:	Thorstein went to the-mound and spoke such words as the-boy, and was then out cast staff and gloves and spoke this:	Thorstein went to the mound and spoke the same words that the boy had, and then a staff and gloves were cast out and a voice asked:
"hverr tekr nú við?"	"who takes now with?"	"Who wants these now?".
"bjálfi, sonr þinn",	"Bjalfi, son yours",	"Bjalfi, your son",
sagði Þorsteinn.	said Thorstein.	said Thorstein.
síðan stígr hann á stafinn og ríður þar eptir, sem piltrinn fór undan.	afterwards climbed he on the-staff and rode there after, as the-boy travelled away-from.	Afterwards he climbed on the staff and rode away after the boy.
þeir kómu að einni móðu og steyptu sér ofan í hana, og var því líkast sem þeir væði reyk.	they came to a large-river and cast he down in it, and was it like as they waded-through smoke.	They came to a large river and cast down into it, and it was like they were wading through smoke.
því næst birti þeim fyrir augum, og kómu þeir að, sem á fell fram af hömrum.	then near revealed they before eyes, and came they to, as a-river falling from off a-steep-cliff.	Then revealed before their eyes, they came to where a river was falling from a steep cliff.
sér Þorsteinn þá byggð mikla og borg stóra.	saw Thorstein then settlements great and a-city great.	Thorstein then saw large settlements and a great city.
þeir stefna til borgarinnar, og sitr þar fólk yfir borðum.	they directed to the-city, and sat there folk across a-table.	They turned to the city, and there people were sat across a table.

The Tale of Thorsteinn House-Power (Old Icelandic)

Old Icelandic	Literal	English
þeir gengu í höllina, og var höll skipuð af fólki, og var þar af engu drukkið utan af silfrkerum.	they went in the-hall, and was the-hall equipped of folk, and were they of nothing drinking except-for of silver.	They walked into the hall, and there were people filling the hall, and they were drinking from nothing but silver cups.
trapiza stóð á gólfi.	table stood on the-floor.	A table stood on the floor.
allt sýndist þeim þar gullligt og ekki drukkið nema vín.	all seemed they there gold and nothing drunk but wine.	Everything seemed to be gold, and everyone drunk nothing but wine.
það þóttist Þorsteinn skilja, að engi maður sá þá.	that thought Thorstein such, that no man see then.	Then Thorstein realised that no man could see them.
félagi hans fór með borðum og henti allt það, sem niður fell.	companion his went along the-tables and caught all that, as down fell.	His companion went along the tables and caught all that fell down from them.
konungr sat þar í hásæti og drottning.	the-king sat there in high-seat and the-queen.	The king sat there in the high seat with the queen.
menn váru glaðir um höllina.	men were glad about the-hall.	The men about the hall were glad.
þessu næst sér Þorsteinn, að maður kom í höllina og kvaddi konung og kveðst vera sendur til hans utan af indíalandi ór fjalli því, er Lúkanus heitir, frá jarli þeim, er þar réð fyrir, og segir konungi, að hann var huldumaður.	this next saw Thorstein, that a-man came into the-hall and called the-king and greetings were sent to him out of India from mountains because, that Lucanus named, from the-earl they, that was advised for, and said the-king, that he was a-hidden-man.	Then Thorstein saw that a man had come into the hall and greeted the king, and he sent greetings from the mountains of India because the earl Lucanus ruled there, and he advised the king that he was an elf-man.
hann færði honum einn gullhring.	he took to-him a gold-ring.	He presented him with a gold ring.
eigi þóttist konungr betri hring sét hafa, og fór hringrinn um höllina til sýnis, og lofuðu hann allir.	not thought the-king better ring seen had, and went the-ring about the-hall to his, and praised it all.	The king thought that he had not seen a better ring, and it was shown around the hall, and praised by all.
hann var sundur tekinn í fjórum stöðum.	it was apart taken in four places.	This ring could be taken apart in four sections.
annan grip sá Þorsteinn, er honum þótti mikils um vert.	another-thing grabbed seeing Thorstein, that to-him thought much about worth.	Another thing grabbed Thorstein's sight, that he thought might be worth a lot.

The Tale of Thorsteinn House-Power (Old Icelandic)

Old Icelandic	Literal	English
það var dúkr sá, er lá á konungs borðinu.	it was table-cloth saw, that laid at the-king's table.	It was the table cloth that he saw, which was laid at the king's table.
hann var með gullligum röndum og í festir þeir tólf gimsteinar, sem beztir eru.	it was with gold stripes and on fastened there twelve precious-stones, that best were.	It had stripes of gold and was fastened with twelve of the best precious stones.
gjarna vildi Þorsteinn dúkinn eiga.	gladly willed Thorstein table-cloth to-own.	Thorstein gladly wished to own the table-cloth.
kemur honum í hug að treysta á konungs hamingju og vita, hvárt hann getr ekki nát hringnum.	came he to think to reckon on the-king's luck and know, whether he get not get-hold-of the-ring.	He came to think about the king's luck and find out whether or not he could get hold of the ring.
nú sér Þorsteinn, að konungrinn ætlar að draga hringinn á hönd sér.	now saw Thorstein, that the-king intended to carry the-ring on hand his.	Now Thorstein saw that the king intended to carry the ring on his hand.
þá greip Þorsteinn hringinn af honum, en annarri hendi tók hann dúkinn, og fór allr matr í saur, en Þorsteinn hljóp á dyrr, en krókstafur hans varð honum eptir í höllinni.	then grabbed Thorstein the-ring off him, then another hand took he the-table-cloth, and went all food in the-mud, then Thorstein ran to the-door, but crooked-stick his was him behind in the-hall.	Then Thorstein grabbed the ring off him, and then with his other hand he took the table cloth, and all the food fell in the mud, and then Thorstein ran to the door, but the crooked stick was behind him in the hall.
verður nú upphlaup mikið, hlaupa menn út síðan og sjá, hvar Þorsteinn ferr, og stefna eptir honum.	became now uproar great, ran men out after and saw, where Thorstein went, and directed after him.	There now became a great uproar, and men ran out afterwards and saw where Thorstein went and started after him.
sér hann nú, að þeir muni geta nát honum.	saw he now, that they would get hold-of him.	He saw now that they would catch him.
hann mælti þá:	he spoke then:	He then spoke:
"ef þú ert svá góður, Óláfur konungr, sem ek treysti mikið til þín, þá veittu mér lið".	"if you are so good, Olaf king, as I trust much to you, then grant me assistance".	"If you are so good king Olaf, as I trust you are, then grant me assistance".
en svá var Þorsteinn frár, að þeir kómust ekki fyrir hann, fyrr en hann kom að ánni, og staldraði hann þá við.	then so was Thorstein swift, that they came not for him, before that he came to the-river, and lingered he then with.	Then Thorstein was so fast, that they could not catch him before he came to the river, where he had to wait.

The Tale of Thorsteinn House-Power (Old Icelandic)

Old Icelandic	Literal	English
þeir slógu hring um hann, en Þorsteinn varðist vel og drap ótal marga, áður förunautr hans kom og færði honum stafinn, og hurfu þeir þegar í móðuna.	they formed a-circle around him, and Thorstein defended well and killed countless many, after companion his came and brought him the-stick, and disappeared they straightaway into the-river.	They formed a circle around him, and Thorstein defended himself well killing a countless many of them, and afterwards his companion came and brought him the stick, and they disappeared straightaway into the river.
komu þeir aptr á inn sama hól sem fyrr gátum vér, þá sól var í vestri.	came they back to the same hill as before opening was, then the-sun was in the-west.	They came back to the same hill where the opening had been before, and then the sun was in the west.
kastaði piltrinn þá inn stafnum og klæðsekk þeim, sem hann hafði fylldan af góðum krásum, og svá gerði Þorsteinn.	cast the-boy then the stick and sack theirs, which he had filled of good food, and so did Thorstein.	The boy cast the stick and their sack, which he had filled with good food, and so did Thorstein.
kollsveinn hljóp inn, en Þorsteinn nam staðar við glugginn.	the-boy ran in, but Thorstein took to-stand by the-skylight.	They boy ran inside, but Thorstein waited by a skylight window.
hann sá þar tvær konur, og vaf önnur guðvef, en önnur ruggaði barni.	he saw then two women, and wove one precious-cloth, and another rocking a-baby.	He then saw two women, and one wove precious cloth, and another was rocking a baby.
sú mælti:	so spoke:	So they spoke:
"hvað dvelr hann bjálfa, bróður þinn?"	"what delays him Bjalfi, brother yours?"	"What delays your brother Bjalfi?".
"ekki hefir hann mér fylgt í dag?"	"not has he me followed to day?"	"Has he not followed me today?",
sagði hann.	said he.	he said.
"hverr hefir þá farið með krókstafinn?"	"who has then gone with the-crooked-stick?"	"Who has gone with the crooked-stick then?" she said.
segir hún.	said she.	"That was Thorstein House-Power",
"það var Þorsteinn Bæjarmagn",	"that was Thorstein House-Power",	said Kollsvein,
segir Kollsveinn, "hirðmaður Óláfs konungs.	said Kollsvein, "court-man Olaf's the-king's.	"a court man of King Olaf's.

The Tale of Thorsteinn House-Power (Old Icelandic)

Old Icelandic	Literal	English
kom hann okkr í mikinn vanda, því að hann hafði ór undirheimum þau þing, að eigi munu slík í Noregi, og var við því búið, að vit mundum drepnir, er hann kastaði stafnum í hendur þeim, og eltu þeir hann til niðrgangs, og þá færði ek honum stafinn, og víst er hann hraustr maðr, því að eigi veit ek, hversu marga hann drap".	came he us in much difficulty, because that he had away-from under-world their assembly, which not would-be such in Norway, and were with therefore prepared, to know would-be killed, when he cast stick in hand theirs, and chased they him to down-going, and then took I to-him the-stick, and certainly was he brave man, because that not know I, how-so many men killed".	He has brought us unto much difficulty by stealing from the assembly in the underworld, the like of which aren't to be found in Norway, and was nearly killed when he threw his stick into their hands, and they were chasing him to his death, and then I took the stick to him, and he certainly was a brave man, because I do not know how many men were killed".
og nú laukst aptr haugrinn.	and now closed back the-mound.	And now the mound closed.
fór Þorsteinn nú til sinna manna, og sigldu þaðan til Noregs, og fann Óláf konung austr í Vík og færði honum gersemi þessi og sagði frá ferðum sínum, og fannst mönnum mikið um.	went Thorstein now to his men, and sailed from-there to Norway, and found Olaf the-king east in Vik and brought him treasures these and said from voyage his, and found men much about.	Thorstein now went to his men, and sailed from there to Norway, and found King Olaf at Vik in the east, and brought him the treasures and told him of his voyage, and people thought much about it.
konungr bauð að gefa Þorsteini lén mikið, en hann kveðst enn vilja fara eina ferð í Austrveg.	the-king offered to give Thorstein a-fee great, but he said but wished travel one voyage to Eastern-Lands.	The king offered to give Thorstein a great fee but he said that he wished to travel on a voyage to the Eastern-Lands.
var hann nú með konungi um vetrinn.	was he now with the-king about winter.	He was now with the king over the winter.

3

að vári bjó Þorsteinn skip sitt.	in spring prepared Thorstein ship his.	In spring Thorstein prepared his ship.
hann hafði snekkju og fjóra menn og tuttugu.	he had a-sailboat and four men and twenty.	He had a sailboat and twenty four men.
og er hann kom við Jamtaland, lá hann í höfn einn dag, og gekk hann á land að skemmta sér.	and when he came to Jamtland, lay he in the-harbour one day, and went he to land to amuse himself.	And when he came to Jamtland, he lay in port one day, and he went ashore to amuse himself.
hann kom í eitt rjóður.	he came to a clearing.	He came to a clearing.

The Tale of Thorsteinn House-Power (Old Icelandic)

Old Icelandic	Literal	English
þar var einn mikill steinn.	there was a large stone.	There was a large stone.
skammt þaðan sá hann einn dverg furðuliga ljótan, og grenjaði upp yfir sik.	a-short-distance from-there saw he a dwarf exceedingly hideous, and howling up over himself.	A short distance from there he saw a dwarf strangely ugly, and he was howling about himself.
sýndist Þorsteini kjaptrinn snúinn út að eyranu, en öðrum megin nefit niður að kjaptinum.	thought Thorstein jaw twisted out at ears, on one side nose below the mouth.	It seemed to Thorstein that his jaw twisted up to the ear on one side and on the other side his nose overlapped his mouth.
Þorsteinn segir, hví hann léti svá heimsliga.	Thorstein said, why he made so foolishly.	Thorstein asked him why he was behaving so foolishly.
"þú, góði maður",	"you, good man",	"You, good man",
sagði hann, "undrast eigi.	said he, "wonder not.	he said,
sér þú eigi þann mikla örn, er þar flýgr?	see you not that great eagle, that there flies?	"it is no wonder.
hann hefir tekið son minn.	he had taken son mine.	Do you not see the great eagle that flies there? He's taken my son.
ætla ek það, að sá ófögnuður sé sendur af Óðni, en ek spring, ef ek missi barnit".	suppose I that, it so unhappy he-is sent of Odin, that I burst, if I lost child".	I think that the unhappy one was sent by Odin, but I will explode if I lose my child".
Þorsteinn skaut eptir erninum, og kom undir vænginn, og datt hann dauður niður, en Þorsteinn henti dvergsbarnit á lopti og færði föðurnum, en dvergrinn varð feginn mjög og mælti:	Thorstein shot after the-eagle, and came down the-wing, and fell he dead down, but Thorstein caught the-dwarf's-boy from-the-sky and brought to-the-father, the dwarf was relieved much and spoke:	Thorstein shot at the eagle, and it came down on the wing, and he fell down dead, but Thorstein caught the dwarf's boy as he fell from the sky, and brought it to his father, and the dwarf was relieved and spoke
"þér á ek að launa lífgjöf og sonr minn, og kjós þér nú fyrir laun í gulli og silfri".	"to-you that I to repay life-gift and son mine, and choose to-you now for to-repay in gold and silver".	"To you I owe a great debt for saving my son's life, and I choose to repay you in gold and silver".
"græð þú fyrst son þinn",	"tend-to you first son yours",	"Tend to your son first",
sagði Þorsteinn "er ek eigi vanr að taka mútur á afli mínu".	said Thorstein "that I not accustomed to take payment for strength mine".	said Thorstein, "because I am not accustomed to taking payment for my strength".

The Tale of Thorsteinn House-Power (Old Icelandic)

Old Icelandic	Literal	English
"eigi væri mér að óskyldara að launa",	"not should-be to-me that less-should to repay",	"That should not make me repay you any less",
segir dvergrinn.	said the-dwarf.	said the dwarf.
"mun þér ekki þykkja framboðligr serkr minn af sauða ullu, en eigi muntu á sundi mæðast og eigi sár fá, ef þú hefir hann næst þér".	"would you not value be-offered shirt mine of wether's wool, that not shall-you to swimming get-tired and not wound get, if you have it next to-you".	"Would you not value if I offered you my shirt of ram's wool, for you shall never get tired when swimming and never be wounded if you wear it next to your skin".
Þorsteinn fór í serkinn, og var honum mátuligr, en honum sýndist dvergnum of lítill.	Thorstein went to the-shirt, and was he fitting, though to-him seemed the-dwarf of small.	Thorstein tried on the shirt, and it fit him, even though it seemed too small for the dwarf.
hann tók og silfrhring ór pungi sínum og gaf Þorsteini og bað hann vel geyma og sagði honum aldri féfátt verða mundu, meðan hann ætti hringinn.	he took also silver-ring from pouch his and gave Thorstein and asked him well retain and said he never lack-of-money become would, as-long-as he had the-ring.	He also took a silver ring from his pouch and gave it to Thorstein and asked him to keep it safe saying that he would never lack money as long as he had the ring.
síðan tók hann einn stein svartan og gaf Þorsteini, "og ef þú felr hann í lófa þér, sér þik engi.	afterwards took he a stone black and gave Thorstein, "and if you fold it in promise to-you, see you none.	Afterwards he took a black stone and gave it to Thorstein: "and if you fold it in your hand in promise, no one shall see you.
eigi hefi ek fleira, það þér megi gagn að vera.	not have I more, that to-you may benefit to be.	I do not have any more that may be of benefit to you.
hall einn vil ek gefa þér til skemmtunar".	piece-of-marble one will I give to-you for amusement".	There is a piece of marble that I will give to you for your amusement".
tók hann þá hallinn ór pungi sínum.	took he then the-piece-of-marble from pouch his.	He took the piece of marble then from his pouch.
fylgdi honum einn stálbroddr.	following it a steel-point.	There followed a steel point.
hallrinn var þríhyrndr.	the-piece-of-marble was three-sided.	The piece of marble was three sided.
hann var hvítr í miðju, en rauður öðrum megin, en gul rönd utan um.	it was white in the-middle, and red other side, and gold around outside about.	It was white in the middle, red on one side, and gold around the outside.
dvergrinn mælti:	the-dwarf said:	The dwarf said:

The Tale of Thorsteinn House-Power (Old Icelandic)

Old Icelandic	Literal	English
"ef þú pjakkar broddinum á hallinn, þar sem hann er hvítr, þá kemur haglhríð svá mikil, að engi þorir móti að sjá.	"if you prick the-point of the-piece-of-marble, there where it is white, then comes hailstorm so great, that none dare to-meet to see.	"If you prick the point of the piece of marble where it is white, then there will come a hailstorm so great that none will dare to look towards it.
en ef þú vilt þíða þann snjó, þá skaltu pjakka þar, sem gulr er hallrinn, og kemur þá sólskin, svá að allt bræðir.	then if you wish thaw then snow, then shall-you prick there, where gold is the-marble, and comes then sunshine, so that all thaws.	Then if you wish to thaw the snow, then you should prick there, where the marble is gold, and then there will come sunshine, so that everything thaws.
en ef þú pjakkar þar í, sem rautt er, þá kemur þar ór eldur og eimyrja með gneistaflaug, svá að engi má móti að sjá.	then if you prick there in, where red is, then comes there out-of fire and embers with a-shower-of-sparks, so that none may meet to see.	Then if you prick there, where it is red, then there will come embers of fire with a shower of sparks, so much that none will dare to look towards
þú mátt og hæfa það, sem þú vilt, með broddinum og hallinum, og hann kemur sjálfur aptr í hönd þér, þegar þú kallar.	you may also hit that, whatever you wish, with the-point and the-marble, and it comes itself back in hand to-you, as-soon-as you call.	You may also hit, whatever you wish, with the point and the marble, and it will come back by itself into your hand, as soon as you call for them.
get ek nú ekki launað þér fleira að sinni".	guess I now not repay you more than this".	I guess now that I cannot repay you more than this".
Þorsteinn þakkar honum gjafirnar.	Thorstein thanked him the-gifts.	Thorstein thanked him for the gifts.
fór hann nú til sinna manna, og var honum þessi ferð betr farin en ófarin.	went he now to his men, and was to-him this journey better gone than unfinished.	He now went to his men, and to him the journey had gone better than when it was unfinished.
þessu næst gefur þeim byr og sigla í Austrveginn.	this next given them fair-wind and sailed to Eastern-Lands.	Next they were given a favourable wind and sailed to the Eastern-Lands.
koma nú á fyrir þeim myrkr og hafvillur, og vita þeir ekki, hvar þeir fara, og var það hálfan mánuð, að þessi villa helzt.	came now to before them fog and open-sea, and knew they not, where they travelled, and was that half a-month, that this lost-way held.	Now a fog came before them in the open sea, and they did not know where they travelled, and this held for half a month.

The Tale of Thorsteinn House-Power (Old Icelandic)

Old Icelandic	Literal	English
# 4	# 4	# 4
það var eitt kvöld, að þeir urðu varir við land.	it was one evening, that they became aware with land.	It was one evening that they were aware that they were close to land.
köstuðu þeir nú akkerum og lágu þar um nóttina.	cast they now anchor and laid there about the-night.	They cast anchor and lay there overnight.
um morguninn var gott veður og sólskin fagrt.	about morning was good weather and sunshine fair.	In the morning the weather was good with fair sunshine.
váru þeir þá komnir á einn fjörð langan, og sjá þeir þar hlíðir fagrar og skóga.	were they then come to a fjord long, and saw they there slope fair and forests.	They came to a long fjord, and saw fair slopes and forests.
engi maður var sá innanborðs, að þetta land þekkti.	no man was saw aboard, that this land knew.	There was no man aboard that saw the land and knew this land.
ekki sáu þeir kvikt, hvárki dýr né fugla.	not saw they living-thing, neither wild-animals nor birds.	They saw no living thing, neither animals nor birds.
reistu þeir nú tjald á landi og bjuggust vel um.	raised they now tents on the-land and settled well about.	They now raised tents on the land and settled there well.
að morgni mælti Þorsteinn til sinna manna:	at morning spoke Thorstein to his men:	At morning Thorstein spoke to his men:
"ek vil gera yður kunnigt um ætlan mína.	"I wish to-make you know about intentions mine.	"I wish to let you know about my intentions.
þér skuluð bíða mín hér sex nætr.	you should await me here six nights.	You should wait for me here for six nights.
ætla ek mér að kanna land þetta".	intend I me to explore the-land this".	It is my intention to explore this land.
þeim þótti mikið fyrir því og vilja með honum fara, en Þorsteinn vill það eigi, "og ef ek kem eigi aptr, áður sjau sólir eru af himni",	they thought much for therefore and wished with him to-travel, but Thorstein wished that not, "and if I come not back, after seven suns they-are of the-sky",	They thought much of this because they also wished to travel with him, but Thorstein did not wish for that, "and if I do not come back before the seventh sunset in the sky",

The Tale of Thorsteinn House-Power (Old Icelandic)

Old Icelandic	Literal	English
segir hann, "þá skuluð þér sigla heim og segja svá Óláfi konungi, að mér mun ekki auðið verða aptr að koma".	said he, "then should you sail home and tell so Olaf the-king, that I should not fated be return to come".	he said, "then you should sail home and tell King Olaf that I am not fated to return home".
gengu þeir þá með honum upp á skóginn.	went they then with him up to the-forests.	They went with him up to the forests.
því næst hvarf hann þeim, og fóru þeir aptr til skips og breyttu eptir því, sem Þorsteinn bauð þeim.	then next disappeared he from-them, and went they back to the-ships and behaved after accordingly, as Thorstein asked them.	Then next he disappeared from their sight, and they went back to the ships and behaved, as Thorstein had asked them.
nú er að segja af Þorsteini, að allan þann dag gengr hann um mörkina og verður við ekki varr.	now is to say that Thorstein, about all the day went he about the-trees and came with not aware.	Now is to say of Thorstein, that all day he went through the trees and was not aware of anything.
en að áliðnum degi kemur hann á eina braut breiða.	then that following day came he to a way broad.	Then the following day he came to a broad road.
hann gekk eptir brautinni, þangað til að aptnaði.	he went after turned-away, from-there to the the-evening.	He turned to follow it until the evening.
gekk hann þá brott af brautinni og víkr að einni stórri eik og stígr upp í hana.	went he then away of turning and moved towards a large oak and climbed up it he.	He turned off the track and moved towards a large oak tree and he climbed up it.
var þar nóg rúm í að liggja.	was there enough room of to lie-down.	There was enough room for him to lie down.
sefur hann þar um nóttina.	slept he there about the-night.	He slept there for the night.
en er sólin kom upp, heyrir hann dunur miklar og manna mál.	when that sunrise came up, heard he a-din great and men's conversations.	When sunrise came, he heard a great din and men talking.
sá hann þá, hvar margir menn ríða.	saw he then, were many men riding.	He then saw that there were many man riding.
þeir váru tveir og tuttugu.	they were two and twenty.	There were twenty two.
þá bar svá skjótt um fram.	then bore so swiftly about from.	They came so swiftly past.
undraðist Þorsteinn mjög vöxt þeira.	surprised Thorstein much grown they-were.	Thorstein was surprised by how large they were.

The Tale of Thorsteinn House-Power (Old Icelandic)

Old Icelandic	Literal	English
hafði hann eigi sét jafnstóra menn fyrr.	had he not seen equally-large men before.	He had not seen men as large before.
Þorsteinn klæðir sik.	Thorstein clothed himself.	Thorstein clothed himself.
líður nú morgininn til þess, að sól er komin í landsuður.	passed now morning to this, that the-sun was coming to the-south-east.	Now the morning passed so that the sun was coming to the South-East.

5

Old Icelandic	Literal	English
nú sér Þorsteinn þrjá menn ríða vel vápnaða og svá stóra, að enga menn sá hann fyrr jafnstóra.	now saw Thorstein three men riding well weaponed and saw great, that none men saw him before equally-as-big.	Now Thorstein saw three men riding well armed and very large, no men had he seen equally as big.
sá var mestr, er í miðit reið, í gullskotnum klæðum á bleikum hesti, en hinir tveir riðu á grám hestum í rauðum skarlatsklæðum.	so was the-most, then in the-middle riding, in gold-trimmed clothes a pale horse, but the-other two rode on grey horses in red scarlet-clothing.	The most large, then riding in the middle, was in gold-trimmed clothes on a pale horse, but the other two rode on grey horses in red scarlet clothing.
en er þeir kómu þar gegnt, sem Þorsteinn var, mælti sá, sem fyrir þeim var, og nam staðar:	and when they came there opposite, where Thorstein was, spoke so, as for they were, and took standing:	And when they came opposite where Thorstein was, they spoke where they were, and stood:
"hvað er kvikt í eikinni?"	"what is alive in the-oak?"	"What is alive in that oak?"
Þorsteinn gekk þá á veginn fyrir þá og heilsaði þeim, en þeir ráku upp hlátr mikinn, og mælti inn mikli maður:	Thorstein went then to the-road before-them then and greeted them, but they drove up laughter much, and spoke the larger man:	Thorstein then went to the road before them and then greeted them, but they erupted with much laughter, and the larger man spoke:
"sjaldsénir eru oss þvílíkir menn, eða hvert er nafn þitt, eða hvaðan ertu?"	"rarely-seen are us the-like men, but what is name yours, and from-where are-you?"	"Rarely have we seen the like of such a man, but what is your name, and where are you from?"
Þorsteinn nefndi sik og kveðst vera kallaður Bæjarmagn, "en kyn mitt er í Noregi.	Thorstein named himself and said being called House-Power, "and kin mine is in Norway.	Thorstein named himself and said about-being called House-Power, "and my kin is in Norway.
er ek hirðmaður Óláfs konungs".	am I court-man Olaf's the-king".	I am a court man of King Olaf".

The Tale of Thorsteinn House-Power (Old Icelandic)

Old Icelandic	Literal	English
inn mikli maður brosti og mælti:	the largest man burst-out-laughing and said:	The largest man burst out laughing and said:
"mest er logit frá hirðprýði hans, ef hann hefir engan vaskligri.	"mostly is a-lie from court his, if he has no-one braver.	"Most about his court must be lies if he has no one braver.
þykki mér þú heldur mega heita Bæjarbarn en Bæjarmagn".	think me you rather may be-named House-Child than House-Power".	I think you may rather be called House-Child than House-Power".
"lát nokkut fylgja nafnfesti",	"have some following naming-gift",	"Give me a naming gift then",
segir Þorsteinn.	said Thorstein.	said Thorstein.
inn mikli maður tók fingrgull og gaf Þorsteini.	the largest man took finger-gold and gave Thorstein.	The largest man took a gold ring from his finger and gave it to Thorstein.
það vá þrjá aura.	that was three ounces.	It was three ounces.
Þorsteinn mælti:	Thorstein spoke:	Thorstein spoke:
"hvert er þitt nafn, eða hverrar ættar ertu, eða í hvert land er ek kominn?"	"what is your name, and whose lineage are-you, and in what land have I come?"	"What is your name, and whose lineage are you, and in what land have I come?"
"Goðmundur heiti ek.	"Godmund named I.	"I am named Godmund.
ræð er þar fyrir, sem á Glæsisvöllum heitir.	ruler am here over, which is Glasir-Plains named.	I rule over here, which is named Glasir-Plains.
þar þjónar til það land, er Risaland heitir.	there serve to that land, which Giant-Land named.	There serves to that land, which is named Giant-Land.
ek er konungsson, en mínir sveinar heitir annarr Fullsterkr, en annarr Allsterkr, eða sáttu enga menn ríða hér um í morgin?"	I am a-king's-son, and my companions named one Full-Strong, and another All-Strong, and saw-you any men riding here about in the-morning?"	I am a king's son and my companions, one is named Full-Strong, and the other All-Strong, and did you see any men riding through here in the morning?"
Þorsteinn mælti:	Thorstein spoke:	Thorstein spoke:
"hér riðu um tveir menn og tuttugu og létu eigi lítinn".	"here rode about two men and twenty and had none little".	"Twenty two men rode through here and none were little".
"þeir eru sveinar mínir",	"they were men mine",	"They were my men",

The Tale of Thorsteinn House-Power (Old Icelandic)

Old Icelandic	Literal	English
segir Goðmundr.	said Godmund.	said Godmund.
"það land liggr hér næst, er Jötunheimar heitir.	"that land lying here next-to, is Giant-Land named.	"That land lying next to here is named Giant-Land.
þar ræður sá konungr, er Geirröður heitir.	there rules so the-king, who Geirrod named.	So there rules the king who is named Geirrod.
undir hann erum vér skattgildir.	under him are we tributaries.	We are tributaries under him.
faðir minn hét Úlfheðinn Trausti.	father mine is-named Ulfhedin Trusty.	My father is named Ulfhedin Trusty.
hann var kallaður goðmundur sem allir aðrir, þeir á Glæsisvöllum búa.	he was called Godmund as all others, they who Glasir-Plains live.	He was called Godmund as are all others who live in Glasir-Plains.
en faðir minn fór í Geirröðargarða að afhenda konungi skatta sína, og í þeiri ferð fekk hann bana.	but father mine went to Geirrod's-Town to of-hand the-king tax his, and on their journey got he death.	But my father went to Geirrod's-Town to hand taxes to the king, but on their journey they got death.
hefir konungr gert mér boð, að ek skylda drekka erfi eptir föður minn og taka slíkar nafnbætr sem faðir minn hafði, en þó unum vér illa við að þjóna jötnum".	has the-king made me an-invite, that I should drink inheritance after father mine and take such name-titles as father mine had, but though happy we badly with that serving giants".	The king has made me an invite, for me to drink to his honour and take such titles that my father had, but we are not happy about serving giants".
"hví riðu yðrir menn undan?",	"why rode your men before?",	"Why did your men ride before?",
segir Þorsteinn.	said Thorstein.	said Thorstein.
"mikil á skilr land vort",	"great is separating land ours",	"There is a great separation of our land",
segir Goðmundr.	said Godmund.	said Godmund.
"sú heitir Hemra.	"so named Hemra.	"It is called Hemra.
hún er svá djúp og ströng, að hana vaða engir hestar nema þeir, sem vér kumpánar eigum.	she is so deep and strong, that she wades no horses except they, which we fellows own.	It is so deep and strong, that no horses can wade it, except for the three which we are on.

The Tale of Thorsteinn House-Power (Old Icelandic)

Old Icelandic	Literal	English
skulu hinir ríða fyrir uppsprettu árinnar, og finnumst vér í kveld".	shall others ride before up-spring the-river, and meet we in the-evening".	The others shall ride before the river spring, and we will meet in the evening".
"það mundi skemmtan að fara með yður",	"that could-be amusement to travel with you",	"It could be an amusement to travel with you",
segir Þorsteinn, "og sjá, hvað þar verður til tíðenda".	said Thorstein, "and see, what there becomes to news".	said Thorstein, "and see what happens".
"eigi veit ek, hversu það hentar",	"not know I, how-so that suits",	"I do not know how that suits",
segir Goðmundr, "því að þú munt kristinn".	said Godmund, "because that you must-be Christian".	said Godmund", because you must be a Christian".
"ek mun mik ábyrgjast",	"I could myself take-care-of",	"I can take care of myself",
segir Þorsteinn.	said Thorstein.	said Thorstein.
"ekki vilda ek þú hlytir vánt af mér",	"not wish I you to-get difficulty from me",	"I do not wish for you to get any difficulty from me",
sagði Goðmundr, "en ef Óláfur konungr vill leggja gæfu á með oss, þá mundi ek framt á treysta, að þú færir".	said Godmund, "but if Olaf the-king will grant luck then with us, then should I provide to trust, that you travel".	said Godmund", but if King Olaf will grant you luck to travel with us, then I shall trust you to travel".
Þorsteinn segist því heita vilja.	Thorstein said accordingly promised he-wished.	Thorstein gave him his word as he wished.
Goðmundur biður hann fara á bak með sér, og svá gerði hann.	Godmund asked him to-travel on the-back with him, and so did he.	Godmund asked him to travel back with him, and so he did.
ríða þeir nú til árinnar.	rode they now to the-river.	They now rode to the river.
var þar eitt hús, og tóku þeir þar önnur klæði og klæddu sik og sína hesta.	was there a house, and took they there other clothes and dressed themselves and their horses.	There was a house, and they took their other clothes and dressed themselves and their horses.
þau klæði váru þeirar náttúru, að ekki festi vatn á þeim, en vatnið var svá kalt, að þegar hljóp drep í, ef nokkut vöknaði.	their clothes were there natured, that not joined the-water to them, about the-water was so cold, that there ran gangrene to, if anything became-wet.	Their clothes were of a nature that the water could not touch them, because the water was so cold, that gangrene ran if anything became wet.

The Tale of Thorsteinn House-Power (Old Icelandic)

Old Icelandic	Literal	English
riðu þeir nú yfir ána.	rode they now across the-river.	They now rode across the river.
hestarnir óðu sterkliga.	the-horses waded strongly.	The horses waded strongly.
hestr Goðmundar rasaði, og varð Þorsteinn vátr á tánni, og hljóp þegar drep í.	horse Godmund's tumbled, and became Thorstein water about toe, and ran there gangrene to.	Godmund's horse tumbled, and Thorstein's toe came into the water, and there ran gangrene.
en er þeir kómu af ánni, breiddu þeir niður klæðin til þerris.	when that they came off the-river, spread they down clothes to dry.	When they came off the river, they spread their clothes to dry.
Þorsteinn hjó af sér tána, og fannst þeim mikið um hreysti hans.	Thorstein hewed off his toe, and found they much about bravery his.	Thorstein cut his toe off, and they thought much of his bravery.
ríða þeir nú sinn veg.	rode they now their way.	They now rode on their way.
bað Þorsteinn þá eigi fela sik, "því að ek kann að gera þann hulinshjálm, að mik sér engi".	asked Thorstein then not hide him, "because that I can to make then helm-of-invisibility, that me see none".	Thorstein asked them not to hide him, "because I have a helm of invisibility, that none see me".
Goðmundur segir það góða kunnáttu.	Godmund said that good skills.	Godmund said that was a good skill.
kómu þeir nú til borgarinnar, og kómu menn Goðmundar í móti honum.	came they now to the-town, and came men Godmund's to meet him.	They now came to the town, and Godmund's men came to meet him.
riðu þeir nú í borgina.	rode they now into the-town.	They now rode into the town.
mátti þar nú heyra alls háttar hljóðfæri, en ekki þótti Þorsteini af setning slegit.	could they now hear all kinds musical-instruments, but not thought Thorstein of the-setting struck.	They could now hear all kinds of musical instruments, but Thorstein did not think much of the settings being played.
Geirröður konungr kom nú í mót þeim og fagnaði þeim vel, og var þeim skipað eitt steinhús eða höll að sofa í og menn til fengnir að leiða hesta þeira á stall.	Geirrod the-king came now to meet them and celebrated they well, and were they directed-to a stone-house and a-hall to sleep in and men to get to led horses there to stable.	King Geirrod now came to meet them and they were well welcomed, and they were directed to a stone house and a hall to sleep in, and men led their horses to a stable.
var Goðmundur leiddur í konungshöll.	was Godmund led to the-king's-hall.	Godmund was led to the king's hall.

The Tale of Thorsteinn House-Power (Old Icelandic)

Old Icelandic	Literal	English
konungr sat í hásæti og jarl sá hjá honum, er Agði hét.	the-king sat on a-high-seat and the-earl so beside him, was Agdi named.	The king sat on a high seat and the earl so beside him, was named Agdi.
hann réð fyrir því heraði, er Grundir heita.	he ruled over therefore district, was Grundir named.	He ruled over the district, which was named Grundir.
það er á millum Risalands og Jötunheima.	it was in between Giant-Land and Giant-Home.	It was in between Giant-Land and Giant-Home.
hann hafði atsetu að Gnípalundi.	he had a-seat at Gnipalund.	He had an estate at Gnipalund.
hann var fjölkunnigr, og menn hans váru tröllum líkari en mönnum.	he was skilled-in-magic, and men his were trolls like than men.	He was skilled in magic, and his men were more like trolls than men.
Goðmundur settist á skörina fyrir öndvegit gagnvart konungi.	Godmund sat beside high-seat before opposite going-from the-king.	Godmund sat beside the high seat opposite the king.
var sá siður þeira, að konungsson skyldi ekki í hásæti sitja, fyrr en hann hafði tekið nafnbætr eptir föður sinn og drukkið væri it fyrsta full.	was so the-custom theirs, that the-king's-son should not in high-seat sit, before that he had taken name-titles after father his and drink-to was the first drunk.	It was their custom, that the king's son should not sit in the high seat, before he had taken his titles and the first drink to honour his father had been drunk.
ríss þar nú upp in vænsta veizla, og drukku menn glaðir og kátir og fóru síðan að sofa.	rose there now up the good feast, and drank men gladly and merry and went then to sleep.	They now rose up and had a good feast, and the men drank gladly and merrily, and then went to sleep.
en er Goðmundur kom í hús sitt, sýndi Þorsteinn sik.	and when Godmund came to the-house his, showed Thorstein himself.	And when Godmund came to his house, Thorstein showed himself.
hlógu þeir að honum.	laughed they at him.	They laughed at him.
Goðmundur sagði mönnum sínum, hverr hann var, og bað þá ekki hafa hann að hlátri.	Godmund told the-men his, who he was, and ordered then not have he to laughter.	Godmund told his men who he was and ordered them not to laugh at him.
og sofa þeir af um nóttina.	and slept they of through the-night.	And they slept through the night.

The Tale of Thorsteinn House-Power (Old Icelandic)

Old Icelandic	Literal	English
6	**6**	**6**
nú er morginn kom, váru þeir snemma á fótum.	now when morning came, were they early about feet.	Now when morning came, they were up early and on their feet.
var Goðmundur leiddur til konungs hallar.	was Godmund led to the-king's hall.	Godmund was led to the king's hall.
konungr fagnaði honum vel.	the-king celebrated him well.	The king welcomed him well.
"viljum vér nú vita",	"wish we now know",	"We wish to know",
segir konungr, "hvárt þú vilt veita mér slíka hlýðni sem faðir þinn, og vil ek þá auka þínar nafnbætr.	said the-king, "whether you wish to-grant me such homage as father yours, and wish I then extra your name-titles.	said the king, "whether you wish to grant me such homage as your father, and then I wish to give you more titles.
skaltu þá halda Risalandi og sverja mér eiða".	shall-you then keep Giant-Land and swear to-me oath".	You shall then keep Giant-Land and swear an oath to me".
Goðmundur svarar:	Godmund answered:	Godmund answered:
"ekki er það lög að krefja svá unga menn til eiða".	"not is that law that demand so young men to oath".	"It is not lawful to demand oaths from a man as young as me".
"það skal vera",	"that shall be",	"So it shall be",
sagði konungr.	said the-king.	said the king.
síðan tók konungr guðvefjarskikkju og lagði yfir Goðmund og gaf honum konungsnafn, tók síðan horn mikið og drakk til Goðmundi.	then took the-king a-precious-cloak and laid over Godmund and gave him the-king's-name, took afterwards horn great and drank to Godmund.	Then the king took a precious cloak and laid it over Godmund and gave him the title of king, and then took a great horn and drank to Godmund.
hann tók við horninu og þakkaði konungi.	he took with the-horn and thanked the-king.	He took the horn and thanked the king.
síðan stóð Goðmundur upp og sté á stokkinn fyrir sæti konungs og strengdi þess heit, að hann skal engum konungi þjóna né hlýðni veita, meðan Geirröður konungr lifði.	afterwards stood Godmund up and stepped onto the-foot-board before seat the-king's and boldly this declared, that he shall no king serve nor homage grant, while Geirrod the-king lived.	Afterwards Godmund stood up and stepped onto the footboard before the king's seat and boldly declared, that he would serve no king nor grant homage, while King Geirrod lived.

The Tale of Thorsteinn House-Power (Old Icelandic)

Old Icelandic	Literal	English
konungr þakkaði honum, sagði sér það þykkja meira vert en þótt hann hefði eiða svarið.	the-king thanked him, told him that valued more worth that though he had oaths sworn.	The king thanked him, and told him that he would have valued more if he had sworn oaths.
síðan drakk Goðmundur af horninu og gekk til sætis síns.	afterwards drank Godmund of the-horn and went to seat his.	Afterwards Godmund drank from the horn and went to his seat.
váru menn þá glaðir og kátir.	were men then glad and merry.	Then the men were glad and merry.
tveir menn eru nefndir með Agða jarli.	two men were named with Agdi the-earl.	Two men were with Earl Agdi.
hét annarr Jökull, en annarr frosti.	named one Jokul, and the-other Frosti.	One was named Jokul, and the other Frosti.
þeir váru öfundsjúkir.	they were jealous.	They were jealous.
Jökull þreif upp uxahnútu og kastaði í lið Goðmundar.	Jokul grabbed up ox-bone and threw at the-company-of Godmund.	Jokul grabbed an ox-bone and threw it at Godmund's company.
Þorsteinn sá það og henti á lopti og sendi aptr, og kom á nasir þeim, er gustr hét, og brotnaði í honum nefit og ór honum allar tennrnar, en hann fell í óvit.	Thorstein saw that and caught in the-air and sent back, and came about nose them, was Gust named, and broke it his nose and through his all teeth, and he fell to unconscious.	Thorstein saw that, caught it in the air and sent it back, and it hit the nose of a man named Gust, and it broke his nose and all his teeth, and he fell unconscious.
Geirröður konungr reiddist og spurði, hverr berði beinum yfir hans borð.	Geirrod the-king rose and asked, who threw the-bone across his table.	Geirrod the king rose up and asked who threw the bone across the table.
sagði hann, að reynt skyldi verða, hverr sterkastr væri í steinkastinu, áður en úti væri.	said he, that test should be, who strongest was in stone-throwing, after then out was.	He said that there should be a test to find out before it was over who was the strongest at stone throwing.
síðan kallar konungr til tvá menn, Drött og Hösvi:	afterwards called the-king to two men, Drott and Hosvir:	Afterwards the king called two men, Drott and Hosvir:
"farið þit og sækið gullhnött minn og berið hann hingað".	"go you-two and seek gold-ball mine and bring it here".	"You two go and seek my gold ball and bring it here".
þeir fóru og kómu aptr með eitt selshöfuð, er stóð tíu fjórðunga.	they went and came back with a seal's-head, and weighed ten quarters.	They went and came back with a seal's head, which weighed ten quarters.

The Tale of Thorsteinn House-Power (Old Icelandic)

Old Icelandic	Literal	English
það var glóanda, svá að sindraði af svá sem ór afli, en fitan draup niður sem glóanda bik.	it was glowing, so that sparkled of so as from a-forge, and fat dripped down as burning pitch.	It was glowing hot, so that sparks came off it as if from a forge, and fat dripped from it like burning pitch.
konungr mælti:	the-king spoke:	The king spoke:
"takið nú knöttinn og kastið hverr að öðrum.	"take now the-ball and throw each to other.	"Now take the ball and throw it to each other.
hverr, sem niður fellir, skal fara útlægr og missa eignir sínar, en hverr eigi þorir að henda, skal heita níðingr".	anyone, who down drops, shall go outlawed and lose property his, and anyone not daring to catch, shall be-named a-coward".	Anyone who drops it shall go outlawed and lose his property, and anyone who does not dare to catch, shall be named a coward.

7

Old Icelandic	Literal	English
nú kastar Dröttr knettinum að Fullsterk.	now threw Drott the-ball at Full-Strong.	Now Drott threw the ball at Full-Strong.
hann greip á móti annarri hendi.	he gripped to meet one hand.	He gripped against it with one hand.
Þorsteinn sá, að honum varð orkufátt, og hljóp undir knöttinn.	Thorstein saw, that he became low-energy, and ran behind the-ball.	Thorstein saw that his strength weakened, and got behind the ball.
þeir snöruðu að Frosta, því að kapparnir stóðu fremstir við hvárntveggja bekkinn.	they threw at Frosti, because that champions stood foremost against either-side of-the-bench.	They threw it at Frosti, because the champions stood in front of the benches on either side.
Frosti tók mót sterkliga, og kom svá nær andliti hans, að kinnbeinit rifnaði.	Frosti took against strongly, and came so near face his, that chin-bone split.	Frosti caught it strongly, and it came so near his face, that it split his chin bone.
hann kastar knettinum að Allsterk.	he threw the-ball at All-Strong.	He threw the ball at All-Strong.
hann tók í móti báðum höndum, og lá við, að hann mundi kikna, áður Þorsteinn studdi hann.	he received it against both hands, and had with, that he would-have bent-backwards, before Thorstein steadied him.	He caught it with both hands, and he would have bent backwards, before Thorstein steadied him.
Allsterkr snaraði að Agða jarli, en hann greip móti báðum höndum.	All-Strong turned-quickly at Agdi the-earl, and he grabbed against both hands.	All-Strong hurled the ball at Earl Agdi, and he caught it with both hands.

The Tale of Thorsteinn House-Power (Old Icelandic)

Old Icelandic	Literal	English
fitan kom í skeggit á honum, og logaði það allt, og var honum til þess annast að afhenda knöttinn og fleygir að Goðmundi konungi.	fat came to beard of his, and blazed that all, and was he to this he-took-care-of that off-handed the-ball and flew-it at Godmund the-king.	Burning fat went on to his beard, and it was all ablaze, and as he had to take care of that, he hurriedly threw the ball at King Godmund.
en Goðmundur snaraði að Geirröði konungi, en hann veik sér undan, og urðu þeir fyrir Dröttr og Hösvir, og fengu þeir bana.	then Godmund flew-it at Geirrod the-king, but he turned himself away, and came they for Drott and Hosvir, and caught them dead.	Then Godmund threw it at King Geirrod, but he turned out of the way, and it came to Drott and Hosvir, and killed them both.
en knöttrinn kom á glerglugg einn og svá út í díki það, sem grafit var um borgina, og hljóp upp eldur logandi.	then the-ball came to glass-window one and so out into the-moat that, which dug was about the-city, and ran up the-flames ablaze.	Then the ball went through a glass window and out into the moat, which was dug around the city, and the flames ran up in a blaze.
var nú lokið þessu gamni.	was now ended this game.	The game was now ended.
tóku menn þá til drykkju.	took men then to drinking.	The men took to drinking.
sagði Agði jarl, að honum hrysi hugr við jafnan, er hann kom í flokk Goðmundar.	said Agdi the-earl, that he trembled thought with every-time, that he came to band Godmund's.	Earl Agdi said that he thought he trembled every time he came to Godmund's company.
um kveldið gekk Goðmundur að sofa og hans menn.	about evening went Godmund to seep and his men.	In the evening Godmund went to sleep and so did his men.
þökkuðu þeir Þorsteini hjástöðu, að þeim hefði slysalaust farið.	thanked they Thorstein beside-standing, to them had accidents-without gone.	They thanked Thorstein for standing by them, so that they were without accidents.
Þorsteinn kvað lítit til reynt, "eða hvað mun til gamans haft á morgin?"	Thorstein said little to test, "but what should to games have in the-morning?"	Thorstein said it was nothing much, "but what sort of games will we have in the morning?"
"konungr mun láta glíma",	"the-king should have wrestling",	"The king shall have wrestling",
segir Goðmundr, "og munu þeir þá hefna sín, því að fjarstætt er um afl várt".	said Godmund, "and should they then avenge themselves, accordingly to far-away from about strength ours".	said Godmund, "and they shall avenge themselves accordingly because their strength is far more than ours".
"konungs gæfa mun styrkja oss",	"the-king's luck should strengthen us",	"The king's luck shall strengthen us",

The Tale of Thorsteinn House-Power (Old Icelandic)

Old Icelandic	Literal	English
segir Þorsteinn.	said Thorstein.	said Thorstein.
"hirðið eigi, þótt þér berizt þangað að, sem ek er fyrir".	"take-care not, though you bear from-there that, which I am before".	"Take care not to bear it there, but bear towards me".
sofa þeir af um nóttina.	slept they of through night.	They slept through the night.
en að morgni fór hverr til sinnar skemmtunar, en matsveinar að dúka borð.	and at morning went each to his entertainment, while food-servants to tablecloths table.	And in the morning each went to his entertainment, while the food servants put the tablecloths on the table.
Geirröður konungr spurði, hvárt menn vildu ekki glíma, en þeir sögðu, að hann skyldi ráða.	Geirrod the-king asked, which men wished not wrestling, and they said, as he should decide.	King Geirrod asked, which men wished to wrestle, and they said that he should decide.
síðan afklæðast þeir og tókust fangbrögðum.	afterwards undressed they and took to-wrestling.	Then they undressed and took to wrestling.
Þorsteinn þóttist eigi sét hafa slíkan atgang, því að allt skalf, þá þeir fellu, og lékst mjög á mönnum Agða jarls.	Thorstein thought not seen had such to-going, because that all shook, then they fell, and played much to men Agdi the-earl's.	Thorstein thought he had not seen such a clash, because everywhere shook, whenever they fell, and this happened often to Earl Agdi's men.
frosti gekk nú fram á gólfit og mælti:	Frosti went now to the floor and spoke:	Frosti now went to the floor and said:
"hverr skal mér á móti?"	"who shall me to meet?"	"Who shall oppose me?"
"til mun verða einhverr",	"to should be someone",	"There will be someone",
sagði Fullsterkr.	said Full-Strong.	said Full-Strong.
ráðast þeir nú á, og váru með þeim miklar sviptingar, og er frosti miklu sterkari.	arranged they now to, and were with they much tussle, and was Frosti much stronger.	They now attacked, and there were great upheavals with them, and Frosti was much stronger.
berast þeir nú að Goðmundi.	bore they now to Godmund.	They now arrived at Godmund.
frosti tekr hann upp á bringu sér og keiktist mjög.	Frosti took him up by the-chest his and bent much.	Frosti took him up by his chest and he had to bend his knees.

The Tale of Thorsteinn House-Power (Old Icelandic)

Old Icelandic	Literal	English
Þorsteinn slær fæti sínum á knésbætr honum, og fell frosti á bak aptr, en Fullsterkr á hann ofan.	Thorstein struck feet his about the-back-of-the-knees his, and fell Frosti on back back, but Full-Strong on him over.	Thorstein struck his foot on the back of his knees, and Frosti fell on his back, and Full-Strong fell on him.
hnakkinn sprakk á Frosta og olnbogarnir.	the-back-of-the-head broke of Frosti and elbows.	The back of Frosti's head was broken, and so were his elbows.
hann stóð seint upp og mælti:	he stood slowly up and spoke:	He slowly stood up and spoke:
"ekki eru þér einir að gamninu, eða hví er svá fúlt í flokki yðrum?"	"not are you alone in the-game, and what is so foul among men yours?"	"You are not alone in this game, and what is it that is so foul among your men?"
"skammt á nefit að kenna ór kjaptinum",	"short is nose to know from the-mouth",	"Your nose is too close to your own mouth",
sagði Fullsterkr.	said Full-Strong.	said Full-Strong.
Jökull stóð þá upp, og Allsterkr réðst þá í móti honum, og var þeira atgangr inn harðasti.	Jokul stood then up, and All-Strong moved then to oppose him, and were they to-going the hardest.	Jokul then stood up, and All-Strong moved to oppose him, and their clash was the hardest yet.
en þó var Jökull sterkari og bar hann að bekk, þar sem Þorsteinn var fyrir.	but though was Jokul stronger and carried him to a-bench, there as Thorstein was before.	But Jokul was stronger and carried him to a bench, where Thorstein was.
Jökull vildi draga Allsterk frá bekknum og togast við fast, en Þorsteinn helt honum.	Jokul wished-to drag All-Strong from the-bench and pulled against hard, but Thorstein held him.	Jokul tried had to drag All-Strong from the bench and pulled hard against him, but Thorstein held him.
Jökull tók svá fast, að hann sté í hallargólfit upp að ökkla, en Þorsteinn hratt Allsterk frá sér, og fell Jökull á bak aptr, og gekk ór liði á honum fótrinn.	Jokul tugged so hard, that he stepped in hall-floor up to ankles, then Thorstein pushed All-Strong away-from him, and fell Jokul on back back, and went out-of dislocated of his leg.	Jokul pulled so hard, that his feet sunk into the hall floor up to his ankles, then Thorstein pushed All-Strong away from him, and Jokul fell back and dislocated his leg.
Allsterkr gekk til bekkjar, en Jökull stóð upp seint og mælti:	All-Strong went to bench, but Jokul stood up slowly and spoke:	All-Strong went back to his bench, but Jokul stood up slowly and spoke:
"ekki sjáum vér alla þessa, sem á bekknum eru".	"not see we all this, which on that-bench they-are".	"We cannot see everyone that is on that bench".

The Tale of Thorsteinn House-Power (Old Icelandic)

Old Icelandic	Literal	English
Geirröður segir Goðmundi, hvárt hann vildi ekki glíma.	Geirrod said-to Godmund, whether he would not wrestle.	Geirrod asked Godmund if he would wrestle.
en hann kveðst aldri glímt hafa, en kveðst eigi vildu synjast.	and he said never wrestled had, but said not would refuse.	And he said that he had never wrestled, but he would not refuse.
konungr bað Agða jarl hefna manna sinna.	the-king ordered Agdi the-earl avenge men his.	The king ordered Earl Agdi to avenge his men.
hann kveðst löngu hafa af lagt, en segir konung ráða skyldu.	he said long had of left, but told the-king advice would.	He said that he had given up long ago, but he would do as the king decided.
síðan afklæddust þeir.	afterwards undressed they.	Then they undressed.
eigi þóttist Þorsteinn sét hafa tröllsligri búk en á Agða.	not thought Thorstein seen had troll-like thick-set than was Agdi.	Thorstein thought that he had not seen such a troll-like thick set man as Agdi.
var hann blár sem hel.	was he black as death.	He was black as death.
Goðmundur reis mót honum.	Godmund rose to-meet him.	Godmund rose to meet him.
var hann hvítr á skinnslit.	was he white in colour.	He was white in colour.
Agði jarl hösvaðist að honum og lagði svá fast krummurnar að síðum hans, að allt gekk niður að beini, og bárust þeir víða um höllina.	Agdi the-earl went-for at him and had so fastened grabbed at sides his, that all went down to the-bone, and bore they widely about the-hall.	Earl Agdi went for him and grabbed at his sides so hard that it went down to the bone, and the carried widely around the hall.
og er þeir kómu þar, sem Þorsteinn var, þá brá Goðmundur jarli til sniðglímu og sneri honum vakrliga.	and when they came there, where Thorstein was, then drew Godmund the-earl to hip-throw and turned him nimbly.	And when they came where Thorstein was, Godmund drew the earl into a hip throw and turned him nimbly.
Þorsteinn lagðist niður fyrir fætr jarli, og fell hann þá og stakk niður nösunum, og brotnaði í honum þjófsnefit og fjórar tennr.	Thorstein lay down before feet the-earl's, and fell he then and struck down on-the-nose, and broke was his thieving-nose and four teeth.	Thorstein lay down before the earl's feet, and then he fell and struck his nose, and his thieving nose was broken, and four teeth.
jarl stóð upp og mælti:	the-earl stood up and spoke:	The earl stood up and spoke:
"þung verða gamalla manna föll, og svá þyngst, að þrír gangi að einum".	"heavy becomes the-old man falling, and so heaviest, when three go against one".	"Heavy becomes the old man falling, and heaviest, when it's three against one".

The Tale of Thorsteinn House-Power (Old Icelandic)

Old Icelandic	Literal	English
fóru menn þá í klæði sín.	went the-men then with-that clothed themselves.	With that the men clothed themselves.

8

Old Icelandic	Literal	English
þessu næst fóru þeir konungr til borða.	this next went they the-king to the-tables.	After this the king and his guests went to the tables.
töluðu þeir Agði jarl um, að þeir mundu einhvern prett við hafa haft, "því að mér býður ávallt hita, er ek kem í þeira flokk".	told they Agdi the-earl about, that they must-be some-way tricked against having had, "because that I invite always heat, when I come in their company".	Earl Agdi and the others said that they must have been tricked in some way, "because I always heat up, when I come in their company".
"látum bíða",	"leave-it abide",	"Let it be",
segir konungr, "sá mun koma, að okkr mun kunngera".	said the-king, "so shall come, that us should wiser".	said the king, "something will come and make us wiser".
tóku menn þá að drekka.	took men then to drinking.	Then the men took to drinking.
þá váru borin inn tvau horn í höllina.	then were brought in two horns into the-hall.	There were then two horns brought into the hall.
þau átti Agði jarl, gersemar miklar, og váru kölluð Hvítingar.	they had Agdi the-earl, treasured much, and were called Whitings.	They belonged to Earl Agdi, who treasured them, and they were called Whitings.
þau váru tveggja álna há og gulli búin.	they were two cubits high and gold prepared.	They were two cubits high and inlaid with gold.
konungr lét sitt hornit ganga á hvárn bekk, "og skal hverr drekka af í einu.	the-king had sat a-horn going to each bench, "and shall each drink of in one.	The king had set a horn on each bench, "and everyone shall drink from it in one.
sá, sem því orkar eigi, skal fá byrlaranum eyri silfrs".	so, that accordingly able-to not, shall pay the-cup-bearer an-ounce-of silver".	So, therefore those not able to shall pay the cup bearer an ounce of silver".
gekk engum af að drekka utan köppunum, en Þorsteinn gað svá til sét, að þeir, sem með Goðmundi váru, varð engi víttr.	went none of to drink out-of the-cups, but Thorstein got so to seen, that they, which with Godmund were, became not bewitched.	No one was able to drink out of the cups, but Thorstein could see that those who were with Godmund did not become bewitched.

The Tale of Thorsteinn House-Power (Old Icelandic)

Old Icelandic	Literal	English
drukku menn nú glaðir það, sem eptir var dagsins, en um kveldið fóru menn að sofa.	drank men now gladly that, as after was of-the-day, then about evening went men to sleep.	People now drank happily what was left of the day, but in the evening they went to sleep.
Goðmundur þakkaði Þorsteini fyrir góða hjástöðu.	Godmund thanked Thorstein for the-good beside-standing.	Godmund thanked Thorstein for his good help.
Þorsteinn spurði, nær endast mundi veizlan.	Thorstein asked, near ending would the-feast.	Thorstein asked, when the feast would end.
"að morgni skulu menn mínir ríða",	"at morning should men mine ride",	"In the morning my men shall ride",
segir Goðmundr.	said Godmund.	said Godmund.
"veit ek, að nú lætr konungr allt við hafa.	"know I, that now acts the-king all against have.	"I know that now the king will act against us with all he has.
eru nú sýndar gersemar.	they-are now shown treasures.	When the treasures are shown.
lætr konungr nú bera inn horn sitt it mikla.	have the-king now brought in a-horn his this great.	Let the king now carry in his great horn.
það er kallað Grímr inn Góði.	that is called Grim the Good.	That is called Grim the Good.
það er gersemi mikil og þó galdrafullt og búið með gull.	that is a-treasure great and though magic-full and inlaid with gold.	It is a great treasure, and magical and rich in gold.
mannshöfuð er á stiklinum með holdi og munni, og það mælir við menn og segir fyrir óorðna hluti og ef það veit ófriðar ván.	a-man's-head is about the-narrow with flesh and a-mouth, and that speaks with men and said for unspoken lot and if that known un-peace is-expected.	A man's head is about the narrow end with flesh and a mouth, and it speaks to men and says unspoken things, and if war is expected.
verður það bani vár, ef konungr veit, að kristinn maður er með oss.	becomes it the-death ours, if the-king knows, that a-Christian man is with us.	It will be the death of us if the king knows that a Christian man is with us.
munum vér eigi þurfa að vera fésparir við hann".	should we not need to be fee-sparing with him".	We should not need to spare wealth with him".
Þorsteinn sagði Grím eigi mæla fleira enn Óláfur konungr vildi, "en ek ætla, að Geirröður sé feigr.	Thorstein said Grim not speak more than Olaf the-king wished, "and I suppose, that Geirrod is fated-to-die.	Thorstein said that Grim would not say to him any more than King Olaf wished, "and I suppose that Geirrod is a doomed man.

The Tale of Thorsteinn House-Power (Old Icelandic)

Old Icelandic	Literal	English
þykki mér ráð, að þér hafið mín ráð heðan af.	seems to-me advice, that you have my counsel from-hence of.	It seems to me to advise, that you do as I advise you from now on.
skal ek sýna mik á morgin".	shall I show myself in the-morning".	I shall show myself in the morning".
en þeir sögðu það hættu ráð.	but they said that dangerous advice.	But they said that it was a dangerous decision.
Þorsteinn sagði, að Geirröður vildi þá feiga, "eða hvað segir þú mér af Grími inum Góða fleira?"	Thorstein said, that Geirrod wished then doomed, "but what say you to-me of Grim the Good more?"	Thorstein said that Geirrod wished them all doomed, "but what else can you tell me about Grim the Good"?
"það er frá honum að segja, að meðalmaður má standa undir bugtinni á honum, en álnar breitt yfir beitina, og er sá mestr drykkjumaður í þeira liði, er drekkr beitina, en konungr drekkr af í einu.	"that is from him to say, that an-average-man may stand under the-curve of him, and a-yard broad across opening, and is so the-greatest drinking-man of their company, that drinks the-opening, but the-king drinks of all in-one.	"The first thing to say, is that an average man can stand under the curve of the horn, and it is a yard across at the opening, and the greatest drinking man in their company can drink deep into the horn, but only the king can drink it all in one.
hverr maður á að gefa Grími nokkura gersemi, en sú virðing þykkir honum sér mest ger, að í einu sé af drukkið.	each man is to give Grim some treasure, but so worthy seems to-him to-see most done, that in one you of drink.	Each man has to give Grim something valuable, but most worthy honour to him is to drink it in one.
en ek veit, að mér ber fyrstum af að drekka, en það er einskis manns þol að drekka það í einu".	but I know, that I bear first of to drink, but that is nothing man endure than drink that in one".	But I know that I have to drink first, but it is no man's endurance to drink it at once".
Þorsteinn mælti:	Thorstein spoke:	Thorstein spoke:
"þú skalt fara í serk minn, því að þér má þá ekki granda, þó að ólyfjan sé í drykknum.	"you shall go in shirt mine, because that you may then not to-injure, though that poison even if drink.	"You shall go in my shirt, because then you shall not come to injury, even if there is poison in the drink.
tak kórónu af höfði þér og gef Grími inum góða og seg í eyra honum, að þú skalt gera honum miklu meira heiður en Geirröður, og síðan skaltu láta sem þú drekkir.	take the-crown off head yours and give Grim the Good and say in ear his, that you shall do him much more honour than Geirrod, and afterwards shall-you lay-out that you drink.	Take the crown off your head, and give it to Grim the Good, and say in his ear that you will do him much more honour than Geirrod, and afterwards shall you drink to that.

The Tale of Thorsteinn House-Power (Old Icelandic)

Old Icelandic	Literal	English
en eitr mun í horninu, og skaltu steypa niður næst þér, og mun þik ekki saka.	then poison should-be in the-horn, ad shall-you cast down near you, and shall you not injury.	Then should the poison be in the horn, you shall cast it down beside you, and you shall not be injured.
en þá er drykkjuskapr er úti, skaltu láta menn þína ríða".	but then when drinking is over, shall-you have men yours ride-away".	But when the drinking is over, have your men ride away".
Goðmundur sagði, að hann skuli ráða.	Godmund said, that he shall decide.	Godmund said, that he shall decide.
"en ef Geirröður deyr, þá á ek alla Jötunheima, en ef hann lifir lengr, verður það bani vár".	"but if Geirrod dies, then with I all Giant-Home, but if he lives longer, becomes that death ours".	"But if Geirrod dies, then I own all the Giant-Home, but if he lives longer, that death will be ours".
síðan sofa þeir af um nóttina.	afterwards slept they of about the-night.	Afterwards they slept through the night.

9

um morguninn eru þeir snemma á fótum og taka sín klæði.	about morning were they soon about feet and took their clothes.	In the morning they got up early and took their clothes.
þá kemur Geirröður konungr til þeira og biður þá drekka velfaranda sinn.	then came Geirrod the-king to them and asked them to-drink well-faring his.	Then King Geirrod came to them and asked them to drink their welfare.
þeir gerðu svá.	they did so.	They did so.
váru fyrst drukkin hornin Hvítingar næst máldrykkju skálum, en þá var drukkið minni Þórs og Óðins.	were first drunk the-horns Whitings next drinking bowls, and then were drunk in-memory Thor's and Odin's.	First the horns called Whitings were drunk from, next the drinking bowls, and they were drunk from in memory of Thor and Odin.
því næst kómu inn margir slagir hljóðfæra, og tveir menn, nokkuru minni en Þorsteinn, þeir báru Grím inn Góða.	then next came in many artful musical-instruments, and two men, somewhat smaller than Thorstein, they carried Grim the Good.	Then many kinds of instruments came in, and two men, somewhat smaller than Thorstein, brought in Grim the Good.
allir stóðu upp og fellu á kné fyrir honum.	all stood up and fell to knees before him.	Everyone stood up and fell on their knees before him.
Grímr var óhýrligr.	Grim was unfriendly-looking.	Grim was hideous.

The Tale of Thorsteinn House-Power (Old Icelandic)

Old Icelandic	Literal	English
Geirröður mælti til Goðmundar:	Geirrod spoke to Godmund:	Geirrod said to Godmund:
"tak við Grími inum Góða, og er þetta þín handsals skál".	"take with Grim the Good, and be this your binding shall".	"Take Grim the Good and let this toast be your binding pledge".
Goðmundur gekk að Grími og tók af sér gullkórónu og setti á hann og mælti í eyra honum, sem Þorsteinn hafði sagt honum.	Godmund went to Grim and took off himself gold-crown and set on him and spoke in ear his, as Thorstein had told him.	Godmund went to Grim, took off his gold crown, set it upon him, and spoke in his ear, as Thorstein had told him.
síðan lét hann renna af horninu ofan í serk sér, og var eitr í.	then had he ran of the-horn over into shirt his, and was poison in.	Then he ran the horn over into his shirt, and poured the poisonous drink in.
hann drakk til Geirröði konungi og kyssti á stikilinn, og fór Grímr hlæjandi frá honum.	he drank to Geirrod the-king and kissed the horn-point, and went Grim smiling went-from him.	He drank to King Geirrod and kissed the point of the horn, and Grim was taken away from him with a smile on his face.
tók Geirröður þá við fullu horninu og bað Grím með góðri heill koma og bað hann kunngera sér, ef nokkurr háski væri nær.	took Geirrod then with the-full horn and asked Grim with luck whole coming and asked him to-announce to-him, if something dangerous was near.	Geirrod took the full horn and asked Grim to bring him good luck and asked him if there was anything dangerous near.
"hefi ek opt sét þik með betra bragði".	"have I often seen you with better looking".	"I have often seen you in a better mood".
tók hann gullmen af sér og gaf Grími, drakk síðan til Agða jarli, og þótti því líkast sem boði felli á sker, er niður rann eptir hálsinum á honum, og drakk af allt.	took he gold-necklace off himself and gave Grim, drank afterwards to Agdi the-earl, and seemed therefore like as breaking wave on a-rock, as down ran after throat of him, and drank of all.	He took a gold necklace off himself and gave it to Grim, and drank afterwards to Earl Agdi, and it was like a wave breaking on a rock, as the drink ran down his throat, and he drank all of it.
Grímr hristi höfuðið, og var hann borinn Agða jarli, og gaf hann honum tvá gullhringa og bað sér miskunnar og drakk síðan af í þremr og fekk byrlaranum.	Grim shook his-head, and was he carried Agdi the-earl, and gave it to-him two gold-rings and asked his mercy and drank afterwards of in three and went the-cup-bearer.	Grim shook his head, and he was carried to Earl Agdi who gave him two gold rings and asked for his mercy, and he drank in three draughts and then returned it to the cup-bearer.
Grímr mælti:	Grim said:	Grim said:

The Tale of Thorsteinn House-Power (Old Icelandic)

Old Icelandic	Literal	English
"svá ergist hverr sem eldist".	"the feebler each who oldest".	"The older the man, the feebler"
þá var hornit fyllt, og skyldu þeir drekka af tveir, Jökull og Fullsterkr.	then was the horn, filled and should they drink of, Jokul and Full-Strong.	The horn was filled again so that Jokul and Full-Strong would drink from it.
Fullsterkr drakk fyrr.	Full-Strong drank before.	Full-Strong drank before.
Jökull tók við og leit í hornit og kvað lítilmannliga drukkið og sló Fullsterk með horninu.	Jokul took with and had in horn and said weakly drank and struck Full-Strong with the-horn.	Jokul took the horn and said that Full-Strong drank like a weakling, and struck him with the horn.
en hann rak hnefann á nasir Jökli, svá að þjófshakan brotnaði, en ór hrutu tennrnar.	but he drove fist to nose Jokul's, so that thievish-chin broken, then out-of erupted the-teeth.	But he drove his first into Jokul's nose, so that his thievish chin was broken, and then teeth erupted out of his mouth.
var þá upphlaup mikið.	was then uproar much.	There was much uproar.
Geirröður bað menn eigi láta þetta spyrjast, að þeir skildi svá illa.	Geirrod asked men not have this was-heard, that they separated so ill.	Geirrod asked the men not to have it heard that they had separated on bad terms.
váru þeir þegar sáttir, og var Grímr inn góði burt borinn.	were they straightaway agreed, and was Grim the Good away carried.	They were reconciled straight away and Grim the Good was carried away.

10

litlu síðar kom maður gangandi í höllina.	little afterwards came a-man walking into the-hall.	A little afterwards a man came walking into the hall.
allir undruðust, hversu lítill hann var.	all wondered, how-so little he was.	Everyone wondered at how little he was.
það var Þorsteinn Bæjarbarn.	that was Thorstein House-Child.	It was Thorstein House-Child.
hann veik að Goðmundi og sagði, að hestar væru til reiðu.	he turned to Godmund and told, him horses were to ride.	He turned to Godmund and told him to prepare the horses to ride.
Geirröður spurði, hvað barn að það væri.	Geirrod asked, who the-child that it was.	Geirrod asked who the child was.

The Tale of Thorsteinn House-Power (Old Icelandic)

Old Icelandic	*Literal*	*English*
Goðmundur segir:	Godmund said:	Godmund said:
"það er smásveinn minn, er Óðinn konungr sendi mér, og er konungs gersemi og kann marga smáleika, og ef yður þætti nokkuru neytr, þá vil ek gefa yður hann".	"that is little-boy mine, that Odin the-king sent me, and is the-king's treasure and knows many small-games, and if you seem some good-use, then will I give you him".	"This is my little boy that king Odin sent me, and is the king's treasure, and he knows many tricks, and if you think he may be of use then I will give him to you".
"það er svipmikill drengr",	"that is a-striking fellow",	"That is a striking fellow",
segir konungr, "og vil ek sjá fimleika hans",	said the-king, "and wish I to-see tricks his",	said the king, "and I wish to see his tricks",
og bað Þorstein leika nokkurn smáleik.	and asked Thorstein play some small-games.	and asked Thorstein to play some tricks.
Þorsteinn tók hall sinn og brodd og pjakkar þar í, sem hvítt er.	Thorstein took marble his and point and pricked there in, where white was.	Thorstein took his marble and point and pricked where it was white.
kemur haglhríð svá mikil, að engi þorir í móti að sjá, og varð svá mikil fönn í höllinni, að tók í ökkla.	came hailstorm so great, that none dared to meet to see, and was so great snow in the-hall, that took at ankles.	There came a hailstorm so great, that none dared to meet it with their eyes, and the snow was so great in the hall that it was up to everyone's ankles".
konungr hló að.	the-king laughed at.	The king laughed at this.
nú stangaði Þorsteinn hallinn, þar sem hann var gulr.	now stabbed Thorstein the-marble, there where it was yellow.	Now Thorstein stabbed at the marble where it was yellow.
kom þá sólskin svá heitt, að snjórinn bráðnaði allr á lítilli stundu.	came then sunshine so hot, that the-snow melted all in little while.	Then came sunshine so hot that the snow melted in a short while.
þar fylgdi sætr ilmr, en Geirröður kvað hann var listamann.	there followed mountain-pastures sweet-smell, and Geirrod said he was a-skilled-craftsman.	There followed the sweet smell of mountain pastures, and Geirrod said that he was a skilled craftsman.
en Þorsteinn segir eptir einn leikinn, er heitir svipuleikr.	then Thorstein said after one trick, that called the-scourge.	Then Thorstein said that there remained one trick which was called the scourge.
konungr segist hann sjá vilja.	the-king said he to-see wished.	The king said he wished to see it.

The Tale of Thorsteinn House-Power (Old Icelandic)

Old Icelandic	Literal	English
Þorsteinn stóð á miðju hallargólfi og pjakkar þar í hallinn, sem rautt er.	Thorstein stood in the-middle hall-floor and pricked there in the-marble, where red was.	Thorstein stood in the middle of the hall floor and pricked the marble where it was red.
stökkva þar ór gneistar.	jumped there of sparks.	Then sparks jumped from it.
síðan hleypr hann um höllina fyrir hvert sæti.	afterwards ran he about the-hall before each seat.	Afterwards he ran about the hall in front of each seat.
tókust þá að vaxa gneistaflaugin, svá að hverr maður varð að geyma sín augu.	took then to grow sparks-flying, so that each man was to to-mind their eyes.	Then the fling sparks grew so that every man had to mind his eyes.
en Geirröður konungr hló að.	then Geirrod the-king laughed at.	Then King Geirrod laughed at this.
tók þá að vaxa eldrinn, svá að öllum þótti við of um.	took then to grow the-fire, so that all thought against of about.	The fires grew so that all thought against it.
Þorsteinn hafði sagt Goðmundi fyrir, að hann skyldi út ganga og fara á hest.	Thorstein had told Godmund before, that he should out go and travel with horses.	Thorstein had told Godmund before, that he should go and travel with the horses.
Þorsteinn hleypr fyrir Geirröð og mælti:	Thorstein ran before Geirrod and said:	Thorstein ran before Geirrod and said:
"vili þér láta auka leikinn?"	"wish you to-have more games?"	"Do you wish to have more games?"
"lát sjá, sveinn",	"let see, boy",	"Let's see, boy",
sagði hann.	said he.	he said.
pjakkar Þorsteinn þá í fastara lagi.	pricked Thorstein then to harder thrust.	Thorstein then pricked harder.
kemur þá í auga Geirröði konungi.	came then in eyes Geirrod's the-king.	Then came sparks into King Geirrod's eyes.
Þorsteinn hleypr til dyranna og snaraði hallinum og broddinum, og kom í sitt auga hvárt á Geirröði konungi, og steyptist hann dauður á gólfit, en Þorsteinn gekk út.	Thorstein ran to the-door and threw the-marble and point, and came to his eyes each that Geirrod the-king, and knocked him dead on the-floor, then Thorstein went out.	Thorstein ran to the door and threw the marble and the point, and each came to King Geirrod's eyes, and he was knocked dead on the floor, then Thorstein went out.
var Goðmundur þá kominn á hest.	when Godmund then came to horses.	Godmund had then come on horseback.

The Tale of Thorsteinn House-Power (Old Icelandic)

Old Icelandic	Literal	English
Þorsteinn bað þá ríða, "því að nú er ekki deigum vært".	Thorstein bid then to-ride, "because that now is not weak short".	Thorstein then bid then that they ride away, "because now is not the time for weakness".
þeir ríða til árinnar.	they rode to the-river.	They rode to the river
var þá aptr kominn hallrinn og broddrinn.	was then back coming the-marble and the-point.	Then the marble and point was coming back.
Þorsteinn segir, að Geirröður var dauður.	Thorstein said, that Geirrod was dead.	Thorstein said that Geirrod was dead.
ríða þeir nú yfir ána og þangað, sem þeir höfðu fundizt.	rode they now across the river from-there, where they had met.	They now rode across the river from there, where they had met.
þá mælti Þorsteinn:	then spoke Thorstein:	Then Thorstein spoke:
"hér munum vér nú skilja, og mun mönnum mínum mál þykkja, að ek komi til þeira".	"forces should we now separate, and should men mine the-matter think, that I come to them".	"Our forces should now separate, and my men think that I should come to them.
"far heim með mér",	"travel home with me",	"Travel home with me",
sagði Goðmundr, "og skal ek launa þér góða fylgd".	said Godmund, "and shall I repay you good following".	said Godmund, "and I shall repay you for your good help".
"síðan mun ek þess vitja",	"afterwards should I this visit",	"Afterwards I should visit",
segir Þorsteinn, "en aptr skalt þú fara með fjölmenni í Geirröðargarða.	said Thorstein, "but back shall you travel with following-men to Geirrod's-Town.	said Thorstein, "but you should travel back to Geirrod's-Town with a following of men.
er nú landið í yðru valdi".	is now the-land in your control".	Now the land is in your control".
"þú munt ráða",	"you should reckon",	"Whatever you reckon"
sagði Goðmundr, "en Óláfi konungi skaltu færa kveðju mína".	said Godmund, "then Olaf the-king shall be-brought greetings mine".	said Godmund, "then King Olaf shall be brought my greetings".

The Tale of Thorsteinn House-Power (Old Icelandic)

Old Icelandic	Literal	English
tók hann þá eitt gullker og silfrdisk og tvítugt handklæði gullofit og sendi konungi, en bað Þorstein vitja sín, og skildu með kærleikum.	took he then a golden-bowl and silver-dish and twenty hand-cloths gold-woven and sent the-king, and asked Thorstein visit him, and separated with friendly-terms.	He then took a golden bowl and a silver dish and twenty gold woven towels also to send to the king, and he asked Thorstein to visit him, and they separated on friendly terms.

11

Old Icelandic	Literal	English
en nú sér Þorsteinn, hvar Agði jarl ferr í allmiklum jötunmóð.	and now saw Thorstein, where Agdi the-earl travelling in all-mighty giant's-wrath.	And now saw Thorstein, where Earl Agdi was travelling in an almighty giant's wrath.
Þorsteinn ferr eptir honum.	Thorstein went after him.	Thorstein went after him.
sér hann þá mikinn húsabæ, er Agði átti.	saw he then great farmstead, which Agdi owned.	He then saw a great farmstead, which Agdi owned.
aldingarður var við grindhliðið, og stóð þar við ein jungfrú.	orchard was with gate, and stood there with a young-woman.	There was an orchard, and at the gate there stood a young woman.
hún var dóttir Agða og hét Goðrún.	she was daughter Agdi's and named Gudrun.	She was Agdi's daughter and was named Gudrun.
mikil var hún og fríð.	tall was she and peaceful.	She was tall and fair.
hún heilsaði föður sínum og spurði tíðenda.	she greeted father hers and asked of-news.	She greeted her father and asked him the news.
"nóg eru tíðendi",	"enough is news",	"There is news enough",
segir hann.	said he.	he said.
"Geirröður konungr er dauður, og hefir Goðmundur af Glæsisvöllum svikit oss alla og hefir leynt þar kristnum manni, og heitir sá Þorsteinn Bæjarmagn.	"Geirrod the-king is dead, and has Godmund of Glasir-Plains tricked us all and has hidden there Christian man, and named so Thorstein House-Power.	"King Geirrod is dead, and Godmund of Glasir-Plains has tricked us all and has hidden a Christian man there, and he is named Thorstein House-Power.
hann hefir ausit eldi í augu oss.	he has thrown fire in eyes ours.	He has thrown fire in our eyes.
skal ek nú drepa menn hans".	shall I now kill men his".	I shall now kill his men".

The Tale of Thorsteinn House-Power (Old Icelandic)

Old Icelandic	Literal	English
kastar hann þar niður hornunum Hvítingum og hljóp til skógar, sem hann væri galinn.	threw he there down the-horn Whitings and ran to the-forest, as-if he was mad.	There he threw down the horn called Whitings and ran to the forest as if he was mad.
Þorsteinn gekk að Goðrúnu.	Thorstein went to Gudrun.	Thorstein went to Gudrun.
hún heilsaði honum og spurði hann að nafni.	she greeted him and asked him of name.	She greeted him and asked him his name.
hann kvaðst Þorsteinn Bæjarbarn heita, hirðmaður Óláfs konungs.	he said Thorstein House-Child named, court-man Olaf's the-king.	He said he was named Thorstein House-Child, a court man of King Olaf.
"stórr mun þar inn stærsti, sem þú ert barnit",	"big must there the biggest, if you are the-child",	"His big must be the biggest, if you are the child",
sagði hún.	said she.	she said.
"viltu fara með mér",	"will-you travel with me",	"Will you travel with me",
segir Þorsteinn, "og taka við trú?"	said Thorstein, "and take with the-faith?"	said Thorstein, "and take the faith?".
"við lítit yndi á ek hér að skiljast",	"with little happiness that I here to separate",	"With little happiness here to separate from", she said,
segir hún, "því að móðir mín er dauð.	said she, "because that mother mine is dead.	"because my mother is dead.
hún var dóttir Óttars jarls af Hólmgörðum, og váru þau ólík að skapsmunum, því að faðir minn er mjög tröllaukinn, og sé ek nú, að hann er feigr.	she was daughter Ottar's the-earl of Novgorod, and were they unlike in mood-mind, as that father mine is much troll-possessed, and see I now, that he is doomed.	She was the daughter of Earl Ottar of Novgorod, and they were unlike in temperament, as my father who is troll-possessed, and I see now that he is doomed.
en ef þú vilt fylgja mér aptr hingað, þá mun ek fara með þér".	then if you will follow me back here, then shall I travel with you".	Then if you will follow back here with me, then I shall travel with you".
síðan tók hún þing sín, en Þorsteinn tók hornin Hvítinga.	afterwards took she things hers, and Thorstein took the-horn Whitings.	Afterwards she took her things, and Thorstein took the horn called Whitings.
síðan gengu þau á skóginn og sáu, hvar Agði fór.	afterwards went they into the-forest and saw, where Agdi went.	Afterwards they went into the forest and saw, where Agdi went.

The Tale of Thorsteinn House-Power (Old Icelandic)

Old Icelandic	Literal	English
hann grenjaði mjög og helt fyrir augun.	he screamed much and held before eyes.	He screamed a lot and held his hands before his eyes.
hafði það saman borið, þegar hann sá skip Þorsteins, hljóp sá verkr í þjófsaugun á honum, að hann sá eigi.	had that together borne, as-soon-as he saw ship Thorstein's, ran so pain in thief's-eyes of his, that he saw not.	That had happened together with, as soon as he saw Thorstein's ship, a pain ran in his thief's eyes, so that he could not see.
var þá komið að sólarfalli, er þau komu til skips.	was then coming to sunset, when they came to ships.	It was approaching sunset, when they came to the ships.
váru menn Þorsteins þá burt búnir, en er þeir sáu Þorstein, urðu þeir fegnir.	when men Thorstein's then away prepared, then when they saw Thorstein, became they joyful.	When Thorstein's men were preparing to journey away, then they saw Thorstein and became joyful.
sté Þorsteinn þá á skip, og sigldu burt.	stepped Thorstein then onto the-ship, and sailed away.	Thorstein stepped onto the ship, and they sailed away.
er eigi getið um ferð hans, fyrr en hann kom heim í Noreg.	is nothing told-of about the-journey his, before that he came home to Norway.	Nothing is told of his journey, before he came home to Norway.

12 | # 12 | # 12

Old Icelandic	Literal	English
þenna vetr sat Óláfur konungr í Þrándheimi.	that winter sat Olaf the-king in Trondheim.	That winter King Olaf sat at Trondheim.
Þorsteinn fann konung að Jólum og færði honum gripi þá, sem Goðmundur sendi honum, og hornin Hvítinga og marga aðra gripi.	Thorstein met the-king at Yule and brought him treasure then, which Godmund sent him, and the-horn Whitings and many other treasures.	Thorstein met the king at Yule and brought him treasure, which Godmund had sent him, and the horn called Whitings, and many other treasures.
sagði hann konungi frá ferðum sínum og sýndi honum Goðrúnu.	told he the-king from voyage his and showed him Gudrun.	He told the king of his voyages and showed him Gudrun.
konungr þakkaði honum, og lofuðu allir hans hreysti og þótti mikils um vert.	the-king thanked him, and praised all his valour and thought much about worthy.	The king thanked him, and praised all his valour and thought much of his worthiness.
síðan lét konungr skíra Goðrúnu og kenna trú.	afterwards had the-king baptised Gudrun and taught the-faith.	Afterwards the king had Gudrun baptised and taught the faith.

The Tale of Thorsteinn House-Power (Old Icelandic)

Old Icelandic	Literal	English
Þorsteinn lék svipuleik um Jólin, og þótti mönnum það skemmtan mikil.	Thorstein played the-scourge about Yule, and thought men that amusement great.	Thorstein played the scourge through Yule, and men thought it was great amusement.
Hvítingar gengu í minnum, og váru tveir menn um hvárt horn.	Whitings went in came, and were two men about each horn.	The Whitings were brought in, and two men shared each horn.
en ker það, sem Goðmundur hafði sent konungi, gekk engum af að drekka utan Þorsteini Bæjarbarni.	the vessel that, which Godmund had sent the-king, went none of of drinking except Thorstein House-Child.	The cup that Godmund had sent the king, was not drunk from except by Thorstein House-Child.
handklæðit brann eigi, þótt því væri í eld kastað, og var hreinna eptir en áður.	hand-cloth burned not, though that was in fire cast, and was cleaner after than before.	The hand-cloth did not burn, even though it was cast in fire, and was cleaner than before.
Þorsteinn talar um við konung, að hann vildi gera brullaup til Goðrúnar, en konungr veitti honum það, og var það sæmilig veizla.	Thorstein talked through with the-king, that he wished to-make wedding-proposal to Gudrun, and the-king granted him that, and was that well feast.	Thorstein talked through with the king, that he wished to make a wedding proposal to Gudrun, and the king granted him that, and was there a splendid feast.
og ina fyrstu nótt, er þau kómu í eina sæng og niður var hleypt fortjaldinu, þá brast upp þilfjöl að höfðum Þorsteins, og var þar kominn Agði jarl og ætlaði að drepa hann.	and the first night, when they came to one bed and down was cast the-curtain, then burst up decks over head Thorstein's, and was then come Agdi the-earl and intended to kill him.	And on the first night, when they came to bed together, the curtain was cast down, and then the decks over Thorstein's head burst open, and there had come Earl Agdi intending to kill him.
en þar laust í móti hita svá miklum, að hann þorði eigi inn að ganga.	but then loosed in opposition heat so great, that he dared not in to go.	But then was released so great a heat against him, that he dared not go in.
sneri hann þá í burtu.	turned he then to away.	He turned away.
þá kom konungr að og sló hann með gullbúnu refði í höfuðið, en hann steyptist niður í jörðina.	then came the-king to and struck him with gold-plated staff about head, then he fell down to the-ground.	Then the king came and struck him with a gold plated staff on the head, then he fell face down on the ground.
helt konungr vörð um nóttina, en um morguninn váru horfin hornin Hvítingar.	held the-king guard about the-night, then about morning were disappeared the-horns Whitings.	The king held guard through the night, and then in the morning the horns called Whitings had disappeared.
gekk veizlan vel fram.	went the-feast well from-there.	The feast went well from there.

The Tale of Thorsteinn House-Power (Old Icelandic)

Old Icelandic	Literal	English
sat Þorsteinn með konungi um vetrinn, og unnust þau Goðrún vel.	sat Thorstein with the-king through winter, and loved they Gudrun well.	Thorstein sat with the king through the winter, and he and Gudrun loved each other well.
um várið beiddi Þorsteinn orlofs að sigla í Austrveginn og finna Goðmund konung.	about spring asked Thorstein vacation to sail to Eastern-Lands and find Godmund the-king.	In the spring Thorstein asked for a vacation to sail to the Eastern-Lands to find King Godmund.
en konungr sagðist það eigi gera, utan hann lofaði að koma aptr.	but the-king said that not to-do, without him pledging to come back.	But the king said that he should not do it without promising to come back.
Þorsteinn hét því.	Thorstein promised accordingly.	Thorstein promised accordingly.
konungr bað hann halda trú sína vel, "og eig meira undir þér en þeim Austr þar".	the-king asked him keep faith his well, "and have more behind you than they Eastern-Lands there".	The king asked him to keep his faith well: "and have more behind you than those in the Eastern-Lands there".
skildust þeir með kærleikum, og báðu allir vel fyrir honum, því að Þorsteinn var orðinn vinsæll.	separated they with friendship, and bid all well for him, because that Thorstein was became popular.	They separated with friendship, and all bid him well, for Thorstein had become popular.
sigldi hann í Austrveg, og er eigi getið annars en sú ferð færist vel.	sailed he to Eastern-Lands, and was nothing told-of other than so travelled the-journey well.	He sailed to the Eastern-Lands, and nothing was told other than that he travelled the journey well.
kom hann á Glæsisvöllu, og fagnaði Goðmundur honum vel.	came he to Glasir-Plains, and welcomed Godmund him well.	He came to Glasir-Plains, and Godmund welcomed him well.
Þorsteinn mælti:	Thorstein spoke:	Thorstein spoke:
"hvað hafið þér frétt ór Geirröðargörðum?"	"what have you news of Geirrod's-Town?"	"What news do you have of Geirrod's-Town?"
"þangað fór ek",	"there travelled I",	"I travelled there",
segir Goðmundr, "og gáfu þeir landið í mitt vald, og ræður þar fyrir Heiðrekr Úlfhamr, sonr minn".	said Godmund, "and gave they land to me power, and rules there over Heidrek Wolf-Skin, son mine".	said Godmund, "and they gave me power over the land, and ruling over there is Heidrek Wolf-Skin, my son".
"hvar er Agði jarl?"	"what of Agdi the-earl?"	"What of Earl Agdi?"
segir Þorsteinn.	said Thorstein.	said Thorstein.

The Tale of Thorsteinn House-Power (Old Icelandic)

Old Icelandic	Literal	English
"hann lét gera sér haug, þá þér fóruð",	"he had done himself a-burial-mound, when you travelled",	"He had made himself a burial mound, when you travelled",
segir Goðmundr, "og gekk þar í með mikið fé, en þeir Jökull og Frosti drukknuðu í ánni Hemru, er þeir fóru frá veizlunni, en ek hefi nú vald yfir heraðinu á Grundum".	said Godmund, "and went there in with much wealth, but they Jokul and Frosti drowned in the-river Hemra, as they travelled from the-feast, then I have now power across the-district of Grundir".	said Godmund", and retired there with much wealth, and Jokul and Frosti drowned in the river Hemra, as they travelled from the feast, and I now have power across the district of Grundir".
"þar er nú mikið undir",	"there is now much under",	"There is now a lot under it",
segir Þorsteinn, "hverju þú vilt mér af skipta, því að mér þykkir Goðrún eiga arf allan eptir föður sinn, Agða jarl".	said Thorstein, "how you will me to give, because that to-me seems Gudrun my-wife inheritance all after father his, Agdi the-earl".	said Thorstein, "how much you wish to let me have, because it seems to me that my wife Gudrun is entitled to all the inheritance after he father, Earl Agdi".
"ef þú vilt vera minn maður",	"if you will be my man",	"If you will be my man",
sagði Goðmundr.	said Godmund.	said Godmund.
"þá muntu ekki vanda um trú mína",	"then should not custom about the-faith mine",	"Then you will not have any problems with my faith",
segir Þorsteinn.	said Thorstein.	said Thorstein.
"það vil ek",	"that will I",	"That I will",
sagði Goðmundr.	said Godmund.	said Godmund.
sídan fóru þeir til Grunda, og tók Þorsteinn heraðið undir sik.	afterwards travelled they to Grundir, and took Thorstein the-district under himself.	Afterwards they travelled to Grundir, and Thorstein took the district under himself.

13

Þorsteinn reisti bú að Gnípalundi, því að Agði jarl hafði gengið aptr og eytt bæinn.	Thorstein raised the-dwelling at Gnipalund, because that Agdi the-earl had come back and devastated the-dwelling.	Thorstein raised the house at Gnipalund, as Earl Agdi had come back and devastated the old house.
gerðist Þorsteinn höfðingi mikill.	became Thorstein a-chieftain great.	Thorstein became a great chieftain.

The Tale of Thorsteinn House-Power (Old Icelandic)

Old Icelandic	Literal	English
Goðrún fæddi sveinbarn mikið litlu síðar, og hét Brynjólfur.	Gudrun raised a-baby-boy large little since, and named Brynjolf.	Gudrun gave birth to a big baby boy, and he was named Brynjolf.
ekki var traust, að Agði jarl glettist eigi við Þorstein.	not was trusted, that Agdi the-earl playing-tricks not against Thorstein.	There was no confidence that Earl Agdi would not play-tricks against Thorstein.
eina nótt gekk Þorsteinn af sæng sinni og sá, hvar að Agði fór.	one night went Thorstein to bed his and saw, where that Agdi moving.	One night Thorstein got out of his bed and saw where Agdi was moving.
hann þorði hvergi inn í hliðin, því að kross var fyrir hverjum dyrum.	he dared neither in the the-gates, because that the-cross was before each doorway.	He dared not enter the gates, for there was a cross at every door.
Þorsteinn gekk til haugsins.	Thorstein went to burial-mound-his.	Thorstein went to the mound.
hann var opinn, og gekk hann inn og tók burt hornin Hvítinga.	it was open, and went he inside and took away the-horns Whitings.	It was open, and he went inside and took away the horns called Whitings.
þá kom Agði jarl í hauginn, en Þorsteinn hljóp út hjá honum og setti kross í dyrrnar, og laukst aptr haugrinn, og hefir ekki orðið vart við Agða síðan.	then came Agdi the-earl into the-mound, and Thorstein ran out beside him and set the-cross in the-door, and closed afterwards the-mound, and has no word was of Agdi since..	Then Earl Agdi came to the mound, but Thorstein ran out beside him and put a cross in the door, and the mound was closed, and Agdi has not been seen since.
um sumarið eptir fór Þorsteinn til Noregs og færði Óláfi konungi hornin Hvítinga.	about summer after went Thorstein to Norway and brought Olaf the-king the-horns Whitings.	The following summer Thorstein went to Norway, and brought King Olaf the horns called Whitings.
síðan fekk hann orlof og sigldi til eigna sinna.	then got he leave to sail to possessions his.	Then he took leave and sailed to his possessions.
bauð konungr honum halda vel trú sína.	asked the-king him hold well faith his.	The king commanded him to keep his faith well.
höfum vér eigi frétt síðan til Þorsteins.	have we not news since of Thorstein's.	We have not heard from Thorstein since.
en þá Óláfur konungr hvarf af Orminum Langa, hurfu hornin Hvítingar.	but when Olaf the-king disappeared from The-Serpent Long, vanished the-horns Whitings.	But when King Olaf disappeared from the Long Serpent, the horns of the Whites disappeared.

The Tale of Thorsteinn House-Power (Old Icelandic)

Old Icelandic	Literal	English
lúkum vér þar þætti Þorsteins Bæjarbarns.	end we there the-story Thorstein's House-Child.	We end there the tale of Thorstein House-Child.

Word List *(Old Icelandic to English)*

Old Icelandic	English
A, a	
að	about, against, as, at, from, him, in, it, of, over, than, that, the, to, towards, when, which
aðra	other
aðrir	others
af	drink, from, from, of, of, off, that, to, to
afhenda	off-handed, of-hand
afklæðast	undressed
afklæddust	undressed
afl	strength
afla	provide
afli	a-forge, strength
Agða	Agdi (name), Agdi (name), Agdi's (name)
Agði	Agdi (name), Agdi (name)
akkerum	anchor
aldingarður	orchard
aldri	never, never
alla	all, all
allan	all
allar	all
allir	all, all
allmiklum	all-mighty
allr	all, all
alls	all
Allsterk	All-Strong (name)
Allsterkr	All-Strong (name)
allt	all, all
andliti	face
annan	another-thing
annarr	another, one, one, the-other
annarri	another, one
annars	other
annast	he-took-care-of
aptnaði	the-evening
aptr	afterwards, back, back, return
arf	inheritance
atgang	to-going
atgangr	to-going
atsetu	a-seat
auðið	fated
auga	eyes, eyes
augu	eyes, eyes
augum	eyes
augun	eyes
auka	extra, more
aura	ounces
ausit	thrown
austr	east, east, Eastern-Lands (place)
Austrveg	Eastern-Lands (place)
Austrveginn	Eastern-Lands (place)
Á, á	
á	a, about, a-river, at, beside, by, for, from, in, into, is, of, on, onto, that, the, then, to, was, who, with
ábyrgjast	take-care-of
áður	after, before
áliðnum	following
álna	cubits
álnar	a-yard
ána	the, the-river
ánni	the-river, the-river
árinnar	the-river, the-river
átti	had, owned
áttu	had
ávallt	always
Æ, æ	
ætla	intend, suppose
ætlaði	intended

Word List (Old Icelandic to English)

Old Icelandic	English
ætlan	intentions
ætlar	intended
ættar	lineage
ætti	had

B, b

Old Icelandic	English
bað	asked, bid, ordered
báðu	bid
báðum	both
bæinn	the-dwelling
Bæjarbarn	House-Child (name)
Bæjarbarni	House-Child (name)
Bæjarbarns	House-Child (name)
Bæjarmagn	House-Power (name)
bak	back, the-back
Bálagarðssíðu	Balagardsida (place)
bana	dead, death
bandvettlinga	mittens
bani	death, the-death
bar	bore, carried
barn	the-child
barni	a-baby
barnit	child, the-child
báru	carried
bárust	bore
bauð	asked, offered
beiddi	asked
beini	the-bone
beinum	the-bone
beitina	opening, the-opening
bekk	a-bench, bench
bekkinn	of-the-bench
bekkjar	bench
bekknum	that-bench, the-bench
ber	bear
bera	bear, brought
berast	bore
berði	threw
berið	bring
berizt	bear
betr	better
betra	better
betri	better
beztir	best
bíða	abide, await
biður	asked
bik	pitch
birti	revealed
bjálfa	Bjalfi
bjálfi	Bjalfi
bjó	lived, prepared
bjuggust	settled
blár	black
bleikum	pale
boð	an-invite
boði	breaking
bóndi	farmer
borð	table
borða	the-tables
borðinu	table
borðum	a-table, the-tables
borg	a-city
borgarinnar	the-city, the-town
borgina	the-city, the-town
borið	borne
borin	brought
borinn	carried
börn	children
brá	drew
bráðnaði	melted
bræðir	thaws
bragði	looking
brann	burned
brast	burst
braut	way
brautinni	turned-away, turning
breiða	broad
breiddu	spread
breitt	broad
breyttu	behaved
bringu	the-chest
brodd	point
broddinum	point, the-point
broddrinn	the-point
bróður	brother
brosti	burst-out-laughing
brotnaði	broke, broken
brott	away
brullaup	wedding-proposal

Word List (Old Icelandic to English)

Old Icelandic	English
Brynjólfur	Brynjolf (name)
bú	the-dwelling
búa	live
bugtinni	the-curve
búið	inlaid, prepared
búin	prepared
búk	thick-set
búnir	prepared
burt	away
burtu	away
býður	invite
byggð	settlements
byr	fair-wind
byrlaranum	the-cup-bearer

D, d

Old Icelandic	English
dag	day
Dagný	Dagny (name)
dagsins	of-the-day
datt	fell
dauð	dead
dauður	dead
degi	day
deigum	weak
deyr	dies
díki	the-moat
djúp	deep
dóttir	daughter
draga	carry, drag
drakk	drank
drap	killed
draup	dripped
dregr	drew
drekka	drink, drinking, they, to-drink
drekkir	drink
drekkr	drinks
drengr	fellow
drep	gangrene
drepa	kill
drepnir	killed
Drött	Drott (name)
drottning	the-queen
Dröttr	Drott (name)
drukkið	drank, drink, drinking, drink-to, drunk
drukkin	drunk
drukknuðu	drowned
drukku	drank
drykkju	drinking
drykkjumaður	drinking-man
drykkjuskapr	drinking
drykknum	drink
dúka	tablecloths
dúkinn	table-cloth, the-table-cloth
dúkr	table-cloth
dunur	a-din
dvelr	delays
dverg	dwarf
dvergnum	the-dwarf
dvergrinn	dwarf, the-dwarf
dvergsbarnit	the-dwarf's-boy
dýr	wild-animals
dyranna	the-door
dyrr	door, the-door
dyrrnar	the-door
dyrum	doorway

E, e

Old Icelandic	English
eða	and, but, or
ef	if
eiða	oath, oaths
eig	have
eiga	my-wife, said-of, to-own
eigi	none, not, nothing
eigna	possessions
eignir	property
eigum	own
eik	oak
eikinni	the-oak
eimyrja	embers
ein	a
eina	a, one
einhvern	some-way
einhverr	someone
einir	alone

Word List (Old Icelandic to English)

Old Icelandic	English
einn	a, one
einni	a
einskis	nothing
einu	in-one, one
einum	a, one
eitr	poison
eitt	a, one
ek	I
ekki	no, not, nothing
eld	fire
eldi	fire
eldist	oldest
eldrinn	the-fire
eldsskara	fire-poker
eldur	fire, the-flames
eltu	chased
en	about, and, but, on, than, that, the, then, though, when, while
endast	ending
enga	any, none
engan	no-one
engi	no, none, not
engir	no
engu	nothing
engum	no, none
enn	but, than
eptir	after, behind
er	am, and, as, be, from, have, is, of, that, then, was, when, which, who
erfi	inheritance
ergist	feebler
erninum	the-eagle
ert	are
ertu	are-you
eru	are, is, they-are, were
erum	are
eyra	ear
eyranu	ears
eyri	an-ounce-of
eytt	devastated

F, f

Old Icelandic	English
fá	get, pay
faðir	father
fæddi	raised
færa	be-brought
færði	brought, took
færir	travel
færist	the-journey
fæti	feet
fætr	feet
fagnaði	celebrated, welcomed
fagr	beautiful
fagrar	fair
fagrt	fair
fangbrögðum	to-wrestling
fann	found, met
fannst	found
far	travel
fara	go, to-travel, travel, travelled, travelling
farið	go, gone
farin	gone
fast	fastened, hard, hard
fastara	harder
fé	wealth
féfátt	lack-of-money
feginn	relieved
fegnir	joyful
feiga	doomed
feigr	doomed, fated-to-die
fekk	got, went
fela	hide
félagi	companion
fell	falling, fell
felli	wave
fellir	drops
fellu	fell
felr	fold
fengnir	get
fengu	caught
fengust	got-they
ferð	journey, the-journey, travelled, voyage
ferðum	voyage

Word List (Old Icelandic to English)

Old Icelandic	English
ferr	travelling, went
fésparir	fee-sparing
festi	joined
festir	fastened
fimleika	tricks
fingrgull	finger-gold
finna	find
finnumst	meet
fitan	fat
fjalli	mountains
fjarstætt	far-away
fjölkunnigr	skilled-in-magic
fjölmenni	following-men
fjóra	four
fjórar	four
fjörð	fjord
fjórðunga	quarters
fjórum	four
fleira	more
flestum	most
fleygir	flew-it
flokk	band, company
flokki	men
flýgr	flies
föður	father
föðurnum	to-the-father
fólk	folk
fólki	folk
föll	falling
fönn	snow
fór	moving, travelled, went
fortjaldinu	the-curtain
fóru	travelled, went
fóruð	travelled
förunautr	companion
fótrinn	leg
fótum	feet
frá	away-from, from, went-from
fram	from, from-there, to
framboðligr	be-offered
framt	provide
frár	swift
fremstir	foremost
frétt	news
frið	peaceful
Frosta	Frosti (name)
frosti	Frosti, Frosti (name)
fugla	birds
full	drunk
Fullsterk	Full-Strong (name)
Fullsterkr	Full-Strong (name)
fullu	the-full
fúlt	foul
fundizt	met
furðuliga	exceedingly
fylgd	following
fylgdi	followed, following
fylgja	follow, following
fylgt	followed
fylldan	filled
fyllt	horn
fyrir	before, before-them, for, over
fyrr	before
fyrst	first
fyrsta	first
fyrstu	first
fyrstum	first

G, g

Old Icelandic	English
gað	got
gæfa	luck
gæfu	luck
gaf	gave
gáfu	gave
gagn	benefit
gagnvart	going-from
galdrafullt	magic-full
galinn	mad
gamalla	the-old
gamans	games
gamni	game
gamninu	the-game
gandreið	witch-ride
ganga	go, going, walk
gangandi	walking
gangi	go
gátum	opening

Word List (Old Icelandic to English)

Old Icelandic	English
Gaulardal	Gaulardale (place)
gef	give
gefa	give
gefur	given
gegnt	opposite
Geirröð	Geirrod (name)
Geirröðargarða	Geirrod's-Town (place)
Geirröðargörðum	Geirrod's-Town (place)
Geirröði	Geirrod (name), Geirrod's (name)
Geirröður	Geirrod (name)
gekk	went
gengið	come
gengr	went
gengu	went
ger	done
gera	do, done, make, to-do, to-make
gerði	did
gerðist	became
gerðu	did
gersema	precious-things
gersemar	treasured, treasures
gersemi	a-treasure, treasure, treasures
gert	made
get	guess
geta	get
getið	told-of
getr	get
geyma	retain, to-mind
gimsteinar	precious-stones
gjafirnar	the-gifts
gjarna	gladly
glaðir	glad, gladly
Glæsisvöllu	Glasir-Plains (place)
Glæsisvöllum	Glasir-Plains (place)
glerglugg	glass-window
glettist	playing-tricks
glíma	wrestle, wrestling
glímt	wrestled
glóanda	burning, glowing
glugginn	the-skylight
gneistaflaug	a-shower-of-sparks
gneistaflaugin	sparks-flying
gneistar	sparks
Gnípalundi	Gnipalund (place)
góða	good, Good (name), the-good
góði	good, Good (name)
Goðmund	Godmund (name)
Goðmundar	Godmund (name), Godmund's (name)
Goðmundi	Godmund (name)
Goðmundr	Godmund (name)
goðmundur	Godmund, Godmund (name)
góðri	luck
Goðrún	Gudrun (name)
Goðrúnar	Gudrun (name)
Goðrúnu	Gudrun (name)
góðum	good
góður	good
gólfi	the-floor
gólfit	floor, the-floor
gott	good
græð	tend-to
grafit	dug
grám	grey
granda	to-injure
greip	grabbed, gripped
grenjaði	howling, screamed
Grím	Grim (name)
Grími	Grim (name)
Grímr	Grim (name)
grindhliðið	gate
grip	grabbed
gripi	treasure, treasures
Grunda	Grundir (place)
Grundir	Grundir (place)
Grundum	Grundir (place)
guðvef	precious-cloth
guðvefjarskikkju	a-precious-cloak
gul	gold
gull	gold
gullbúnu	gold-plated
gullhnött	gold-ball
gullhring	gold-ring
gullhringa	gold-rings
gulli	gold

Word List (Old Icelandic to English)

Old Icelandic	English
gullker	golden-bowl
gullkórónu	gold-crown
gullligt	gold
gullligum	gold
gullmen	gold-necklace
gullofit	gold-woven
gullskotnum	gold-trimmed
gulr	gold, yellow
gustr	Gust

H, h

Old Icelandic	English
há	high
hæfa	hit
hægt	possible
hættu	dangerous
hafa	had, had, have, having
hafði	had
hafið	have
haft	had, have
hafvillur	open-sea
haglhríð	hailstorm
Hákon	Hakon (name)
halda	hold, keep
hálfan	half
hall	marble, piece-of-marble
hallar	hall
hallargólfi	hall-floor
hallargólfit	hall-floor
hallinn	the-marble, the-piece-of-marble
hallinum	the-marble
hallrinn	the-marble, the-piece-of-marble
háls	the-neck
hálsinum	throat
hamingju	luck
hana	he, it, she
handklæði	hand-cloths
handklæðit	hand-cloth
handsals	binding
hann	he, him, it, men
hans	him, his
harðasti	hardest
harðúðigr	hard-minded
hásæti	a-high-seat, high-seat
háski	dangerous
hátíð	festival
háttar	kinds
haug	a-burial-mound
hauginn	the-mound
haugrinn	the-mound
haugsins	burial-mound-his
heðan	from-hence
hefði	had
hefi	have
hefir	had, has, have
hefna	avenge
Heiðrekr	Heidrek (name)
heiður	honour
heill	whole
heilsaði	greeted
heim	home
heiminum	the-world
heimsliga	foolishly
heit	declared
heita	be-named, named, promised
heiti	named
heitir	called, named
heitt	hot
hel	death
heldur	rather
helt	held
helzt	held
Hemra	Hemra (place)
Hemru	Hemra (place)
henda	catch
hendi	hand
hendur	hand
hentar	suits
henti	caught
hér	forces, here
heraði	district
heraðið	the-district
heraðinu	the-district
hernaði	raiding
hest	horses
hesta	horses

Word List (Old Icelandic to English)

Old Icelandic	English
hestar	horses
hestarnir	the-horses
hesti	horse
hestr	horse
hestum	horses
hét	is-named, named, promised
heyra	hear
heyrir	heard
himni	the-sky
hingað	here
hinir	others, the-other
hirðið	take-care
hirðmaður	court-man
hirðmönnum	court-men
hirðprýði	court
hita	heat
hjá	beside
hjástöðu	beside-standing
hjó	hewed
hlæjandi	smiling
hlátr	laughter
hlátri	laughter
hlaupa	ran
hleypr	ran
hleypt	cast
hliðin	the-gates
hlíðir	slope
hljóðfæra	musical-instruments
hljóðfæri	musical-instruments
hljóp	ran
hló	laughed
hlógu	laughed
hluti	lot
hlýðni	homage
hlytir	to-get
hnakkinn	the-back-of-the-head
hnefann	fist
höfði	head
höfðingi	a-chieftain
höfðu	had
höfðum	head
höfn	the-harbour
höfuðið	head, his-head
höfum	have
hól	hill
holdi	flesh
hólinn	the-mound
hóll	mound
höll	a-hall, the-hall
höllina	the-hall
höllinni	the-hall
Hólmgörðum	Novgorod (place)
hólnum	the-mound
hömrum	a-steep-cliff
hönd	hand
höndum	hands
honum	he, him, his, it, to-him
horfin	disappeared
horn	a-horn, horn, horns
hornin	the-horn, the-horns
horninu	horn, the-horn
hornit	a-horn, horn, the
hornunum	the-horn
hösvaðist	went-for
Hösvi	Hosvir (name)
Hösvir	Hosvir (name)
hratt	pushed
hraustr	brave
hreinna	cleaner
hreysti	bravery, valour
hring	a-circle, ring
hringinn	the-ring
hringnum	the-ring
hringrinn	the-ring
hristi	shook
hrutu	erupted
hrysi	trembled
hug	think
hugr	thought
huldumaður	a-hidden-man
hulinshjálm	helm-of-invisibility
hún	she
hurfu	disappeared, vanished
hús	house, the-house
húsabæ	farmstead
húsum	houses
hvað	what, who
hvaðan	from-where
hvar	were, what, where
hvarf	disappeared

Word List (Old Icelandic to English)

Old Icelandic	English
hvárki	neither
hvárn	each
hvárntveggja	either-side
hvárt	each, whether, which
hvárttveggja	either
hvergi	neither
hverju	how
hverjum	each
hvern	everyone
hverr	anyone, each, who
hverrar	whose
hversu	how-so
hvert	each, what
hví	what, why
Hvítinga	Whitings (name)
Hvítingar	Whitings (name)
Hvítingum	Whitings (name)
hvítr	white
hvítt	white

I, i

Old Icelandic	English
illa	badly, ill
ilmr	sweet-smell
in	the
ina	the
indíalandi	India
inn	in, inside, the
innanborðs	aboard
inum	the
it	the, this

Í, í

Old Icelandic	English
í	about, all, among, at, if, in, into, it, of, on, the, to, was, with-that

J, j

Old Icelandic	English
jafnan	every-time
jafnstóra	equally-as-big, equally-large
jafnstórr	equally-big
Jamtaland	Jamtland (place)
jarl	earl, the-earl
jarli	the-earl, the-earl's
jarls	the-earl, the-earl's
Járnskeggja	Iron-Beard (name)
Jökli	Jokul's (name)
Jökull	Jokul (name)
Jólin	Yule (name)
Jólum	Yule (name)
jörðina	the-ground
jötnum	giants
Jötunheima	Giant-Home (place)
Jötunheimar	Giant-Land (place)
jötunmóð	giant's-wrath
jungfrú	young-woman

K, k

Old Icelandic	English
kærleikum	friendly-terms, friendship
kallað	called
kallaður	called
kallar	call, called
kalt	cold
kann	can, knows
kanna	explore
kapparnir	champions
Karkr	Kark (name)
kastað	cast
kastaði	cast, threw
kastar	threw
kastið	throw
kátir	merry
kaupferðir	trading-voyages
kaupferðum	trading-journeys
keiktist	bent
kem	come
kempa	warrior
kemur	came, comes
kenna	know, taught
kenndur	recognised
ker	vessel
keyrir	the-stick
kikna	bent-backwards

Word List (Old Icelandic to English)

Old Icelandic	English
kinnbeinit	chin-bone
kjaptinum	mouth, the-mouth
kjaptrinn	jaw
kjós	choose
klæddu	dressed
klæði	clothed, clothes
klæðin	clothes
klæðir	clothed
klæðsekk	sack
klæðum	clothes
kné	knees
knésbætr	the-back-of-the-knees
knettinum	the-ball
knöttinn	the-ball
knöttrinn	the-ball
kollóttan	bald-headed
Kollsveinn	Kollsvein (name), the-boy
kölluð	called
kom	came
koma	came, come, coming
komi	come
komið	coming
komin	coming
kominn	came, come, coming
komnir	come
komu	came
kómu	came
kómust	came
kona	wife
konung	the-king
konungi	king, the-king
konungnum	the-king
konungr	king, the-king
konungrinn	the-king
konungs	the-king, the-king's
konungshöll	the-king's-hall
konungsnafn	the-king's-name
konungsson	a-king's-son, the-king's-son
konur	women
köppunum	the-cups
kórónu	the-crown
köstuðu	cast
krásum	food
krefja	demand
kristinn	a-Christian, Christian
kristnum	Christian
krókstaf	crooked-staff
krókstafinn	the-crooked-stick
krókstafur	crooked-stick
kross	the-cross
krummurnar	grabbed
kumpánar	fellows
kunnáttu	skills
kunngera	to-announce, wiser
kunnigt	know
kvað	said
kvaddi	called
kvaðst	said
kveðju	greetings
kveðst	greetings, said
kveld	the-evening
kveldið	evening
kvikt	alive, living-thing
kvöld	evening
kyn	kin
kyssti	kissed

L, l

Old Icelandic	English
lá	had, laid, lay
lætr	acts, have
lagði	had, laid
lagðist	lay
lagi	thrust
lagt	left
lágu	laid
land	land, the-land
landi	the-land
landið	land, the-land
landsuðri	South-East
landsuður	the-south-east
Langa	Long (name)
langan	long
lát	have, let
láta	have, lay-out, to-have
látum	leave-it
laukst	closed
laun	to-repay
launa	repay

Word List (Old Icelandic to English)

Old Icelandic	English
launað	repay
laust	loosed
leggja	grant
leiða	led
leiddur	led
leika	play
leikinn	games, trick
leit	had
lék	played
lékst	played
lén	a-fee
lendur	landed
lengr	longer
lét	had
léti	made
létu	had
leynt	hidden
lið	assistance, the-company-of
liði	company, dislocated
líður	passed
lifði	lived
lífgjöf	life-gift
lifir	lives
liggja	lie-down
liggr	lying
líkari	like
líkast	like
listamann	a-skilled-craftsman
lítill	little, small
lítilli	little
lítilmannliga	weakly
lítinn	little
lítit	little
litlu	little
ljótan	hideous
lófa	promise
lofaði	pledging
lofuðu	praised
lög	law
logaði	blazed
logandi	ablaze
logit	a-lie
lokið	ended
löngu	long
lopti	the-air, the-sky
Lúkanus	Lucanus (name)
lúkum	end

M, m

Old Icelandic	English
má	may
maður	a-man, man
mæðast	get-tired
mæla	speak
mælir	speaks
mælt	spoke
mælti	said, spoke
mál	conversations, the-matter
máldrykkju	drinking
manna	man, men, men, men's
manni	man
manns	man
mannshöfuð	a-man's-head
mánuð	a-month
marga	many
margir	many
matr	food
matsveinar	food-servants
mátt	may
mátti	could
mátuligr	fitting
með	along, with
meðalmaður	an-average-man
meðan	as-long-as, while
mega	may
megi	may
megin	side
meira	more
menn	men, the-men
mér	I, me, to-me
mest	most, mostly
mestr	the-greatest, the-most
miðit	the-middle
miðju	the-middle
mik	me, myself
mikið	great, large, much
mikil	great, tall
mikill	great, large

Word List (Old Icelandic to English)

Old Icelandic	English
mikils	much
mikinn	great, much
mikla	great
miklar	great, much
mikli	larger, largest
miklu	much
miklum	great
millum	between
mín	me, mine, my
mína	mine
mínir	mine, my
minn	mine, my
minni	in-memory, smaller
minnum	came
mínu	mine
mínum	mine
miskunnar	mercy
missa	lose
missi	lost
mitt	me, mine
mjög	great, much
móðir	mother
móðu	large-river
móðuna	the-river
mönnum	men, the-men
morgin	morning, the-morning
morgininn	morning
morginn	morning
morgni	morning
morguninn	morning
mörkina	the-trees
mót	against, meet, to-meet
móti	against, meet, oppose, opposition, to-meet
mun	could, must, shall, should, should-be, would
mundi	could-be, should, would, would-have
mundu	must-be, would
mundum	would-be
muni	would
munni	a-mouth
munt	must-be, should
muntu	shall-you, should
munu	should, would-be
munum	should
mútur	payment
myrkr	fog

N, n

Old Icelandic	English
nær	near
næst	near, next, next-to
nætr	nights
nafn	name
nafnbætr	name-titles
nafnfesti	naming-gift
nafni	name
nam	took
nasir	nose
nát	get-hold-of, hold-of
náttúru	natured
né	nor
neðra	under
nefit	nose
nefndi	named
nefndir	named
nema	but, except
neytr	good-use
níðingr	a-coward
niðrgangs	down-going
niður	below, down
nóg	enough
nokkura	some
nokkurn	some
nokkurr	something
nokkuru	some, somewhat
nokkut	anything, some
Noreg	Norway (place)
Noregi	Norway (place)
Noregs	Norway (place)
nösunum	on-the-nose
nótt	night
nóttina	night, the-night
nú	now

Word List (Old Icelandic to English)

Old Icelandic	English

O, o

of	of
ofan	down, over
ofmagni	to-overpower
og	ad, also, and, filled, river, to
okkr	us
olnbogarnir	elbows
opinn	open
opt	often
orðið	word
orðinn	became
orðum	words
orkar	able-to
orkufátt	low-energy
orlof	leave
orlofs	vacation
Orminum	The-Serpent (name)
oss	ours, us

Ó, ó

óaflátssamr	un-indulgent
Óðinn	Odin (name)
Óðins	Odin's (name)
Óðni	Odin (name)
óðu	waded
ófarin	unfinished
ófögnuður	unhappy
ófriðar	un-peace
óhýrligr	unfriendly-looking
Óláf	Olaf (name)
Ólafi	Olaf (name)
Óláfs	Olaf's (name)
Óláfur	Olaf (name)
ólík	unlike
ólyfjan	poison
óorðna	unspoken
ór	away-from, from, of, out-of, through
óskyldara	less-should
ótal	countless
óþýður	unfriendly

Old Icelandic	English
Óttars	Ottar's (name)
óvæginn	ruthless
óvit	unconscious

Ö, ö

öðrum	one, other
öfundsjúkir	jealous
ökkla	ankles
öllum	all
öndvegit	opposite
önnur	another, one, other
örn	eagle

P, p

pilt	boy
piltrinn	the-boy
pjakka	prick
pjakkar	prick, pricked
prett	tricked
pungi	pouch

R, r

ráð	advice, counsel
ráða	advice, decide, reckon
ráðast	arranged
ræð	ruler
ræður	rules
rak	drove
ráku	drove
rann	ran
rasaði	tumbled
rauðum	red
rauður	red
rautt	red
réð	advised, ruled
réðst	moved
refði	staff
reið	riding
reiddist	rose

Word List (Old Icelandic to English)

Old Icelandic	English
reiðu	ride
reis	rose
reisti	raised
reistu	raised
renna	ran
reyk	smoke
reynt	test
ríða	ride, ride-away, riding, rode, to-ride
riðu	rode
ríður	rode
rifnaði	split
ríki	kingdom
Risaland	Giant-Land (place)
Risalandi	Giant-Land (place)
Risalands	Giant-Land (place)
ríss	rose
rjóðrinu	the-clearing
rjóður	clearing
rönd	around
röndum	stripes
röskr	brave
ruggaði	rocking
rúm	room

S, s

Old Icelandic	English
sá	saw, see, seeing, so, there
sækið	seek
sæmilig	well
sæng	bed
sæti	seat
sætis	seat
sætr	mountain-pastures
sagði	said, said, told, told
sagðist	said
sagt	told, told
saka	injury
sama	same
saman	together
sár	wound
sat	sat
sáttir	agreed
sáttu	saw-you
sáu	saw
sauða	wether's
saur	the-mud
sé	even, he-is, is, see, you
sefur	slept
seg	say
segir	said, said-to, say, told
segist	said
segja	say, tell
seint	slowly
selshöfuð	seal's-head
sem	as, as-if, if, that, whatever, where, which, who
sendi	sent
sendiferðir	missions
sendur	sent
sent	sent
sér	he, him, himself, his, saw, see, to-him, to-see
serk	shirt
serkinn	the-shirt
serkr	shirt
sét	seen
setning	the-setting
setti	set
settist	sat
sex	six
sídan	afterwards
síðan	after, afterwards, since, since., then
síðar	afterwards, since
síðum	sides
siður	the-custom
sigla	sail, sailed
sigldi	sail, sailed
sigldu	sailed
Sigurðarson	Son-of-Sigurd (name)
sik	him, himself, his, themselves
silfrdisk	silver-dish
silfrhring	silver-ring
silfri	silver
silfrkerum	silver
silfrs	silver

Word List (Old Icelandic to English)

Old Icelandic	English
sín	hers, him, their, themselves
sína	his, their
sínar	his
sindraði	sparkled
sinn	his, occasion, their
sinna	his
sinnar	his
sinni	his, this
síns	his
sínum	hers, his
sitja	sit
sitr	sat
sitt	his, sat
sjá	saw, see, to-see
sjaldsénir	rarely-seen
sjálfur	itself
sjau	seven
sjáum	see
skal	shall
skál	shall
skalf	shook
skalt	shall
skaltu	shall, shall-you
skálum	bowls
skammt	a-short-distance, short
skapsmunum	mood-mind
skarlatsklæðum	scarlet-clothing
skatta	tax
skattgildir	tributaries
skaut	shot
skeggit	beard
skemmta	amuse
skemmtan	amusement
skemmtunar	amusement, entertainment
sker	a-rock
skildi	separated
skildu	separated
skildust	separated
skilja	separate, such
skiljast	separate
skilr	separating
skinnslit	colour
skip	a-ship, ship, the-ship
skipað	directed-to
skips	ships, the-ships
skipta	give
skipuð	equipped
skíra	baptised
skjótt	swiftly
skóga	forests
skógar	the-forest
skóginn	the-forest, the-forests
skörina	high-seat
skorinn	cut
skuli	shall
skulu	shall, should
skuluð	should
skyldi	should
skyldu	and, would
slær	struck
slagir	artful
slegit	struck
slík	such
slíka	such
slíkan	such
slíkar	such
slikum	such
sló	struck
slógu	formed
slysalaust	accidents-without
smáleik	small-games
smáleika	small-games
smásveinn	little-boy
snarað	twisted
snaraði	flew-it, threw, turned-quickly
snekkju	a-sailboat
snemma	early, soon
sneri	turned
sniðglímu	hip-throw
snjó	snow
snjórinn	the-snow
snöruðu	threw
snúinn	twisted
sofa	seep, sleep, slept
sögðu	said
sól	the-sun
sólarfalli	sunset
sólin	sunrise

Word List (Old Icelandic to English)

Old Icelandic	English
sólir	suns
sólskin	sunshine
son	son
sonr	son
sprakk	broke
spring	burst
spurði	asked
spyrjast	was-heard
staðar	standing, to-stand
stærsti	biggest
staf	staff
stafinn	the-staff, the-stick
stafnum	stick
stakk	struck
stálbroddr	steel-point
staldraði	lingered
stall	stable
standa	stand
stangaði	stabbed
sté	stepped
stefna	directed
stein	stone
steinhús	stone-house
steinkastinu	stone-throwing
steinn	stone
sterkari	stronger
sterkastr	strongest
sterkliga	strongly
sterkr	strong
steypa	cast
steyptist	fell, knocked
steyptu	cast
stígr	climbed
stikilinn	horn-point
stiklinum	the-narrow
stóð	stood, weighed
stóðu	stood
stöðum	places
stokkinn	the-foot-board
stökkva	jumped
stóra	great
stórr	big
stórri	large
strengdi	boldly
stríðlyndur	obstinate
ströng	strong
studdi	steadied
stundu	while
stundum	awhile
styrkja	strengthen
sú	so
sumarið	summer
sundi	swimming
sundur	apart
svá	saw, so, the
svarar	answered
svarið	sworn
svartan	black
sveinar	companions, men
sveinbarn	a-baby-boy
sveinn	boy
sverja	swear
svikit	tricked
svipmikill	a-striking
sviptingar	tussle
svipuleik	the-scourge
svipuleikr	the-scourge
sýna	show
sýndar	shown
sýndi	showed
sýndist	seemed, thought
sýnis	his
synjast	refuse

T, t

Old Icelandic	English
tak	take
taka	take, took
takið	take
talar	talked
tána	toe
tánni	toe
tekið	taken
tekinn	taken
tekr	takes, took
tennr	teeth
tennrnar	teeth, the-teeth
tíðenda	news, of-news
tíðendi	news
til	for, of, to

Word List (Old Icelandic to English)

Old Icelandic	English	*Old Icelandic*	English
tíma	time	*þegar*	as-soon-as, straightaway, then, there
tíu	ten		
tjald	tents	*þeim*	from-them, theirs, them, then, they
togast	pulled		
tók	received, took, tugged	*þeir*	should, them, there, they
tókst	took		
tóku	took	*þeira*	their, theirs, them, there, they, they-were
tókust	took		
töldust	considered	*þeirar*	there
tólf	twelve	*þeiri*	their
töluðu	told	*þekkti*	knew
trapiza	table	*þenna*	that
traust	trusted	*þér*	to-you, you, yours
Trausti	Trusty (name)	*þerris*	dry
trautt	scarcely	*þess*	this
treysta	reckon, trust	*þessa*	this
treysti	trust	*þessi*	these, this
tröllaukinn	troll-possessed	*þessu*	this
tröllsligri	troll-like	*þetta*	this
tröllum	trolls	*þíða*	thaw
trú	faith, the-faith	*þik*	you
Tryggvason	Tryggvason (name)	*þilfjöl*	decks
tuttugu	twenty	*þín*	you, your
tvá	two	*þína*	yours
tvær	two	*þínar*	your
tvau	two	*þing*	assembly, things
tveggja	two	*þinn*	yours
tveir	of, two	*þit*	you-two
tvítugt	twenty	*þitt*	your, yours
		þjófsaugun	thief's-eyes
		þjófshakan	thievish-chin
		þjófsnefit	thieving-nose

Þ, þ

Old Icelandic	English
þá	them, then, when
það	it, that
þaðan	from-there
þær	there, those
þætti	seem, the-story
þakkaði	thanked, thanked
þakkar	thanked
þangað	from-there, there
þann	that, the, then
þar	here, then, then, there, they, was
þau	their, they
þjóna	serve, serving
þjónar	serve
þó	though
þökkuðu	thanked
þol	endure
þorði	dared
þorir	dare, dared, daring
Þormóður	Thormod (name)
Þórs	Thor's (name)
Þorstein	Thorstein (name)
Þorsteini	Thorstein (name)
Þorsteinn	Thorstein (name)
Þorsteins	Thorstein's (name)

Word List (Old Icelandic to English)

Old Icelandic	English
þótt	though
þótti	seemed, thought
þóttist	thought
þræli	servant
Þrándheimi	Trondheim (place)
þreif	grabbed
þremr	three
þríhyrndr	three-sided
þrír	three
þrjá	three
þú	you
þung	heavy
þurfa	need
því	accordingly, as, because, it, that, then, therefore
þvílíkir	the-like
þykki	seems, think
þykkir	seems
þykkja	think, value, valued
þyngst	heaviest

U, u

Old Icelandic	English
ullu	wool
um	about, around, through
undan	away, away-from, before
undir	behind, down, under
undirheimum	under-world
undraðist	surprised
undrast	wonder
undruðust	wondered
unga	young
unnust	loved
unum	happy
upp	up
upphlaup	uproar
uppi	up
uppsprettu	up-spring
urðu	became, came
utan	except, except-for, out, out-of, outside, without
uxahnútu	ox-bone

Ú, ú

Old Icelandic	English
úlfaldi	camel
Úlfhamr	Wolf-Skin (name)
Úlfheðinn	Ulfhedin (name)
út	out
úti	out, over
útlægr	outlawed

V, v

Old Icelandic	English
vá	was
vaða	wades
væði	waded-through
vænginn	the-wing
vænsta	good
væri	should-be, was, would
vært	short
væru	were
vaf	wove
vakrliga	nimbly
vald	power
valdi	control
ván	is-expected
vanda	custom, difficulty
vanr	accustomed
vánt	difficulty
vápnaða	weaponed
var	was, were, when
vár	ours
varð	became, was
varðist	defended
vári	spring
várið	spring
varir	aware
varr	aware
vart	was
várt	ours
váru	were, when
vaskligri	braver
vatn	the-water
vatnið	the-water

Word List (Old Icelandic to English)

Old Icelandic	English
vátr	water
vaxa	grow
veður	weather
veg	way
veginn	the-road
veik	turned
veit	know, known, knows
veita	grant, to-grant
veitti	granted
veittu	grant
veizla	feast
veizlan	the-feast
veizlunni	the-feast
vel	well
velfaranda	well-faring
vér	was, we
vera	be, being, were
verða	be, become, becomes
verður	became, becomes, came
verkr	pain
vert	worth, worthy
vestri	the-west
vetr	winter
vetrinn	winter
vettlingana	mitten
við	against, by, of, to, with
víða	widely
Vík	Vik (place)
víkr	moved
vil	will, wish
vilda	wish
vildi	willed, wished, wished-to, would
vildu	wished, would
vili	wish
vilja	he-wished, wished
viljum	wish
vill	will, wished
villa	lost-way
vilt	will, wish
viltu	will-you
vín	wine
vinsæll	popular
virðing	worthy
víst	certainly
vit	know
vita	knew, know
vitja	visit
víttr	bewitched
vöknaði	became-wet
vön	want
vörð	guard
vort	ours
vöttum	gloves
völxt	grown

Y, y

Old Icelandic	English
yðrir	your
yðru	your
yðrum	yours
yður	you
yfir	across, over
yndi	happiness
Yrjum	Yrjar (place)

Ý, ý

Old Icelandic	English
ýmist	either

Word List *(English to Old Icelandic)*

English	Old Icelandic

A, a

English	Old Icelandic
a	á, ein, eina, einn, einni, einum, eitt
a-baby	barni
a-baby-boy	sveinbarn
a-bench	bekk
abide	bíða
ablaze	logandi
able-to	orkar
aboard	innanborðs
about	á, að, en, í, um
a-burial-mound	haug
accidents-without	slysalaust
accordingly	því
accustomed	vanr
a-chieftain	höfðingi
a-Christian	kristinn
a-circle	hring
a-city	borg
a-coward	níðingr
across	yfir
acts	lætr
ad	og
a-din	dunur
advice	ráð, ráða
advised	réð
a-fee	lén
a-forge	afli
after	áður, eptir, síðan
afterwards	aptr, sídan, síðan, síðar
against	að, mót, móti, við
Agdi (name)	Agða, Agði
Agdi's (name)	Agða
agreed	sáttir
a-hall	höll
a-hidden-man	huldumaður
a-high-seat	hásæti
a-horn	horn, hornit
a-king's-son	konungsson
a-lie	logit
alive	kvikt
all	alla, allan, allar, allir, allr, alls, allt, í, öllum
all-mighty	allmiklum
All-Strong (name)	Allsterk, Allsterkr
alone	einir
along	með
also	og
always	ávallt
am	er
a-man	maður
a-man's-head	mannshöfuð
among	í
a-month	mánuð
a-mouth	munni
amuse	skemmta
amusement	skemmtan, skemmtunar
an-average-man	meðalmaður
anchor	akkerum
and	eða, en, er, og, skyldu
an-invite	boð
ankles	ökkla
another	annarr, annarri, önnur
another-thing	annan
an-ounce-of	eyri
answered	svarar
any	enga
anyone	hverr
anything	nokkut
apart	sundur
a-precious-cloak	guðvefjarskikkju
are	ert, eru, erum
are-you	ertu
a-river	á
a-rock	sker
around	rönd, um
arranged	ráðast
artful	slagir
as	að, er, sem, því
a-sailboat	snekkju
a-seat	atsetu
a-ship	skip

Word List (English to Old Icelandic)

English	*Old Icelandic*	English	*Old Icelandic*
a-short-distance	*skammt*	before-them	*fyrir*
a-shower-of-sparks	*gneistaflaug*	behaved	*breyttu*
as-if	*sem*	behind	*eptir, undir*
asked	*bað, bauð, beiddi, biður, spurði*	being	*vera*
		below	*niður*
a-skilled-craftsman	*listamann*	be-named	*heita*
as-long-as	*meðan*	bench	*bekk, bekkjar*
assembly	*þing*	benefit	*gagn*
assistance	*lið*	bent	*keiktist*
as-soon-as	*þegar*	bent-backwards	*kikna*
a-steep-cliff	*hömrum*	be-offered	*framboðligr*
a-striking	*svipmikill*	beside	*á, hjá*
at	*á, að, í*	beside-standing	*hjástöðu*
a-table	*borðum*	best	*beztir*
a-treasure	*gersemi*	better	*betr, betra, betri*
avenge	*hefna*	between	*millum*
await	*bíða*	bewitched	*víttr*
aware	*varir, varr*	bid	*bað, báðu*
away	*brott, burt, burtu, undan*	big	*stórr*
		biggest	*stærsti*
away-from	*frá, ór, undan*	binding	*handsals*
awhile	*stundum*	birds	*fugla*
a-yard	*álnar*	Bjalfi	*bjálfa, bjálfi*
		black	*blár, svartan*

B, b

English	*Old Icelandic*	English	*Old Icelandic*
		blazed	*logaði*
		boldly	*strengdi*
back	*aptr, bak*	bore	*bar, bárust, berast*
badly	*illa*	borne	*borið*
Balagardsida (place)	*Bálagarðssíðu*	both	*báðum*
bald-headed	*kollóttan*	bowls	*skálum*
band	*flokk*	boy	*pilt, sveinn*
baptised	*skíra*	brave	*hraustr, röskr*
be	*er, vera, verða*	braver	*vaskligri*
bear	*ber, bera, berizt*	bravery	*hreysti*
beard	*skeggit*	breaking	*boði*
beautiful	*fagr*	bring	*berið*
be-brought	*færa*	broad	*breiða, breitt*
became	*gerðist, orðinn, urðu, varð, verður*	broke	*brotnaði, sprakk*
		broken	*brotnaði*
became-wet	*vöknaði*	brother	*bróður*
because	*því*	brought	*bera, borin, færði*
become	*verða*	Brynjolf (name)	*Brynjólfur*
becomes	*verða, verður*	burial-mound-his	*haugsins*
bed	*sæng*	burned	*brann*
before	*áður, fyrir, fyrr, undan*	burning	*glóanda*

143

Word List (English to Old Icelandic)

English	Old Icelandic
burst	*brast, spring*
burst-out-laughing	*brosti*
but	*eða, en, enn, nema*
by	*á, við*

C, c

English	Old Icelandic
call	*kallar*
called	*heitir, kallað, kallaður, kallar, kölluð, kvaddi*
came	*kemur, kom, koma, kominn, komu, kómu, kómust, minnum, urðu, verður*
camel	*úlfaldi*
can	*kann*
carried	*bar, báru, borinn*
carry	*draga*
cast	*hleypt, kastað, kastaði, köstuðu, steypa, steyptu*
catch	*henda*
caught	*fengu, henti*
celebrated	*fagnaði*
certainly	*víst*
champions	*kapparnir*
chased	*eltu*
child	*barnit*
children	*börn*
chin-bone	*kinnbeinit*
choose	*kjós*
Christian	*kristinn, kristnum*
cleaner	*hreinna*
clearing	*rjóður*
climbed	*stígr*
closed	*laukst*
clothed	*klæði, klæðir*
clothes	*klæði, klæðin, klæðum*
cold	*kalt*
colour	*skinnslit*
come	*gengið, kem, koma, komi, kominn, komnir*
comes	*kemur*
coming	*koma, komið, komin, kominn*
companion	*félagi, förunautr*
companions	*sveinar*
company	*flokk, liði*
considered	*töldust*
control	*valdi*
conversations	*mál*
could	*mátti, mun*
could-be	*mundi*
counsel	*ráð*
countless	*ótal*
court	*hirðprýði*
court-man	*hirðmaður*
court-men	*hirðmönnum*
crooked-staff	*krókstaf*
crooked-stick	*krókstafur*
cubits	*álna*
custom	*vanda*
cut	*skorinn*

D, d

English	Old Icelandic
Dagny (name)	*Dagný*
dangerous	*hættu, háski*
dare	*þorir*
dared	*þorði, þorir*
daring	*þorir*
daughter	*dóttir*
day	*dag, degi*
dead	*bana, dauð, dauður*
death	*bana, bani, hel*
decide	*ráða*
decks	*þilfjöl*
declared	*heit*
deep	*djúp*
defended	*varðist*
delays	*dvelr*
demand	*krefja*
devastated	*eytt*
did	*gerði, gerðu*
dies	*deyr*
difficulty	*vanda, vánt*
directed	*stefna*
directed-to	*skipað*
disappeared	*horfin, hurfu, hvarf*
dislocated	*liði*

144

Word List (English to Old Icelandic)

English	Old Icelandic
district	heraði
do	gera
done	ger, gera
doomed	feiga, feigr
door	dyrr
doorway	dyrum
down	niður, ofan, undir
down-going	niðrgangs
drag	draga
drank	drakk, drukkið, drukku
dressed	klæddu
drew	brá, dregr
drink	af, drekka, drekkir, drukkið, drykknum
drinking	drekka, drukkið, drykkju, drykkjuskapr, máldrykkju
drinking-man	drykkjumaður
drinks	drekkr
drink-to	drukkið
dripped	draup
drops	fellir
Drott (name)	Drött, Dröttr
drove	rak, ráku
drowned	drukknuðu
drunk	drukkið, drukkin, full
dry	þerris
dug	grafit
dwarf	dverg, dvergrinn

E, e

English	Old Icelandic
each	hvárn, hvárt, hverjum, hverr, hvert
eagle	örn
ear	eyra
earl	jarl
early	snemma
ears	eyranu
east	austr
Eastern-Lands (place)	Austr, Austrveg, Austrveginn
either	hvárttveggja, ýmist
either-side	hvárntveggja
elbows	olnbogarnir
embers	eimyrja
end	lúkum
ended	lokið
ending	endast
endure	þol
enough	nóg
entertainment	skemmtunar
equally-as-big	jafnstóra
equally-big	jafnstórr
equally-large	jafnstóra
equipped	skipuð
erupted	hrutu
even	sé
evening	kveldið, kvöld
everyone	hvern
every-time	jafnan
exceedingly	furðuliga
except	nema, utan
except-for	utan
explore	kanna
extra	auka
eyes	auga, augu, augum, augun

F, f

English	Old Icelandic
face	andliti
fair	fagrar, fagrt
fair-wind	byr
faith	trú
falling	fell, föll
far-away	fjarstætt
farmer	bóndi
farmstead	húsabæ
fastened	fast, festir
fat	fitan
fated	auðið
fated-to-die	feigr
father	faðir, föður
feast	veizla
feebler	ergist
fee-sparing	fésparir
feet	fæti, fætr, fótum
fell	datt, fell, fellu, steyptist

Word List (English to Old Icelandic)

English	Old Icelandic
fellow	drengr
fellows	kumpánar
festival	hátíð
filled	fylldan, og
find	finna
finger-gold	fingrgull
fire	eld, eldi, eldur
fire-poker	eldsskara
first	fyrst, fyrsta, fyrstu, fyrstum
fist	hnefann
fitting	mátuligr
fjord	fjörð
flesh	holdi
flew-it	fleygir, snaraði
flies	flýgr
floor	gólfit
fog	myrkr
fold	felr
folk	fólk, fólki
follow	fylgja
followed	fylgdi, fylgt
following	áliðnum, fylgd, fylgdi, fylgja
following-men	fjölmenni
food	krásum, matr
food-servants	matsveinar
foolishly	heimsliga
for	á, fyrir, til
forces	hér
foremost	fremstir
forests	skóga
formed	slógu
foul	fúlt
found	fann, fannst
four	fjóra, fjórar, fjórum
friendly-terms	kærleikum
friendship	kærleikum
from	á, að, af, er, frá, fram, ór
from-hence	heðan
from-them	þeim
from-there	fram, þaðan, þangað
from-where	hvaðan
Frosti	frosti
Frosti (name)	Frosta, Frosti
Full-Strong (name)	Fullsterk, Fullsterkr

G, g

English	Old Icelandic
game	gamni
games	gamans, leikinn
gangrene	drep
gate	grindhliðið
Gaulardale (place)	Gaulardal
gave	gaf, gáfu
Geirrod (name)	Geirröð, Geirröði, Geirröður
Geirrod's (name)	Geirröði
Geirrod's-Town (place)	Geirröðargarða, Geirröðargörðum
get	fá, fengnir, geta, getr
get-hold-of	nát
get-tired	mæðast
Giant-Home (place)	Jötunheima
Giant-Land (place)	Jötunheimar, Risaland, Risalandi, Risalands
giants	jötnum
giant's-wrath	jötunmóð
give	gef, gefa, skipta
given	gefur
glad	glaðir
gladly	gjarna, glaðir
Glasir-Plains (place)	Glæsisvöllu, Glæsisvöllum
glass-window	glerglugg
gloves	vöttum
glowing	glóanda
Gnipalund (place)	Gnípalundi
go	fara, farið, ganga, gangi
Godmund	goðmundur
Godmund (name)	Goðmund, Goðmundar, Goðmundi, Goðmundr, Goðmundur
Godmund's (name)	Goðmundar
going	ganga
going-from	gagnvart

Word List (English to Old Icelandic)

English	Old Icelandic	English	Old Icelandic
gold	*gul, gull, gulli, gullligt, gullligum, gulr*	hailstorm	*haglhríð*
		Hakon (name)	*Hákon*
gold-ball	*gullhnött*	half	*hálfan*
gold-crown	*gullkórónu*	hall	*hallar*
golden-bowl	*gullker*	hall-floor	*hallargólfi, hallargólfit*
gold-necklace	*gullmen*	hand	*hendi, hendur, hönd*
gold-plated	*gullbúnu*	hand-cloth	*handklæðit*
gold-ring	*gullhring*	hand-cloths	*handklæði*
gold-rings	*gullhringa*	hands	*höndum*
gold-trimmed	*gullskotnum*	happiness	*yndi*
gold-woven	*gullofit*	happy	*unum*
gone	*farið, farin*	hard	*fast*
good	*góða, góði, góðum, góður, gott, vænsta*	harder	*fastara*
		hardest	*harðasti*
Good (name)	*Góða, Góði*	hard-minded	*harðúðigr*
good-use	*neytr*	has	*hefir*
got	*fekk, gað*	have	*eig, er, hafa, hafið, haft, hefi, hefir, höfum, lætr, lát, láta*
got-they	*fengust*		
grabbed	*greip, grip, krummurnar, þreif*		
		having	*hafa*
grant	*leggja, veita, veittu*	he	*hana, hann, honum, sér*
granted	*veitti*		
great	*mikið, mikil, mikill, mikinn, mikla, miklar, miklum, mjög, stóra*	head	*höfði, höfðum, höfuðið*
		hear	*heyra*
greeted	*heilsaði*	heard	*heyrir*
greetings	*kveðju, kveðst*	heat	*hita*
grey	*grám*	heaviest	*þyngst*
Grim (name)	*Grím, Grími, Grímr*	heavy	*þung*
gripped	*greip*	Heidrek (name)	*Heiðrekr*
grow	*vaxa*	he-is	*sé*
grown	*vöxt*	held	*helt, helzt*
Grundir (place)	*Grunda, Grundir, Grundum*	helm-of-invisibility	*hulinshjálm*
		Hemra (place)	*Hemra, Hemru*
guard	*vörð*	here	*hér, hingað, þar*
Gudrun (name)	*Goðrún, Goðrúnar, Goðrúnu*	hers	*sín, sínum*
		he-took-care-of	*annast*
guess	*get*	hewed	*hjó*
Gust	*gustr*	he-wished	*vilja*
		hidden	*leynt*
		hide	*fela*
		hideous	*ljótan*

H, h

English	Old Icelandic
had	*ætti, átti, áttu, hafa, hafði, haft, hefði, hefir, höfðu, lá, lagði, leit, lét, létu*
high	*há*
high-seat	*hásæti, skörina*
hill	*hól*

147

Word List (English to Old Icelandic)

English	Old Icelandic	English	Old Icelandic
him	að, hann, hans, honum, sér, sik, sín	inside	inn
		intend	ætla
himself	sér, sik	intended	ætlaði, ætlar
hip-throw	sniðglímu	intentions	ætlan
his	hans, honum, sér, sik, sína, sínar, sinn, sinna, sinnar, sinni, síns, sínum, sitt, sýnis	into	á, í
		invite	býður
		Iron-Beard (name)	Járnskeggja
		is	á, er, eru, sé
his-head	höfuðið	is-expected	ván
hit	hæfa	is-named	hét
hold	halda	it	að, hana, hann, honum, í, það, því
hold-of	nát		
homage	hlýðni	itself	sjálfur
home	heim		
honour	heiður		
horn	fyllt, horn, horninu, hornit		

J, j

English	Old Icelandic
Jamtland (place)	Jamtaland
jaw	kjaptrinn
jealous	öfundsjúkir
joined	festi
Jokul (name)	Jökull
Jokul's (name)	Jökli
journey	ferð
joyful	fegnir
jumped	stökkva

English	Old Icelandic
horn-point	stikilinn
horns	horn
horse	hesti, hestr
horses	hest, hesta, hestar, hestum
Hosvir (name)	Hösvi, Hösvir
hot	heitt
house	hús
House-Child (name)	Bæjarbarn, Bæjarbarni, Bæjarbarns
House-Power (name)	Bæjarmagn
houses	húsum
how	hverju
howling	grenjaði
how-so	hversu

K, k

English	Old Icelandic
Kark (name)	Karkr
keep	halda
kill	drepa
killed	drap, drepnir
kin	kyn
kinds	háttar
king	konungi, konungr
kingdom	ríki
kissed	kyssti
knees	kné
knew	þekkti, vita
knocked	steyptist
know	kenna, kunnigt, veit, vit, vita
known	veit
knows	kann, veit

I, i

English	Old Icelandic
I	ek, mér
if	ef, í, sem
ill	illa
in	á, að, í, inn
India	indíalandi
inheritance	arf, erfi
injury	saka
inlaid	búið
in-memory	minni
in-one	einu

Word List (English to Old Icelandic)

English	Old Icelandic
Kollsvein (name)	Kollsveinn

L, l

English	Old Icelandic
lack-of-money	féfátt
laid	lá, lagði, lágu
land	land, landið
landed	lendur
large	mikið, mikill, stórri
larger	mikli
large-river	móðu
largest	mikli
laughed	hló, hlógu
laughter	hlátr, hlátri
law	lög
lay	lá, lagðist
lay-out	láta
leave	orlof
leave-it	látum
led	leiða, leiddur
left	lagt
leg	fótrinn
less-should	óskyldara
let	lát
lie-down	liggja
life-gift	lífgjöf
like	líkari, líkast
lineage	ættar
lingered	staldraði
little	lítill, lítilli, lítinn, lítit, litlu
little-boy	smásveinn
live	búa
lived	bjó, lifði
lives	lifir
living-thing	kvikt
long	langan, löngu
Long (name)	Langa
longer	lengr
looking	bragði
loosed	laust
lose	missa
lost	missi
lost-way	villa
lot	hluti
loved	unnust
low-energy	orkufátt
Lucanus (name)	Lúkanus
luck	gæfa, gæfu, góðri, hamingju
lying	liggr

M, m

English	Old Icelandic
mad	galinn
made	gert, léti
magic-full	galdrafullt
make	gera
man	maður, manna, manni, manns
many	marga, margir
marble	hall
may	má, mátt, mega, megi
me	mér, mik, mín, mitt
meet	finnumst, mót, móti
melted	bráðnaði
men	flokki, hann, manna, menn, mönnum, sveinar
men's	manna
mercy	miskunnar
merry	kátir
met	fann, fundizt
mine	mín, mína, mínir, minn, mínu, mínum, mitt
missions	sendiferðir
mitten	vettlingana
mittens	bandvettlinga
mood-mind	skapsmunum
more	auka, fleira, meira
morning	morgin, morgininn, morginn, morgni, morguninn
most	flestum, mest
mostly	mest
mother	móðir
mound	hóll
mountain-pastures	sætr
mountains	fjalli
mouth	kjaptinum

Word List (English to Old Icelandic)

English	Old Icelandic
moved	réðst, víkr
moving	fór
much	mikið, mikils, mikinn, miklar, miklu, mjög
musical-instruments	hljóðfæra, hljóðfæri
must	mun
must-be	mundu, munt
my	mín, mínir, minn
myself	mik
my-wife	eiga

N, n

English	Old Icelandic
name	nafn, nafni
named	heita, heiti, heitir, hét, nefndi, nefndir
name-titles	nafnbætr
naming-gift	nafnfesti
natured	náttúru
near	nær, næst
need	þurfa
neither	hvárki, hvergi
never	aldri
news	frétt, tíðenda, tíðendi
next	næst
next-to	næst
night	nótt, nóttina
nights	nætr
nimbly	vakrliga
no	ekki, engi, engir, engum
none	eigi, enga, engi, engum
no-one	engan
nor	né
Norway (place)	Noreg, Noregi, Noregs
nose	nasir, nefit
not	eigi, ekki, engi
nothing	eigi, einskis, ekki, engu
Novgorod (place)	Hólmgörðum
now	nú

O, o

English	Old Icelandic
oak	eik
oath	eiða
oaths	eiða
obstinate	stríðlyndur
occasion	sinn
Odin (name)	Óðinn, Óðni
Odin's (name)	Óðins
of	á, að, af, er, í, of, ór, til, tveir, við
off	af
offered	bauð
off-handed	afhenda
of-hand	afhenda
of-news	tíðenda
often	opt
of-the-bench	bekkinn
of-the-day	dagsins
Olaf (name)	Óláf, Óláfi, Óláfur
Olaf's (name)	Óláfs
oldest	eldist
on	á, en, í
one	annarr, annarri, eina, einn, einu, einum, eitt, öðrum, önnur
on-the-nose	nösunum
onto	á
open	opinn
opening	beitina, gátum
open-sea	hafvillur
oppose	móti
opposite	gegnt, öndvegit
opposition	móti
or	eða
orchard	aldingarður
ordered	bað
other	aðra, annars, öðrum, önnur
others	aðrir, hinir
Ottar's (name)	Óttars
ounces	aura
ours	oss, vár, várt, vort
out	út, utan, úti
outlawed	útlægr

Word List (English to Old Icelandic)

English	Old Icelandic	English	Old Icelandic
out-of	ór, utan		
outside	utan	**Q, q**	
over	að, fyrir, ofan, úti, yfir		
own	eigum	quarters	fjórðunga
owned	átti		
ox-bone	uxahnútu	**R, r**	

P, p

English	Old Icelandic	English	Old Icelandic
		raiding	hernaði
		raised	fæddi, reisti, reistu
pain	verkr	ran	hlaupa, hleypr, hljóp, rann, renna
pale	bleikum		
passed	líður	rarely-seen	sjaldsénir
pay	fá	rather	heldur
payment	mútur	received	tók
peaceful	fríð	reckon	ráða, treysta
piece-of-marble	hall	recognised	kenndur
pitch	bik	red	rauðum, rauður, rautt
places	stöðum	refuse	synjast
play	leika	relieved	feginn
played	lék, lékst	repay	launa, launað
playing-tricks	glettist	retain	geyma
pledging	lofaði	return	aptr
point	brodd, broddinum	revealed	birti
poison	eitr, ólyfjan	ride	reiðu, ríða
popular	vinsæll	ride-away	ríða
possessions	eigna	riding	reið, ríða
possible	hægt	ring	hring
pouch	pungi	river	og
power	vald	rocking	ruggaði
praised	lofuðu	rode	ríða, riðu, ríður
precious-cloth	guðvef	room	rúm
precious-stones	gimsteinar	rose	reiddist, reis, ríss
precious-things	gersema	ruled	réð
prepared	bjó, búið, búin, búnir	ruler	ræð
prick	pjakka, pjakkar	rules	ræður
pricked	pjakkar	ruthless	óvæginn
promise	lófa		
promised	heita, hét	**S, s**	
property	eignir		
provide	afla, framt	sack	klæðsekk
pulled	togast	said	kvað, kvaðst, kveðst, mælti, sagði, sagðist, segir, segist, sögðu
pushed	hratt		
		said-of	eiga

Word List (English to Old Icelandic)

English	Old Icelandic	English	Old Icelandic
said-to	segir	should-be	mun, væri
sail	sigla, sigldi	show	sýna
sailed	sigla, sigldi, sigldu	showed	sýndi
same	sama	shown	sýndar
sat	sat, settist, sitr, sitt	side	megin
saw	sá, sáu, sér, sjá, svá	sides	síðum
saw-you	sáttu	silver	silfri, silfrkerum, silfrs
say	seg, segir, segja	silver-dish	silfrdisk
scarcely	trautt	silver-ring	silfrhring
scarlet-clothing	skarlatsklæðum	since	síðan, síðar
screamed	grenjaði	since.	síðan
seal's-head	selshöfuð	sit	sitja
seat	sæti, sætis	six	sex
see	sá, sé, sér, sjá, sjáum	skilled-in-magic	fjölkunnigr
seeing	sá	skills	kunnáttu
seek	sækið	sleep	sofa
seem	þætti	slept	sefur, sofa
seemed	sýndist, þótti	slope	hlíðir
seems	þykki, þykkir	slowly	seint
seen	sét	small	lítill
seep	sofa	smaller	minni
sent	sendi, sendur, sent	small-games	smáleik, smáleika
separate	skilja, skiljast	smiling	hlæjandi
separated	skildi, skildu, skildust	smoke	reyk
separating	skilr	snow	fönn, snjó
servant	þræli	so	sá, sú, svá
serve	þjóna, þjónar	some	nokkura, nokkurn, nokkuru, nokkut
serving	þjóna	someone	einhverr
set	setti	something	nokkurr
settled	bjuggust	some-way	einhvern
settlements	byggð	somewhat	nokkuru
seven	sjau	son	son, sonr
shall	mun, skal, skál, skalt, skaltu, skuli, skulu	Son-of-Sigurd (name)	Sigurðarson
shall-you	muntu, skaltu	soon	snemma
she	hana, hún	South-East	landsuðri
ship	skip	sparkled	sindraði
ships	skips	sparks	gneistar
shirt	serk, serkr	sparks-flying	gneistaflaugin
shook	hristi, skalf	speak	mæla
short	skammt, vært	speaks	mælir
shot	skaut	split	rifnaði
should	mun, mundi, munt, muntu, munu, munum, skulu, skuluð, skyldi, þeir	spoke	mælt, mælti
		spread	breiddu
		spring	vári, várið
		stabbed	stangaði

Word List (English to Old Icelandic)

English	Old Icelandic
stable	stall
staff	refði, staf
stand	standa
standing	staðar
steadied	studdi
steel-point	stálbroddr
stepped	sté
stick	stafnum
stone	stein, steinn
stone-house	steinhús
stone-throwing	steinkastinu
stood	stóð, stóðu
straightaway	þegar
strength	afl, afli
strengthen	styrkja
stripes	röndum
strong	sterkr, ströng
stronger	sterkari
strongest	sterkastr
strongly	sterkliga
struck	slær, slegit, sló, stakk
such	skilja, slík, slíka, slíkan, slíkar, slikum
suits	hentar
summer	sumarið
sunrise	sólin
suns	sólir
sunset	sólarfalli
sunshine	sólskin
suppose	ætla
surprised	undraðist
swear	sverja
sweet-smell	ilmr
swift	frár
swiftly	skjótt
swimming	sundi
sworn	svarið

T, t

English	Old Icelandic
table	borð, borðinu, trapiza
table-cloth	dúkinn, dúkr
tablecloths	dúka
take	tak, taka, takið
take-care	hirðið
take-care-of	ábyrgjast
taken	tekið, tekinn
takes	tekr
talked	talar
tall	mikil
taught	kenna
tax	skatta
teeth	tennr, tennrnar
tell	segja
ten	tíu
tend-to	græð
tents	tjald
test	reynt
than	að, en, enn
thanked	þakkaði, þakkar, þökkuðu
that	á, að, af, en, er, sem, það, þann, þenna, því
that-bench	bekknum
thaw	þíða
thaws	bræðir
the	á, að, ána, en, hornit, í, in, ina, inn, inum, it, svá, þann
the-air	lopti
the-back	bak
the-back-of-the-head	hnakkinn
the-back-of-the-knees	knésbætr
the-ball	knettinum, knöttinn, knöttrinn
the-bench	bekknum
the-bone	beini, beinum
the-boy	kollsveinn, piltrinn
the-chest	bringu
the-child	barn, barnit
the-city	borgarinnar, borgina
the-clearing	rjóðrinu
the-company-of	lið
the-crooked-stick	krókstafinn
the-cross	kross
the-crown	kórónu
the-cup-bearer	byrlaranum
the-cups	köppunum
the-curtain	fortjaldinu
the-curve	bugtinni
the-custom	siður

Word List (English to Old Icelandic)

English	Old Icelandic	English	Old Icelandic
the-death	bani	the-marble	hallinn, hallinum, hallrinn
the-district	heraðið, heraðinu	the-matter	mál
the-door	dyranna, dyrr, dyrrnar	the-men	menn, mönnum
the-dwarf	dvergnum, dvergrinn	the-middle	miðit, miðju
the-dwarf's-boy	dvergsbarnit	the-moat	díki
the-dwelling	bæinn, bú	the-morning	morgin
the-eagle	erninum	the-most	mestr
the-earl	jarl, jarli, jarls	the-mound	hauginn, haugrinn, hólinn, hólnum
the-earl's	jarli, jarls	the-mouth	kjaptinum
the-evening	aptnaði, kveld	themselves	sik, sín
the-faith	trú	the-mud	saur
the-feast	veizlan, veizlunni	then	á, en, er, síðan, þá, þann, þar, þegar, þeim, því
the-fire	eldrinn		
the-flames	eldur		
the-floor	gólfi, gólfit	the-narrow	stiklinum
the-foot-board	stokkinn	the-neck	háls
the-forest	skógar, skóginn	the-night	nóttina
the-forests	skóginn	the-oak	eikinni
the-full	fullu	the-old	gamalla
the-game	gamninu	the-opening	beitina
the-gates	hliðin	the-other	annarr, hinir
the-gifts	gjafirnar	the-piece-of-marble	hallinn, hallrinn
the-good	góða	the-point	broddinum, broddrinn
the-greatest	mestr	the-queen	drottning
the-ground	jörðina	there	sá, þær, þangað, þar, þegar, þeir, þeira, þeirar
the-hall	höll, höllina, höllinni		
the-harbour	höfn		
the-horn	hornin, horninu, hornunum	therefore	því
the-horns	hornin	the-ring	hringinn, hringnum, hringrinn
the-horses	hestarnir	the-river	ána, ánni, árinnar, móðuna
the-house	hús		
their	sín, sína, sinn, þau, þeira, þeiri	the-road	veginn
theirs	þeim, þeira	the-scourge	svipuleik, svipuleikr
the-journey	færist, ferð	these	þessi
the-king	konung, konungi, konungnum, konungr, konungrinn, konungs	The-Serpent (name)	Orminum
		the-setting	setning
		the-ship	skip
the-king's	konungs	the-ships	skips
the-king's-hall	konungshöll	the-shirt	serkinn
the-king's-name	konungsnafn	the-sky	himni, lopti
the-king's-son	konungsson	the-skylight	glugginn
the-land	land, landi, landið	the-snow	snjórinn
the-like	þvílíkir	the-south-east	landsuður
them	þá, þeim, þeir, þeira	the-staff	stafinn

Word List (English to Old Icelandic)

English	Old Icelandic	English	Old Icelandic
the-stick	keyrir, stafinn	to-drink	drekka
the-story	þætti	toe	tána, tánni
the-sun	sól	to-get	hlytir
the-table-cloth	dúkinn	together	saman
the-tables	borða, borðum	to-going	atgang, atgangr
the-teeth	tennrnar	to-grant	veita
the-town	borgarinnar, borgina	to-have	láta
the-trees	mörkina	to-him	honum, sér
the-water	vatn, vatnið	to-injure	granda
the-west	vestri	told	sagði, sagt, segir, töluðu
the-wing	vænginn		
the-world	heiminum	told-of	getið
they	drekka, þar, þau, þeim, þeir, þeira	to-make	gera
		to-me	mér
they-are	eru	to-meet	mót, móti
they-were	þeira	to-mind	geyma
thick-set	búk	took	færði, nam, taka, tekr, tók, tókst, tóku, tókust
thief's-eyes	þjófsaugun		
thieving-nose	þjófsnefit	to-overpower	ofmagni
thievish-chin	þjófshakan	to-own	eiga
things	þing	to-repay	laun
think	hug, þykki, þykkja	to-ride	ríða
this	it, sinni, þess, þessa, þessi, þessu, þetta	to-see	sér, sjá
		to-stand	staðar
Thormod (name)	Þormóður	to-the-father	föðurnum
Thor's (name)	Þórs	to-travel	fara
Thorstein (name)	Þorstein, Þorsteini, Þorsteinn	towards	að
		to-wrestling	fangbrögðum
Thorstein's (name)	Þorsteins	to-you	þér
those	þær	trading-journeys	kaupferðum
though	en, þó, þótt	trading-voyages	kaupferðir
thought	hugr, sýndist, þótti, þóttist	travel	færir, far, fara
		travelled	fara, ferð, fór, fóru, fóruð
three	þremr, þrír, þrjá		
three-sided	þríhyrndr	travelling	fara, ferr
threw	berði, kastaði, kastar, snaraði, snöruðu	treasure	gersemi, gripi
		treasured	gersemar
throat	hálsinum	treasures	gersemar, gersemi, gripi
through	ór, um		
throw	kastið	trembled	hrysi
thrown	ausit	tributaries	skattgildir
thrust	lagi	trick	leikinn
time	tíma	tricked	prett, svikit
to	á, að, af, fram, í, og, til, við	tricks	fimleika
		troll-like	tröllsligri
to-announce	kunngera	troll-possessed	tröllaukinn
to-do	gera		

155

Word List (English to Old Icelandic)

English	Old Icelandic
trolls	tröllum
Trondheim (place)	Þrándheimi
trust	treysta, treysti
trusted	traust
Trusty (name)	Trausti
Tryggvason (name)	Tryggvason
tugged	tók
tumbled	rasaði
turned	sneri, veik
turned-away	brautinni
turned-quickly	snaraði
turning	brautinni
tussle	sviptingar
twelve	tólf
twenty	tuttugu, tvítugt
twisted	snarað, snúinn
two	tvá, tvær, tvau, tveggja, tveir

U, u

English	Old Icelandic
Ulfhedin (name)	Úlfheðinn
unconscious	óvit
under	neðra, undir
under-world	undirheimum
undressed	afklæðast, afklæddust
unfinished	ófarin
unfriendly	ópýður
unfriendly-looking	óhýrligr
unhappy	ófögnuður
un-indulgent	óaflátssamr
unlike	ólík
un-peace	ófriðar
unspoken	óorðna
up	upp, uppi
uproar	upphlaup
up-spring	uppsprettu
us	okkr, oss

V, v

English	Old Icelandic
vacation	orlofs
valour	hreysti
value	þykkja
valued	þykkja
vanished	hurfu
vessel	ker
Vik (place)	Vík
visit	vitja
voyage	ferð, ferðum

W, w

English	Old Icelandic
waded	óðu
waded-through	væði
wades	vaða
walk	ganga
walking	gangandi
want	vön
warrior	kempa
was	á, er, í, þar, vá, væri, var, varð, vart, vér
was-heard	spyrjast
water	vátr
wave	felli
way	braut, veg
we	vér
weak	deigum
weakly	lítilmannliga
wealth	fé
weaponed	vápnaða
weather	veður
wedding-proposal	brullaup
weighed	stóð
welcomed	fagnaði
well	sæmilig, vel
well-faring	velfaranda
went	fekk, ferr, fór, fóru, gekk, gengr, gengu
went-for	hösvaðist
went-from	frá
were	eru, hvar, væru, var, váru, vera
wether's	sauða
what	hvað, hvar, hvert, hví
whatever	sem
when	að, en, er, þá, var, váru
where	hvar, sem

Word List (English to Old Icelandic)

English	*Old Icelandic*
whether	hvárt
which	að, er, hvárt, sem
while	en, meðan, stundu
white	hvítr, hvítt
Whitings (name)	Hvítinga, Hvítingar, Hvítingum
who	á, er, hvað, hverr, sem
whole	heill
whose	hverrar
why	hví
widely	víða
wife	kona
wild-animals	dýr
will	vil, vill, vilt
willed	vildi
will-you	viltu
wine	vín
winter	vetr, vetrinn
wiser	kunngera
wish	vil, vilda, vili, viljum, vilt
wished	vildi, vildu, vilja, vill
wished-to	vildi
witch-ride	gandreið
with	á, með, við
without	utan
with-that	í
Wolf-Skin (name)	Úlfhamr
women	konur
wonder	undrast
wondered	undruðust
wool	ullu
word	orðið
words	orðum
worth	vert
worthy	vert, virðing
would	mun, mundi, mundu, muni, skyldu, væri, vildi, vildu
would-be	mundum, munu
would-have	mundi
wound	sár
wove	vaf
wrestle	glíma
wrestled	glímt

English	*Old Icelandic*
wrestling	glíma

Y, y

English	*Old Icelandic*
yellow	gulr
you	sé, þér, þik, þín, þú, yður
young	unga
young-woman	jungfrú
your	þín, þínar, þitt, yðrir, yðru
yours	þér, þína, þinn, þitt, yðrum
you-two	þit
Yrjar (place)	Yrjum
Yule (name)	Jólin, Jólum

A Word Comparison of Old Norse and Old Icelandic Words

Old Norse	Old Icelandic	English
áðr	áður	after
áðr	áður	after
áðr	áður	before
aldingarðr	aldingarður	orchard
at	að	about
at	að	against
at	að	as
at	að	at
at	að	from
at	að	him
at	að	in
at	að	it
at	að	of
at	að	over
at	að	than
at	að	that
at	að	the
at	að	to
at	að	towards
at	að	when
at	að	which
auðit	auðið	fated
biðr	biður	asked
borit	borið	borne
brynjólfr	Brynjólfur	Brynjolf (name)
búit	búið	inlaid
búit	búið	prepared
býðr	býður	invite
dauðr	dauður	dead
drukkit	drukkið	drank
drukkit	drukkið	drink
drukkit	drukkið	drinking
drukkit	drukkið	drink-to
drukkit	drukkið	drunk
drykkjumaðr	drykkjumaður	drinking-man
eldr	eldur	fire
eldr	eldur	the-flames
farit	farið	gone
gat	gað	got
gefr	gefur	given
geirröðr	Geirröður	Geirrod (name)
gengit	gengið	come
getit	getið	told-of
goðmundr	goðmundur	Godmund
goðmundr	Goðmundur	Godmund (name)
góðr	góður	good
grindhliðit	grindhliðið	gate
heiðr	heiður	honour
heldr	heldur	rather
hendr	hendur	hand
heraðit	heraðið	the-district
hingat	hingað	here
hirðmaðr	hirðmaður	court-man
höfuðit	höfuðið	head
höfuðit	höfuðið	his-head
huldumaðr	huldumaður	a-hidden-man
hvat	hvað	what
hvat	hvað	who
kallaðr	kallaður	called
kallat	kallað	called
kastat	kastað	cast
kemr	kemur	came
kemr	kemur	comes
kenndr	kenndur	recognised
komit	komið	coming
krókstafr	krókstafur	crooked-stick
kveldit	kveldið	evening
landit	landið	land
landit	landið	the-land
landsuðr	landsuður	the-south-east
launat	launað	repay
leiddr	leiddur	led
lendr	lendur	landed
líðr	líður	passed
lokit	lokið	ended
maðr	maður	a-man

A Word Comparison of Old Norse and Old Icelandic

Old Norse	Old Icelandic	English	Old Norse	Old Icelandic	English
maðr	maður	man	verðr	verður	became
meðalmaðr	meðalmaður	an-average-man	verðr	verður	becomes
mikit	mikið	great	verðr	verður	came
mikit	mikið	large	yðr	yður	you
mikit	mikið	much			
mjök	mjög	great			
mjök	mjög	much			
niðr	niður	below			
niðr	niður	down			
ófögnuðr	ófögnuður	unhappy			
ok	og	ad			
ok	og	also			
ok	og	and			
ok	og	filled			
ok	og	river			
ok	og	to			
Óláfr	Óláfur	Olaf (name)			
orðit	orðið	word			
óþýðr	óþýður	unfriendly			
ræðr	ræður	rules			
rauðr	rauður	red			
ríðr	ríður	rode			
rjóðr	rjóður	clearing			
sefr	sefur	slept			
sendr	sendur	sent			
siðr	siður	the-custom			
sjálfr	sjálfur	itself			
skipat	skipað	directed-to			
snarat	snarað	twisted			
stríðlyndr	stríðlyndur	obstinate			
sumarit	sumarið	summer			
sundr	sundur	apart			
svarit	svarið	sworn			
tekit	tekið	taken			
þangat	þangað	from-there			
þangat	þangað	there			
þat	það	it			
þat	það	that			
Þormóðr	Þormóður	Thormod (name)			
várit	várið	spring			
vatnit	vatnið	the-water			
veðr	veður	weather			

www.ingramcontent.com/pod-product-compliance
Lightning Source LLC
Chambersburg PA
CBHW051410070526
44584CB00023B/3366